Romantic Poems, Poets, and Narrators

Romantic Poems, Poets, and Narrators

JOSEPH C. SITTERSON, JR.

THE KENT STATE UNIVERSITY PRESS

Kent, Ohio, and London

©2000 by The Kent State University Press, Kent, Ohio 44242
Library of Congress Catalog Card Number 99-54424
ISBN 0-87338-655-8
Manufactured in the United States of America

06 05 04 03 02 01 00 5 4 3 2 1

Library of Congress Cataloging-in-Publication Data
Sitterson, Joseph C., 1945–
    Romantic poems, poets, and narrators / Joseph C. Sitterson, Jr.
        p.   cm.
    Includes bibliographical references and index.
    ISBN 0-87338-655-8 (alk. paper) ∞
        1. English poetry—19th century—History and criticism—Theory, etc. 2. Keats, John,
1795–1821—Criticism and interpretation—History. 3. Wordsworth, William, 1770–1850.
Intimations of immortality. 4. Coleridge, Samuel Taylor, 1772–1834. Rime of the ancient
mariner. 5. Blake, William, 1757–1827. Songs of experience. 6. Wordsworth, William, 1770–1850.
Prelude. 7. Romanticism—Great Britain. 8. Point of view (Literature) 9. First person
narrative. 10. Persona (Literature) 11. Narration (Rhetoric) I. Title.
PR590.S57   2000
821'.709145—dc21   99-54424

British Library Cataloging-in-Publication data are available.

To my mother,

and in memory of my father

Contents

Acknowledgments

I have worked on this book a long time. In doing so, I have depended upon many colleagues and friends, in many ways. They include Paul Betz, Stuart Curran, Leona Fisher, Elaine Hadley, Lisa Nanney, Jason Rosenblatt, Donna Sitterson, Jim Slevin, Penn Szittya, Dennis Todd, Wilfried Ver Eecke, and members of the Washington Area Romanticists' Group. Sue Lanser, Michael Ragussis, and Mark Reed, in particular, have at different times read and responded thoughtfully to the entire manuscript.

I thank Georgetown University for sabbatical leave and summer grant support. I thank also the editors of the following journals for permission to reprint parts of this book that appeared in their publications in substantially different forms: *JEGP, PLL, PMLA, South Atlantic Review,* and *SP.*

Introduction

Canonical Romantic poems have accumulated an unusually rich and complex history of readings over the past half-century, much of which is being ignored or misrepresented in contemporary criticism, theoretical and practical alike. If, as Jerome McGann has argued, "meaning, in a literary event, is a function not of 'the poem itself' but of the poem's historical relations with its readers and interpreters," then more is at stake than the history of criticism.[1] Throughout this book I shall be representing these relations in terms very different than those deriving from, as Chris Baldick puts it, "market-driven notions of obsolescence and supersession" along with a "model of Oedipal conflict between individual critics"—both of which, he continues, encourage us "to believe that any older form of criticism is, once challenged by a newer rival, simply either bankrupted or buried."[2]

The recent critical history of Romantics studies in particular may seem exemplary: new criticism is bankrupted by deconstruction, which in turn is bankrupted by new historicism; or, Cleanth Brooks is buried by Paul de Man, who in turn is buried by McGann. Baldick's own argument is, to the contrary, that "critical discussion at any given time" is characterized by "the simultaneous currency of several incongruous styles, methods, and schools of thought, some of them old enough to be 'discredited' to all except their practitioners, some of them too new and unfamiliar to be digested by many outside the circle of the latest vanguard"; he proposes briefly an alternative model, "the geological image of sedimented mineral deposits, one lying athwart and atop the other without actually erasing it" (8–9). The advantage of his model is that it captures, albeit only descriptively, the "incongru[ity]" and the "uncomfortable co-existence" (8) of differing critical theories and practices. But the model is an inert one, and its advantage thus also a disadvantage, because it keeps such theories and practices separate.

If instead we want a dynamic model, but one less binary and final than the economic and psychological ones he critiques, perhaps we should turn to Kenneth Burke's "unending conversation," a "heated discussion" that both precedes and outlives any actual participant.[3] This model places every reading in a conversational, and perhaps argumentative, "present." It obscures, in its turn, the historicity of each theory and practice, but its advantage is that each can remain potentially a participant in something more than, rather than a silent witness to, a monolog. It is a model that underlies the readings I offer here of poems much of whose significant interpretation now appears mutually incommensurate, because its practitioners are split (again to use Baldick's description) between those seeking to dominate one another in "a cut-throat intellectual bazaar of contending critical 'schools' whose only point of agreement is that the critical methods of twenty years ago are too shop-soiled to be put on sale at all" (7), and those ignoring the bazaar, "who have not felt obliged to abandon their traditional conceptions of mimesis, aesthetic unity, and authorial intention, to learn the new language of fractured subject-positions and counterhegemonic discursive formations" (205). This book is addressed to those readers who, wherever they situate themselves in relation to this split, are at least uneasy if not deeply unhappy about its existence.

The major Romantic poets often seem to claim their own sort of domination, in the form of prophetic or bardic certainty about themselves and their world. In the poems read here, they do present characters, narrators, or dramatized readers who desire such mastery, but I shall be arguing that the poets characteristically represent it to be impossible. At the same time they see attempting it to be necessary, because they cannot otherwise understand its limits. Mastery and awareness of its impossibility thus coexist in necessary tension, within each individual text's subjects—its author, its narrator, its characters, its readers.

Each of these subjects is both stable and unstable, centered and decentered. "The subject," in other words, is not the stable voice hypothesized by authorial intention;[4] at the same time, the subject is not the wholly decentered and empty shifter "I"—caught, as Jacques Lacan puts it, in the signifying chain. It is both. Even though it cannot be reduced to one or the other alternative, however, subjectivity is not achieved on some higher plane of synthesis. In their coexistent stability and instability, readers are like textual subjects, so that as a reader of Romantic texts I shall inevitably encounter limits to my understanding of those texts. A primary, recurrent argument in this book is against the usually implicit claim of different theoretical models or methods, produced by such reading subjects, to transcend such limits. In an interesting displacement, the recent critical history of every poem studied here reveals that readers are less concerned with the problematics of their own interpretive mastery than with the question of narrative mastery or understanding within the poetry—a concern all these poems share thematically, allusively, or generically.

Like Romantic authors, narrators, and characters, then, we are not masters of our world. But we cannot come to terms with, understand, or even locate our limits without exploring the possibility of mastery. (As I am implying here, mastery and understanding are not synonyms. "Mastery" may include what we might call a complete or final understanding, but it also suggests the desire for a kind of control or domination that fuels it, a desire sometimes in but hidden by the word "understanding.") Such exploration here will be on two levels, necessarily not always distinct from one another in the following chapters. On one level, this book explores limits within the poems and finds those limits often to be deliberate, reflecting the poets' understanding of subjectivity (in themselves and their characters, and by implication their readers); this constitutes a fundamental disagreement with arguments that such limits reflect only the poets' *lack* of understanding—of history, of language, of subjectivity. Here my argument corroborates similar ones made by David Simpson and Susan Wolfson, among others, that the Romantic poets often knew what they were doing better than their contemporary demystifiers (if also better than their critics who assign them essentially unproblematic roles as prophets).[5] On another level, this book explores limits in modern critical readings of the poems, and it finds those limits often to reflect our own permanent implication in the limits of understanding subjectivity, an implication that the poets understand deeply. In making this last statement, I do not mean to dismiss such readings. My intention is less to offer radically new readings than to clarify relations among existing and apparently conflicting readings—relations that amount to more than an eclectic pluralism or a conventionalism based on a notion of interpretive community.[6] This means inevitably that I shall be moving back and forth between poem and interpretation. This movement requires as much respect for interpretive text as for poetic text, so that at times I shall be considering the former in as much detail as the latter. Consequently, it may help if I present an outline of my overall argument, with an emphasis here on the poetic texts.

Chapter 1 looks at Blake's "Introduction" to the *Songs of Experience* in terms of its relation to Old and New Testament allusions and to its readers. The poem is both intertextual and reader directed, and by way of its biblical allusions it offers us two incompatible readings of the bard's understanding of himself and his message. One reading takes the vision of the bard, the poem's speaker, to be both coherent and truly visionary. The other takes that vision to be contaminated by the bard's misunderstanding of what he sees. I argue that even though these two readings are incompatible, they not only coexist but reflect Blake's own understanding of prophetic ambivalence and uncertainty, and of our responsibility as readers for interpretive choices necessitated by that uncertainty. Blake's own strategy, then, enables us to see that we can read his poetry as both prophetic and problematic—reflecting his and our own moments of insight coupled with attendant uncertainty.

When prophetic identity in Blake is seen as a problem, it is most often avoided through a carefully formalist separation of the poet from his speakers, whose confusions or inadequacies become ironized, thus showing how far those speakers are from Blake's (and by implication from his readers') complete mastery of the world. When that identity is seen as a solution instead of a problem, Blake and his speakers are conflated, and the poems become embodiments of a Blakean system that achieves such mastery. But we do not have to reject systems or confine ourselves to a deifying formalism if we problematize prophetic identity; instead, we can see such a system as a theoretical ideal toward which Blake (as well as his narrators) is always moving—an ideal that also, with Blake's awareness of paradox, is designed (as are his poems, and their multiple textual forms) to free us from systems. But we never free ourselves wholly, and only within systems is such a relative freedom possible.

Coleridge's awareness of the intertwining of insight and uncertainty appears to take a more anxious form than Blake's, resulting in his habitual poetic self-effacement. (It is dramatized most directly in "Kubla Khan," where the speaker's uncertainty over the validity of his prophetic vision becomes the explicit subject of the last third of the poem: in one sense the vision is validated in words, though not in air; in another, it remains a fantasy. Self-effacement is dramatized less directly, but equally centrally, in "Frost at Midnight," where the poem's confidence hinges on a midpoint turn in the speaker's mood that is as inexplicable as it is powerful; the mystery of that turn's origin reminds us, if not the speaker, that his despairing mood of isolation might recur in a similar turn and that his imagined future education for his infant might be only a fantasy.) In *The Rime of the Ancient Mariner,* this self-effacement, when combined with the traditional generic effacement of the ballad narrator, may be seen both as a considered refusal to play an authoritative role as narrator and as a reflection of Coleridge's personal uncertainty about such a role, and also, finally, as a displacement of narrative authority onto an embedded narrator, the Mariner. This self-effacement leaves such an interpretive gap that readers are tempted to fix on any source of authority they can find in the poem: the Mariner, especially, or the glossator. Like chapter 1 then, chapter 2 studies allusions—in this case, to Neoplatonism, in the gloss. I argue that the allusions are deliberately frustrating. That is, whatever his additional unease with the role of omniscient narrator, Coleridge not only intends the allusions to characterize the glossator's search for mastery of the Mariner's story but also intends the glossator's Neoplatonic understanding to be unable to account for that story. Such attempted mastery is doubly present in the poem, since the Mariner too seeks it and, like the glossator, fails. Neither the Mariner's interpretive frame of ordinary Catholicism nor the glossator's Neoplatonic contextualizing is able to account for the Mariner's experience.

If it is argued, as by McGann's historicist reading of the poem, that the determining contemporary context for the poem's meaning is the interpretive frame of Coleridge's own systematic theology, then such attempted mastery is triply present—and, I argue, along with such reading, also inadequate. The desire of modern readers to achieve a similar mastery usually takes the form of oversimplifying the Mariner, as well as Coleridge's relation to him. I outline that desire, especially as it appears in readings of the poem that take psychoanalysis as the discipline best able to understand subjectivity. Such readings assume that neither the Mariner nor Coleridge understands his experience; my argument is that Coleridge understands better than his protagonist, and finally that Coleridge recognizes limits to understanding that such readings mistakenly believe they can ignore or transcend. At the same time, a careful study of psychoanalytic theory in relation to the Mariner's experience enables us to see the extent to which that experience does not match the paradigm of the Romantic imagination projected onto the poem by readers whose interpretive mastery takes a specifically Christian form.

Chapter 3 shows that Wordsworth recognizes limits to his own self-understanding even in the poem that seems to claim it as his autobiographical possession, *The Prelude.* Such a claim, unsurprisingly, seems most explicit at the poem's end, and readers of the Snowdon episode there tend to agree that the narrator now believes he has understood and mastered what was earlier mysterious; they differ radically, however, about whether that belief indicates the narrator's maturity or his self-deception. Some readers find a mature, fully self-conscious and self-understanding subject; others find an ego in self-deceptive triumph over a discontinuous and fragmented true subject. I argue that the narrator understands more fully at *The Prelude*'s end but also that he understands, and is no longer frustrated by, the limits of his understanding.

Psychoanalytic readings of the poem in particular do not admit that the poet recognizes such limits. Believing they are better able to account for complex subjectivity, they claim a mastery over Wordsworth's text and his understanding of it that reminds us of the same claim made by similar readings of Coleridge's poem. Such a claim denies or obscures the limits to interpretive understanding that, I argue, inhere in the very psychoanalytic theory to which they appeal for certainty.

Chapter 4 reads the Intimations Ode, again in terms of Wordsworth's understanding and its self-acknowledged limits, as they are evidenced, first, in the poem itself, where uncertainty and tension between understanding and its limits are central; second, in the poem's allusions to earlier odes in the generic tradition that, unlike Wordsworth's ode, claim certainty; and, third, in the poem's placement as last in Wordsworth's collected poetry, implying closure yet also denying it.

Like "prophecy" for many Blake readers, "ode" for some Wordsworth readers becomes a generic guarantor of meaning. I argue instead that Wordsworth deliberately situates his Ode in a generic line that, perhaps more obviously than Blake's prophetic genre, problematizes the speaker's mastery of himself and his subject. Also, like Blake, Wordsworth makes this problem a central concern of the poem. Where in *The Prelude* the problem is perhaps the central thematic (rather than generic) focus of the poem, which originates in the narrator's articulated need for self-understanding, in the Intimations Ode it is the poem's generic as well as thematic focus.

Chapter 5 reads Keats's *Lamia* in terms of its narrator: Is the narrator ironic or self-deluded? Is Keats in control of the narrator or identifying with him? In my reading I am led to a single Platonic allusion in the poem, "Platonic shades," the study of which enables us to see finally that "Keats" is not a stable subject in complete, formalist control of a dramatized, unreliable, shifting narrator. It allows us to see also that the narratological questions raised above cannot be answered in mutually exclusive ways: all of their formulations are in varying degrees accurate ways of conceptualizing the relation between Keats and his narrator. The investigation into Keats's deliberate use of Plato also provides an example of the interpretive use of literary history on a less social and economic level than that on which many historicists currently work. This older kind of historicism gets short shrift from theorists, perhaps because in the past it often sought to unify its subject into what newer historicism, acutely conscious of its postmodernity, rejects as the liberal humanist myth of the transcendent Romantic self. But this level of the personal is one that newer historicism cannot ignore in favor of its larger historical arenas without a consequent marginalizing of the complex subject, who is not only the author but one locus of the poem's central theme of desire and mastery.

Like Wordsworth before him, Keats makes the issue of narrative mastery explicit in *Lamia*, albeit as the narrator's story of others, not of himself. But his story of others is also close to Keats's life, and this closeness helps us to see the poem's narrator both as part of Keats's strategy and as caught up in Keats's sense of his own identity.

Although readers have been interested in the question of narrative mastery in Romantic texts, they have not been especially interested in Romantic subjects in terms of those subjects' own *understanding and representation* of their decenteredness and incomplete mastery. I say this despite agreeing with Alan Liu's comment that "as regards Romantic studies, subjectivity is the *donnée* of the field. The whole domain may be said to pivot around the imaginative 'self,' which faces in one way toward the transcendental but in the other—as historicizing Romanticists increasingly point out—toward the material."[7] (A "given," it is worth remembering, is precisely what is not always examined.) "Transcendental" and "material" accurately describe the two directions in which the "self" faces. They also describe, not incidentally, the shift in critical attention—from the transcendental to the material, or more generally, from the transcendental to how that transcendental is undermined, perhaps by the material (for historicist readers), perhaps by the linguistic (for deconstructive readers).

Here, however, I am primarily interested in the verb "faces." For de Man the word is inextricably tied to figuration. In his essay on autobiography, he argues that "Autobiography" is "a figure of reading or of understanding that occurs, to some degree, in all texts. The autobiographical moment happens as an alignment between the two subjects involved in the process of reading [that is, author and reader] in which they determine each other by mutual reflexive substitution." This "specular moment," he goes on to say, "is the manifestation, on the level of the referent, of a linguistic structure." "Our topic," he concludes, therefore "deals with the giving and taking away of faces, with face and deface, *figure*, figuration and dis-figuration."[8] I shall be arguing that the specular moment is *also* the manifestation, on the level of "a linguistic structure," of "the referent." I do not want to ignore the extent to which history *or* language gives face to the subject, but I do want to emphasize here that the nominal form of the verb belies the impersonality that de Man's "figuration" and Liu's "subjectivity" and his quotes around "self" imply, an impersonality that would enable us as readers to remove the Romantic poets from our world: in the one (transcendental) case to a world of stable and centered, autonomous subjects; in the other (material, linguistic) case to a world of unstable and decentered subjects, "what is actually the series of the conglomeration of *positions*, subject-positions, provisional and not necessarily indefeasible, into which a person is called momentarily by the discourses and the world that he/she inhabits."[9]

I shall be arguing throughout this book that the fundamental subject-position into which each Romantic poet finds himself called, and into which his poetry repeatedly and not momentarily calls each careful and self-conscious reader, is the difficult one of facing both ways, toward what Liu calls the transcendental and the material. To represent this double-facing seems as difficult as maintaining it seems awkward; indeed both are pushed toward impossibility by the metaphor itself, which appears imaginable less in a human sense than in the mythological sense of "Janus faced." But it may make better human sense if we think about ways in which we might orient ourselves toward those subject-positions in which we find ourselves. Putting it like this implies yet another subject aware of its subject-positions, but I mean not that the subject transcends those positions, only that I know of no other way to talk about self-consciousness in this context. This has been a problem at least since Hume, on whose observation in *A Treatise of Human Nature* that "when I enter most intimately into what I call *myself*, I always stumble on some particular perception or other," Paul Ricoeur comments, "Here, then, is *someone* who claims to be unable to find anything but a datum stripped of selfhood; *someone* who penetrates within himself, seeks and declares to have found nothing. . . . With the question Who?—who is seeking, stumbling, and not finding, and who perceives?—the self returns just when the same slips away."[10]

Without defining either one exclusively in terms of the other, I shall be trying to situate the poets' subjectivities in relation to their contexts. My argument will be that the Romantic poets can represent claims about the nature of world and self that imply a bardic or transcendent position while recognizing that their desire for such transcendence is itself not transcendent but, instead, subject to what Liu calls the material. Implied in this argument is that the poems studied here are intrinsically especially interesting in this regard, in that they deliberately embody or seek interactions among their authors, characters, and readers, interactions possible specifically and only through the reader's careful and thoughtful engagement with their minute particulars—"close reading." Put another way, I shall be arguing for a Romantic aesthetics that seeks to go beyond formalism but that in doing so recognizes the truth of Geoffrey Hartman's remark that the only path beyond formalism is through it, not around it.[11] De Man has asserted "the necessary presence of a totalizing principle as the guiding impulse of the critical process. In the New Criticism, this principle consisted of a purely empirical notion of the integrity of literary form," but "as it refines its interpretations more and more," he concludes, "This unitarian criticism finally becomes a criticism of ambiguity, an ironic reflection on the absence of the unity it had postulated." In trying to go beyond formalism here, I want first to show this metamorphosis taking place in formalist readings that are themselves becoming increasingly neglected or noticed only for their supposedly misguided unitarianism, and second to say something more about ambiguity and irony than that they are intrinsic, "distinctive structures of literary language."[12] Unless something more can be said, it seems to me that formalism, deconstruction, and historicism have little to say to one another, at least about subjectivity. In this context it is both telling and troubling that although Liu has found in "the critical vocabulary of the New Historicism . . . a massive borrowing from New Criticism," the terms whose presence he documents are "paradox," "irony," "ambiguity," "tension," "contradiction," and "fusion" ("Formalism" 758, n. 5); nowhere is there mention of "author," "speaker," "narrator," or "point of view"—terms equally crucial to formalist readings of narrative and lyric alike.

The directions in which "the imaginative 'self'" might face used to be argued about textually in such formalist terms as "author" and "speaker," in such a way as to avoid the problem of double-facing. That is, when the self was perceived as facing the transcendent, the author and speaker were conflated as successfully bardic; when the self was perceived as facing the material, the consequent limitations of the self were ascribed not to the author but to the speaker. Habitually, if not inevitably, formalism has depended upon a unified subject—sometimes to the point of aesthetic deification—responsible for its speaker, in order to maintain a clear distinction between the two.

This clear distinction is not always so clear. Robert Elliott argues that only "writers who attack the persona are likely to think the term entails a complete separation between the author and the pose he assumes: the mask having nothing to do with the wearer of the mask. Proponents have a much more flexible idea of the relation between persona and author, mask and wearer becoming almost indistinguishable at times."[13] However, the explicit presence of this flexibility is rare in formalist readings of poems—rare enough, in fact, that to find a good example takes us outside Romantic poetry altogether, to Brooks's reading of Marvell's "Horatian Ode." Arguing that "the tension between the speaker's admiration for the kingliness which has won Cromwell the power and his awareness that the power can be maintained only by a continual exertion of these talents for kingship—this tension is never relaxed," Brooks emphasizes that this "total attitude" of the poem is "dramatic"—an emphasis recurrent, with the same words ("tension," "total attitude," "dramatic"), throughout his readings in *The Well Wrought Urn*. Uncharacteristically, Brooks then goes on to say that "The total attitude realized in the 'Ode' does not seem to me monstrously inhuman in its complexity. It could be held by human beings"; and again, "The attitude of the 'Ode' is not inhuman in its Olympian detachment[;] . . . something like it could be held by a human being."[14] But Brooks's repeated explicitness about the poet here may be possible only because for him this poet turns out to be identical to his speaker in their shared "Olympian detachment." When that supreme New Critical virtue does not appear to be present in both, Brooks is much less explicit.

It remains true that formalist theory has tended to suppose a complete separation between author and speaker, and has not been able to account for flexibility. Formalist practice is another matter: not explicitly, because the example above is rare, but implicitly, by in effect admitting this flexibility whenever that practice oscillates (or vacillates) between "the poet" and "the speaker" as its text's speaking subject. Indeed the same implicit admission, in the same sort of oscillation, characterizes some poststructuralist practice that is less rigorous than its theory. One good example is J. Hillis Miller's reading of Hardy's poetry. Miller attributes "the curious and mostly ignored claim Hardy repeatedly makes that his poems in the first person are dramatic monologues" to his assertion that "Hardy experienced in his own life a form of th[e] dissolution" of self explicable by way of "Hume and Nietzsche[, who] dissolve the self by seeing it as a verbal fiction based on taking figures of speech literally"; it follows that "Hardy is, like each human mind for Hume, a null place where diverse impressions happen to have congregated." At this point, to Miller we might echo Ricoeur's response to Hume: with the question, Who?—who is repeatedly making a claim, and who experiences dissolution—the self returns just when the same slips away. Miller frames his argument as an attack against "biographical explanations," which he equates with "the biographical mode of obtaining unity" that is both "too deep because it makes the error of referring the poems back to a ground that is [mistakenly] presumed to underlie them all, to unify them," and "too superficial in that [it] divert[s] the mind from exploring what the poems really say."[15] But Miller's own critique of such a biographical reading of Hardy is itself biographical—except with a deeper sense of a complex and even disunified "Hardy" who is nevertheless conscious of such disunity.

The question now is: How do we speak of speakers and narrators, when we are now conceptualizing them in relation to decentered and disunified subjects who create them, and when correspondingly we have no reason to suppose such speakers to be themselves necessarily more unified than their creators? This question needs to be asked across generic lines in the Romantic period, and across such periodic lines as well, although I do not now ask it in these contexts. It is challenging enough here to apply it to these very different narrators: the explicitly autobiographical narrator of *The Prelude;* the implicitly autobiographical speaker of the Intimations Ode; the explicit, dramatized, nonautobiographical narrator of *Lamia;* the implicit, minimally dramatized narrator of *The Rime of the Ancient Mariner;* and the dramatized, perhaps autobiographical speaker of the "Introduction" to *Songs of Experience.*

1 "Introduction" to
the *Songs of Experience*

The Infection of Time

Modern criticism of Blake's "Introduction" to the *Songs of Experience* reveals in miniature the persistent tendency to simplify, in different ways, the complex subjectivity of Romantic speakers. Some readers set apart the speaker from the author in the name of formalism; others subsume the one in the other in the name of authorial intention. (Still others conceive of a poststructuralist subject so dispersed in and by its contexts that for them the problem of author and speaker seems to disappear. I discuss such a conception later in this chapter, excluding it here in order to clarify the issue of subjectivity in relation to Blake's poem.) The former simplification retains the poet as omniscient, ironizing the Bard as a deluded prophet to the extent that he is not omniscient. The latter collapses all distinctions between poet and speaker, assuming either a unitary, systematic intention shared by the poet and the Bard, or a divided, confused intention in which the poet is as deluded as his speaker. (We can understand such simplification as the result of our need to master another's subjectivity; that, however, does not make it any more adequate to such subjectivity than the oversimplifying acts we perform in daily life on others and even ourselves.) Such simplification is not necessarily simple; interpretations on both sides of the "ironic narrator" problem can be subtle and learned. But they tend to be on one or the other side: the

Bard is either right or wrong, prophetic or deluded; in Mary Lynn Johnson's otherwise useful review of interpretations of the *Songs of Innocence and of Experience*, "the speaker of the 'Introduction' is" either "a reliable witness of Experience— prophetic, visionary, and imaginative," or "authoritarian, error-prone, hypo-critical, or worse."[1] Here I do not intend a transcendent third position, whatever that might be. Instead, I shall argue that finally it does make sense to see the Bard in both ways rather than in only one, to say that the Bard can be at the same time right and wrong, about the same things.

To understand the problem, let us look in some detail at how the poem has been read, adhering to Blake's own well-known principle that "Ideas cannot be Given but in their minutely Appropriate Words."[2] Northrop Frye's has remained the most important of these readings for several decades.[3] It accounts for much more of the poem's detail than any other reading—seeing it, in accord with Blake's own apparent aesthetics, as "a Vision; a perfect Whole . . . in its Minute Particulars; Organized"; it also contextualizes the poem and its speaker persua-sively in relation to other Blake poems, and in relation to Frye's influential Blakean system.[4]

For Frye the Bard is "in the tradition of the Hebrew prophets, who derive their inspiration from Christ as Word of God, and whose life is a listening for and speaking with that Word" (25).

Hear the voice of the Bard!
Who Present, Past, & Future sees
Whose ears have heard,
The Holy Word,
That walk'd among the ancient trees.
(*E* 18)

The first stanza for Frye establishes unequivocally the speaker's identity as a rightly confident prophet "Who Present, Past, & Future sees" and who therefore transcends "our ordinary experience of time" (24). This transcendence enables the Bard to describe what he hears not as "the voice of the Lord God walking in the garden in the cool of the day" (Genesis 3.8) but, building on John's identifica-tion of Word, God, and Jesus (John 1.1, 14), as "The Holy Word, / That walk'd among the ancient trees . . . in the evening dew." Like Blake the Bard knows, implies Frye, that "the worst theological error we can make [is] putting God at the beginning of a temporal sequence"; instead, knowing like Blake that "there is no God but Jesus," he replaces God the Father with Jesus, who "in *Paradise Lost,*" says Frye, "created the unfallen world, placed man in Eden, and discovered man's fall" (24–25). It is, then, not just the Bard's confidence in his own vision ("Hear the voice of the Bard!") but his typologically transformed allusion that serves as evidence for his prophetic identity.

If the Bard really does understand all this as clearly as Frye his reader, we might ask why he nevertheless addresses Earth not with the Good News of the Gospel ("Jesus supposes every Thing to be Evident to the Child & to the Poor & Unlearned Such is the Gospel" [*E* 664]) but with this complex—even in Frye's account—typological reformulation of the Genesis beginning. We might indeed ask why he begins with any version of that biblical book, since God's words and actions from this point on in Genesis condemn man.

There are additional disquieting details or implications in the Bard's account, matters that have led other readers to question the degree of his understanding.[5]

> Calling the lapsed Soul
> And weeping in the evening dew;
> That might controll,
> The starry pole;
> And fallen fallen light renew!

The most obvious problem here is syntactical complexity or confusion: who is "Calling the lapsed Soul"? Frye minimizes the problem, with some covert adverbial uncertainty: "'Calling' refers primarily to Christ, the Holy Word calling Adam in the garden, and the 'lapsed soul' is presumably Adam." If Christ is "calling," it must be he who is "weeping"—"the Jesus of the Gospels who wept over the death of man as typified in Lazarus [John 11.35]." While he admits the initial syntactic ambiguity, then, Frye resolves it by merging the speaker and the Holy Word on the basis of Blake's belief that "there is no God but Jesus, who is also Man": "calling" can thus refer syntactically both to "the Holy Word" and to "the voice of the Bard" at the same time. "Both the calling and the weeping, of course, are repeated by the Bard; the denunciations of the prophet and the elegiac vision of the poet of experience derive from God's concern over fallen man" (25).

The stanza raises a second syntactic question: who "might controll, / The starry pole" and "renew" the "fallen light"? Frye is unequivocal: "In the last three lines the grammatical antecedent of 'That' is 'Soul,'" and this "lapsed Soul" he identifies with fallen man, capable of responding to the prophet's words although not himself prophetic (25–26). But syntactic ambiguity remains: "That might controll" also parallels "That walk'd among the ancient trees" only three lines earlier; thus it might be the "Holy Word," not fallen man, "That might controll" and "renew." Frye avoids the ambiguity, as indeed he must, having conflated Christ and his prophet. It would not make sense, in his argument's terms, that Christ and his prophet *"might* controll, / The starry pole," additionally because accepting this ambiguity would also conflate prophet and fallen man—in which case, how would the two differ, and what grounds would we have for believing the one to be authentically prophetic and the other wrong, or at least mired in Experience? If this poem is "an introduction to some of the main principles of Blake's thought" (23), then this last question's implied skepticism has radical implications not only for how Blake's speaker understands Blake's system but for how we and Blake understand it.[6]

Here is one way of putting the problem. If the Bard is alluding only to the Old Testament (as overtly he seems to be doing, since the clear allusion is to Genesis 3), the Bard seems to be asserting Blake's negative father-priest-king concept of divinity, and we should be careful about believing what he claims and says, since his vision is at least partly mistaken, whatever its truth to experience. To the extent that the Bard is alluding to the New Testament Christ who weeps for man's sin, the Bard is asserting Blake's vision as Frye describes it and is not being ironized. If both allusive contexts come into play, the function of allusion here becomes complex, irreducibly so in terms of the text alone, in fact reducible only by choices for which we as readers are responsible. In the typological terms that most readers of the poem assume Blake to have adopted, to what extent can we gain a New Testament perspective on an Old Testament story of generation?

But the question needs to be rephrased. Typology for Blake does not provide a stable basis for interpretation. Frye's "tradition of the Hebrew prophets, who derive their inspiration from Christ as the Word of God," may have become paradigmatic for how we understand the narrators in Blake's longer poems, but this "tradition" is a problem: "prophet" is not necessarily a fixed state of self, inevitably reliable in its understanding of self or world, in Blake or in the Bible. That is, "prophecy" may be as much of a human problem as it is a generic solution for reading both texts—indeed it is already a problem in Frye's conflation of Old and New Testament prophecy. Zachary Leader argues that "bard" poses a similar problem: its link with both prophecy and Druids "associate[s it] not only with antiquity, poetic high-seriousness, and prophecy, but with a Dark Age of religious and military barbarism" (*Reading Blake's "Songs"* 139). Blake sometimes distinguishes between the two testaments—"Wherefore did Christ come was it not to abolish the Jewish Imposture . . . [he was] in opposition to the Jewish Scriptures which are only an Example of the wickedness & deceit of the Jews" (*E* 614). But he does not consistently oppose them to one another: "The *Jewish &*

Christian Testaments are An original derivation from the Poetic Genius"; "The *Old & New* Testaments are the Great Code of Art" (*E* 1, 274; emphasis added). Instead, he distinguishes between reading the Bible, and presumably other texts, as art and reading it as something else. His aphorism "Prayer is the Study of Art" (*E* 274) suggests his belief in the first kind of reading; his comment on Homer might cause us to rethink our relation to reading for (and his relation to writing for) a unitary system of any kind: "As Unity is the cloke of folly so Goodness is the cloke of knavery Those who will have Unity exclusively in Homer come out with a Moral like a sting in the tail. . . . It is the same with the Moral of a whole Poem as with the Moral Goodness of its parts Unity & Morality, are secondary considerations & belong to Philosophy & not to Poetry" (*E* 269–70).

Let the question formerly phrased in terms of New and Old Testament perspectives then be rephrased: To what extent can we gain a different perspective on Experience than that of an ironized Bard, with whom we are mired in Experience? We shall need eventually to apply this question to Blake as well as to his speaker and to ourselves. For now, I am arguing that it is inadequate to the poem's complexity of viewpoint and understanding to reduce it, and our role as readers of it, to one of the following situations: either the Bard possesses fully and securely a prophetic vision, and our responsibility as readers is to attain his level of understanding; or the Bard is radically mistaken, a limited prophet deluded into taking Experience (and the father-priest-king God of the Old Testament) as the limits of reality, and our responsibility as readers is to understand the ways in which he is ironized and his partial vision undermined by Blake, whose superior understanding we come to share. Instead, we might see a Bard who is striving for prophetic insight, who is claiming it with a rhetoric that may or may not match the depth of that insight, but whose vision is complex and uncertain enough to call into question the adequacy of—*not* invalidate—that insight.

Harold Bloom was the first (and until Leader the only) reader to characterize the Bard in this way. "This Bard of Experience has considerable capacity for vision, and has much in common with Blake, but he is *not* Blake, and his songs are limited by his perspective"; he is "capable of imaginative redemption [but] still stand[s] in need of it." (Despite his momentary insight, Bloom both distances Blake in his omniscience from the Bard and identifies himself with that omniscience as reader, able to know which songs have as their speaker the Bard, which have "various other Redeemed speakers," and which have Blake himself, where "he allows himself a full Reprobate awareness.")[7] We must see the Bard as someone striving for prophetic understanding, partly caught within his culture and therefore partly caught between two readings of the human condition, that is, two cultural conceptions of humanity's relation to divinity: child-worshipper-subject to father-priest-king, and adult to Christ, or adult to oneself, understanding and taking responsibility for the universality of one's own image of deity that does not impinge on another's subjectivity.

If Blake is right that his readers stand in the same need of imaginative redemption as his Bard, then we must apply Bloom's insight more rigorously than does Bloom himself to the Bard and to Blake—and to ourselves, unless we are to assume that omniscience we so quickly grant the poet. This does not mean that we give up trying to understand Blake's poems on the grounds that, after all, we too are mired in Experience and might as well live with our confusion. It does mean that we try to become more self-aware as readers—specifically, that we recognize truths or readings that do not fit our masterful interpretive structures, while at the same time recognizing that we must create or at least work within such structures if we are to know anything at all.[8]

Blake recommends as much, when he writes, "The wisest of the Ancients consider'd what is not too Explicit as the fittest for Instruction, because it rouzes the faculties to act," and adds, "What is it sets Homer Virgil & Milton in so high a rank of Art. Why is the Bible more Entertaining & Instructive than any other book. Is it not because they are addressed to the Imagination which is Spiritual Sensation & but mediately to the Understanding or Reason" (*E* 702–3. Because Blake is writing here to John Trusler—"falln out with the Spiritual World" [*E* 702] and, says Blake to George Cumberland, in that "Class of Men" that Blake "despair[s] of Ever pleasing" [*E* 703]—he may be modifying his real opinions. But the rest of his letter evidences no such compromise.) In this context I take Understanding or Reason to be what produces masterful interpretive structures, Urizen's "solid without fluctuation" (*U* 4.11; *E* 71), and I emphasize that Blake does not deny that the greatest art appeals to reason. He wants to awaken human faculties, of which reason is one. It may take another faculty than reason to recognize reason's limits, but without reason's attempts to master the world and its texts, we cannot articulate the very structures whose limitations we must discover.

My emphasis on how we read the "Introduction" thus is not just an attempt at hermeneutical accommodation. It also reflects Blake's educative poetics and his likely sense of his audience. This reflection can be corroborated if we extrapolate from Heather Glen's contextualizing of Blake's *Songs* in its time.[9] Glen shows that Blake chose his genre because it was popular, "aim[ing the *Songs*] at a known (and growing) market of parents from the polite classes" (9), and at the same time because in that genre "real imaginative life (albeit of an ephemeral, sensationalistic kind) was consistently being subordinated to 'instructive' purposes" (14)—purposes that Blake continually "worked to frustrate" (17). "Blake is using the form of the late eighteenth-century child's song not as a vehicle for 'ideas' counter to those which it usually expresses, but in order to expose and subvert that whole mode of making sense of the world which it characteristically embodied" (18). By doing so, Blake "celebrates individuality and difference" (18), that is, he celebrates the complexity of human subjects, which is flattened out by any educational philosophy that tries to teach doctrine.

Blake's opposition to received doctrine of all sorts is familiar enough—but his celebration of complexity is not, inasmuch as critical readings of Blake so often ignore its application to their own arguments. The important exception here is Tilottama Rajan: because "the *Songs* are spoken by a heteroglossia of different voices," she argues, "they suggest to us that experience or experiment may have priority over any preestablished system."[10] But even Glen appears to ignore her insight into Blake's celebration of individuality and difference and to give in to the desire to contain each collection, when she generalizes about their speakers: "The characteristic poetic shape [of *Experience*] is not one of echoing harmony, the end of the poem confirming and yet pointing outward from the beginning [*Innocence*], but one of linear progression toward a final disillusion which echoes nothing and leads nowhere" (165); "The most confidently authoritative voices . . . are shown not merely to be closed to that upon which they would pronounce, but those least able to change that which they deplore" (31).

Most readers of the *Songs* show the same desire. John Holloway argues that in *Innocence,* "objects began to merge into each other in harmonious oneness"; in *Experience,* "separateness and repulsion pervade it everywhere" (65). Nick Shrimpton argues that *Innocence* and *Experience* "cohere around the single theme of protection": in the former, "th[e] act of protection underlies many different relationships"; in the latter, "the same acts become acts rather of oppression and domination" (28). Even Leader, whose sense of the Bard's complexity is most acute, creates a unifying narrative of (psychic?) maturation to encompass the collection: "The youthful Bard of the experienced title-page grows into the lamed and embittered, though still powerful, old man of 'London,' a Bard who does not yet realize, as he will by the final plate, the dangers into which he has fallen" (*Reading Blake's "Songs"* 197). Indeed Leader, more thoroughly than any other reader, has maintained such a unifying formalist distinction in the *Songs*—that is, "If the Bard is to *Experience* as the Piper is to *Innocence,* then he is the creator of its Songs" (144). (The distinction has been made by other readers—for example, Gleckner 64–65—but has been applied inconsistently.)

Leader's inclusion of the illuminated plates of the *Songs* as evidence for the unifying narrative he proposes does not, oddly, make the identity of the Bard an even more complex problem than I have made it out to be, since he uses the plates as representational corroboration of that narrative (the speaker of "London" is a "lamed . . . old man"), as visual confirmation of his resolution of the ambiguity inescapable within an exclusively formalist reading. But the plates can make the Bard's identity more complex—paradoxically so complex, I shall argue here, that the problem in effect has disappeared from critical view.

Nelson Hilton argues that in his creation of the plates, "In the careful work of retouching, in the continual awareness of mirror-writing, Blake participated in, and manifested, a vision of the word as object, as other, and as divine, [as] an eternal living form with its own personality, family, and destiny." Consequently, "each word signifies so amply that . . . each word finds relation to another[, and w]hile this relational process occurs initially in the mind of the *perceiver*, it can develop through and toward structures in the 'mind' of the *text*, and then further to relations in the 'mind,' or *episteme*, of *English and collective imagination*" (emphasis added). Here "Blake" *and* his speakers have disappeared from critical view and have been replaced by other "minds," deriving from Hilton's initial personification of "the word." There is persuasive evidence, not only in Blake's methods of composition but in his texts—for example, Hilton quotes from *Jerusalem:* "every Word & Every Character / Was Human" (*J* 98.35–36; *E* 258)—for such personifying. But the very attention to those compositional processes that helps to justify such personifying supposes a composing subject whose identity now appears to be irrelevant, literally having been dispersed and transmuted into individual words: "The word has a spirit of its own, more expansive than the individual mind through which it speaks or is read. Like Jesus—the Divine Imagination, Blake would say—the word is the reality in the midst of us sent to reintegrate our fallen and disparate identities."[11]

The Word alone may or may not be that imaginative reality capable of reintegrating us. It remains the case that in spite of his rigorously poststructuralist (or potentially Christian) attention to the Word, Hilton's own reading of the "Introduction" evidences an inevitable return of the repressed subjects, speaker and poet—but not to *critical* view. Hilton later reads the poem carefully, but in terms of speaker and poet unproblematically: "The stern Bard confirms *his* own lack of faith and 'turning away,' as his voice introduces the *Songs of Experience* in a lament. . . . The powerful echoes of Jeremiah and Hosea blind us to the fact, which 'EARTH's Answer' reiterates, that it is the Bard . . . who has turned away to his own words to lament and mourn Earth's condition" (29). (Hilton says that the "fact" of the Bard's misunderstanding is corroborated by "Earth's Answer." I do not consider that poem here, because I would argue instead, as Rajan suggests [*Supplement of Reading* 229–30], that Earth is at least as problematic a source of unironized truth as the Bard; Earth may be a dramatized reader of the Bard's speech, but not therefore the most accurate one. Working out in detail such an argument would complicate in degree, but not in kind, my argument here.)[12] Also, shortly thereafter: "One of the prophet's duties is not to despair; but that, as Blake knew, is sometimes beyond human control. It is as if, in writing so many varied lamentations, Blake exorcises his doubts and despairs in order to hold on to a larger perspective" (34). We have returned to the simplification of the ironized speaker and omniscient, or at least ironizing, poet.

I am arguing here that we are incapable of reading words, at least words that make claims on us ("Hear the voice of the Bard!"), without attributing them to a human subject, however vaguely it is intuited. I am also arguing that this attribution does not necessarily assume a unified subject whose coherence is accessible to us outside of those words (an assumption equivalent to the intentional fallacy): to the extent that we construct that subject on the basis of the words, we may find a subject at least as decentered as it is centered (decentered even in formalist readings, as poet and speaker). Michel Foucault's claim that the question "What difference does it make who is speaking?" is or should be only a "stirring of an indifference" is a provocative attempt to pry us away from even that construction, it seems to me; to that extent it is a misleading ending to his otherwise profound contextualizing of the "author-function."[13]

Perhaps I have elided here a key distinction, between fallen readers and those able to respond to the Word without referring it to a human subject (however complex). Hilton's implied distinction finds some support in Robert Essick's argument that Blake deliberately "merg[es] authorial intention with the accidents of the medium" to reflect what Essick calls "performative" or "kerygmatic" language in his works: "The structure of this sign is not dyadic (signifier/signified) but triadic, requiring for its completion the signifier (physical gesture or sound), the signified (blessing), and the recipient believer whose condition is changed by his inclusion within the signifying process."[14] But later these "triadic interchanges" are "among author, text, and reader, as in the kerygmatic sign," with Blake's intention being the "creat[ion of] a hermeneutic community" (223). Once again, whether such a community is created or not, the reader is imagined as responding not to signs but to signs from another human subject.

Furthermore, Essick also concludes that "the proliferation of variety in colour and texture through multiple printings of the illuminated books," together with his "rhetorical versification" and "idiosyncratic punctuation that indicates vocal pauses and emphases," for Blake "insured an equivalent performative diversity" to that of the orator and reflects Blake's repeated textual emphasis on "the spoken word" (173–74). All of this suggests that Blake encourages his readers to imagine speakers for these utterances, even while at the same time complicating and even frustrating that imaginative act by some of the same strategies—in particular, multiple printings—that encourage it. (Here we should take note of Joseph Viscomi's convincing argument that the interpretive effects of multiple printings have been significantly overestimated. He demonstrates that "nearly all copies of illuminated books written by 1795 were produced either by 1795 or after 1818," that they were "not printed one at a time, a few a year, throughout [Blake's] life, but produced in highly concentrated periods," during each of which "color differences among edition copies were relatively minimal, the inevitable result of hand-coloring and coloring by two different hands. Coloring and printing variations among edition copies were not intended to alter the text or to make each copy a unique version of the book." "Such variations among copies of the same edition, then, do not represent a rethinking of the poem or page but a sensitivity to the generative powers of execution, to the logic of the tools, materials, and processes—and to the original contributions of an assistant.")[15]

Such frustration is related to different strategies, too—in particular, the allusive ambiguity I have emphasized earlier, and in W. J. T. Mitchell's words the frequent "independence of design from text," or "illustrations which do not illustrate." Indeed, my conclusion about the Bard's ambiguity in the text of the "Introduction" parallels closely Mitchell's about the Bard's ambiguity in the frontispiece of *Songs of Experience:* "The implication that the child on the Bard's head is Christ is certainly consistent with the symbolism of *Songs of Innocence and Experience,*" and yet a "darker reading of the winged child"—as the "burden of alienated consciousness which emerges in the state of Experience"—"is not really incompatible with our earlier association of the child with Christ; it serves rather as a way of complicating the image, and rendering what Blake saw as the ambiguity of the poet's relation to his own inspiration in the state of Experience."[16] Notice once again that Mitchell here envisions this ambiguity in terms of human subjects: however nonillustrative or independent the design may be of the text, like the text it encourages us to respond to a human subject.

All the generalizations cited earlier about the *Songs of Experience* imply that any ambiguity we might claim for that collection is only local and is overridden by Blake's ironic and total understanding of the limits of Experience. But Blake knew that ambiguity pervades Experience, and if he really does represent (and celebrate) diversity, we ought not to expect a stable irony in the *Songs of Experience,* an irony that always and consistently undercuts its speakers, an irony that in effect provides us an educational key to a rational analysis of the poems.

Instead, what Glen sees to be true in the "Introduction" to *Songs of Innocence* can apply also to all the poems in both collections: ambiguities in the poem's final stanza that become marks of our own interpretive uncertainties in reading the poems.[17]

> And I made a rural pen,
> And I stain'd the water clear,
> And I wrote my happy songs
> Every child may joy to hear.

The suggestion that writing supposes a cultural contamination of unmediated experience, even if writing is necessary to more permanent understanding, representation, and communication of experience than is afforded face to face; the suggestion that even the "happy songs" may or may not bring joy to children; and the omission of what they might bring to adults—all are insights we ought to apply to the *Songs of Experience* as well. We have been forced to recognize the ambiguities of Innocence because we readers are not Innocent, and because contextualizing Blake culturally and generically here, as Glen has done, shows that Blake knows well that his immediate audience (parents of children, not children) is not Innocent either. So we have come to see that "The Little Black Boy" and the "Chimney Sweeper," especially, both represent the imaginative visions of their speakers and also represent their social and cultural exploitation by an adult world. Neither cancels out the other, just as the clear pastoral of the Piper's song coexists with its cultural stain, as "that which is constantly changing and directly 'heard'" is "shap[ed]" "into fixed and visible form" (66).[18]

Applying this insight to the *Songs of Experience* might enable us to see that here too Blake knows that words, like their speakers, exist in the world of Experience; consequently the Bard's vision is both shaped and contaminated by his words, which include his ambiguous syntax and referents, and his Old and New Testament allusions. That is, the Bard—and every other speaker in (or reader of) the *Songs*—must imagine in the terms of his received culture, even if the speaker (or reader) wants to leave that culture behind. This is because we cannot master the language necessary to our imaginations. As M. M. Bakhtin puts it, "Language is not a neutral medium that passes freely and easily into the private property of the speaker's intentions; it is populated—overpopulated—with the intentions of others. Expropriating it, forcing it to submit to one's own intentions and accents, is a difficult and complicated process."[19] We need to add that this process of expropriation is not just difficult but impossible to complete, since language remains never wholly private, completely under one's control. For Blake, the main danger is passively accepting language, permeated with cultural meanings and "the intentions of others"; "the worst thing one can do with words," in George Orwell's final argument in "Politics and the English Language" (with which Blake would agree), "is to surrender to them." In particular, the "invasion of one's mind by ready-made phrases"—and by "ready-made" Orwell means "made by others"—"can only be prevented if one is constantly on guard against them, and every such phrase anaesthetizes a portion of one's brain."[20] In this sense Blake's struggle with "the stubborn structure of the Language" (*J* 36.59; *E* 183) is his struggle with system: each provides ready-made meanings all too easily naturalized into "reality." But it is also important to understand that Blake does not hold out an alternative, private language, free of accreted public meanings. In this sense Blake's struggle is *with* as well as *against* the stubborn structure of language.

Readers have rarely extended this understanding, that language shapes as it contaminates, to the Bard's "Introduction." (They have done so only locally, within the poem, where they have seen the ambiguity of "giv'n" in the poem's final stanza, without however explaining how that ambiguity might derive from the Bard: "The starry floor / The watry shore / Is giv'n thee till the break of day." Here "giv'n" suggests "gift" and "imposition"; the first accords with the Bard's vision as genuine, the second with it as deluded.) Nor have they often extended it to other poems of Experience, like "The Tyger" and "London," preferring instead to decide that each is or is not ironic, that the speaker of "The Tyger" is or is not intellectually deluded about divinity, that the speaker of "London" is or is not visionary. Edward Larrissy suggests that "to oscillate between two readings, one ironic and the other 'straight,' may be the fullest response one can have to these poems" (63). Such oscillation better fits the dual nature of language we have been discussing here than does either reading alone. Larrissy's reading of "London" in particular (42–55) is exemplary here. He adds that "This uncertainty [between "ironic" and "straight" readings] is pointed up by Blake's indecision about where to place some of the songs," referring to Blake's moving of four songs ("The Little Girl Lost," "The Little Girl Found," "The School Boy," and "The Voice of the Ancient Bard") from *Innocence* to *Experience* (63). Attributing these changes to such uncertainty does seem to make more sense than attributing them to mere confusion on Blake's part, or to lack of significance in the groupings, or to elaborate covering generalizations about *Innocence* versus *Experience*. Viscomi, however, argues that "the various plate orders of these copies of *Experience,* like in copies of *Innocence,* may reflect nothing more than Blake having collated copies of his books from various piles of impressions at different times—or with true indifference" (273).[21]

The importance of a reader-oriented reading of the "Introduction" to *Experience* is corroborated also if we understand Blake's reasoning underlying his well-known insistence on line over color in art—"the more distinct, sharp, and wirey the bounding line, the more perfect the work of art" (*E* 550)—and especially if we understand how, as Morris Eaves explains, that insistence differs from the coincidentally similar neoclassical preference for line.[22] In neoclassical aesthetics, "at its most superficial the argument about the primacy of line over color is an argument about the audience for art." "[L]ine is for an intelligent and educated elite" because it is "the language of the intellect" and thus "reveals the scientific truth underneath natural appearances" (11, 12, 15). "[C]olor has the sort of popular appeal that can sell a picture," because it is "the language of the senses" and thus is "associated with mere appearances and subjective impressions" (11, 12, 14). For Blake, however, line is the language of imagination: "Art is outline because mental forms are clearly defined when clearly imagined" (30). His emphasis on line in the *Songs,* when coupled with his focus on lower-class subjects—as subjects, not objects[23]—and a middle-class audience suggests not only his interest in their lives but his respect for their intellect and his hope for their potential to be educated. It does not indicate an appeal to an educated elite, while at the same time it does not indicate the pandering to popularity that Blake's theoretical remarks about color suggest is color's corollary.

In spite of the consistency of Blake's theoretical statements about the value of line over color, in his analysis of Blake's actual use of color Eaves suggests there is an "oppressive shadow-world of the state of experience . . . that seems to be the special province of certain [of Blake's] color prints, [a world that] may clarify itself in a lack of clarity. The clearest vision of experience may be a chiaroscurist vision that would not be clarified, only falsified, by . . . outline. It may be essential to see that the world of experience seen clearly is obscure" (42) and, I have been suggesting, radically ambiguous. Such ambiguity may be represented in two late but very different copies of the frontispiece to *Songs of Experience:* although both are highly colored, one emphasizes outline, while for the other, as Andrew Lincoln comments, "clarity and subtlety of line seem less important than the textured impression created by areas of dense colour."[24]

What Blake sees as this complex cultural significance of line and color he sometimes presents as a transcendentally ahistorical theory, finding the emphasis on color over line to be the same flaw in "Reynolds & Gainsborough," who "Blotted & Blurred," as in "Such Idiots as Rubens. Correggio & Titian" (*E* 636, 654). But it derives also from, in his words, "Having spent the Vigour of my Youth & Genius under the Opression of Sr Joshua & his Gang of Cunning Hired Knaves Without Employment" (*E* 636). That is, it derives from his professional existence as an engraver in an artworld where financial reward depended on aristocratic patronage—"The Rich Men of England form themselves into a Society. to Sell & Not to Buy Pictures" (*E* 642)—and the approval of the

Royal Academy. Such approval was unlikely to come from what Stewart Crehan analyzes as an "elitist, pro-royalist reaction against middle-class independence [and] artisan traditions," in which engravers "were excluded from membership,"[25] and "only Portrait Painting," emphasizing color over line, was "applauded & rewarded by the Rich & Great" (E 636).

Blake's interest in children's books as a possibly profitable alternative to such painting, like his emphasis on line, may thus be seen as deriving *both* from his educative beliefs *and* from the economic realities of his artworld. But for Blake, education is not simply a more complex form of the indoctrination implied by his eighteenth-century generic models, whose purpose was ultimately to instruct. By "more complex form" here I mean specifically that Blake does not seek to replace what he attacks as the father-priest-king system with his own, as outlined masterfully by Frye. For all the critical emphasis on Blake as prophet, there is a peculiar absence of emphasis on the complexity and even uncertainty of prophetic identity in Blake, and his understanding of it—an uncertainty overtly present in his antecedents, Milton and the biblical prophets.[26] To prophesy that "If you go on So / the result is So" (E 617), even if you believe yourself right, and even if you are proven right, does not provide you with a settled identity as omniscient prophet. Blake's letters are as full of struggle and depression as of prophetic confidence, and the coexistence of the two moods should lead us to one of two conclusions: either Blake was self-deluded in his claim to be a prophet, or we are mistaken in identifying "prophet" as transhistorical Genius. I am arguing that Blake deliberately idealizes the "prophet" only as a useful fiction and realizes it only as a problematic and complex, untranscendent characterization.

Despite some of his more confident pronouncements on the subject, no more in his poetry than in his letters did Blake confidently and unquestioningly assume the role of prophet: the entire epic *Milton* concerns explicitly the problematic nature of the prophet, and it may be worth noting that in that poem the most notoriously difficult part is the Bard's Song. Obscurity in a Blake poem may be a sign of its speaker's confusion rather than his prophetic insight—as Leader remarks, "Prophets, of course, despite their penchant for the declamatory mode, are notoriously obscure (think of Ezekiel and Isaiah), especially when, like the Bard, they are confused" (*Reading Blake's "Songs"* 157). Obscurity may also be a sign of *both*. Here, indeed, is the crux of my argument: Blake does not regard the prophet, any prophet, as transcendent. He aspires to full understanding, of himself and his world and his divinity, but aspiration is not achievement. Nor is it failure; we must recognize also that the Bard of Experience may be at the same time authentic and ironized by Blake. "Blake" here is not a figure for the deified poet in total formalist mastery of an ironized speaker, or for the deified poet identified with the fully authentic prophetic narrator; the poet ironizes his speaker while at the same time identifying with him. We do the same, when self-reflective at least, in our professional lives—when, for example, we present ourselves as understanding our texts, or our audience, in our scholarship or teaching, while recognizing limits to that understanding. (Here I mean something other than unself-conscious identification with or bad-faith posturing in the role of master.)

Even when readers admit such complex irony in the songs, their tendency is to privilege the opening poems and their speakers, as somehow outside the ironies of the songs they introduce; Glen may imply such privileging when she quotes the opening lines of the two poems as evidence that Blake's collection "makes a deeply serious claim for poetry as a dynamic and recreative mode of knowledge" (339). But on what basis can the Bard be removed from his world in this way? Other bards in Blake are not so removed—Los in *The Book of Urizen*, for example (whose attempt at self-removal contributes to the general mess in that poem), or Blake in *Milton*. Blake's other "introductions" to longer works characteristically frustrate the attempt to see in them keys to unlock the meanings of those works: "Thel's Motto" to *The Book of Thel*, for example, or "The Argument" to *The Marriage of Heaven and Hell*, or the "Preludium" to *America, A Prophecy* or to *The Book of Urizen*. (This characteristic also argues against unifying the *Songs* on the basis of a consistent viewpoint in each; such a unification assumes that if we can understand the Piper, or the Bard, we can understand all the poems in each collection.)

We should also ask, on what basis can Blake be removed from his poetic world, or Blake's poetic world from his social and cultural world? Readers have done one or the other frequently enough, either by invoking formalist aesthetics or by invoking Blake's own often-stated critical perspective on his cultural world. We ought to admit that doing so has provided a powerful perspective for interpreting Blake in this century, leading to formalist and symbolic-mythic insights that have helped us read his poetry.

More recently, historicist critics have begun objecting to such removal, reconsidering Blake and the other Romantic poets as, in Shelley's words, "creations of their age," not just as "creators."[27] This reconsideration ought to help us see poet-speaker relations in a different way than we have been able to do in the past; but so far I believe such critics have in fact not confronted formalist readings and have virtually ignored systematic readings, of which Frye's is exemplary, as mere Romantic constructs. These formalist and systematic readings have in common a belief that the poet is a creator, and the current critical refusal or inability to respond to either kind of reading seems based on the contrary belief that the subject is *only* a creation and not a creator—in Foucault's words, "Confronted by a power that is law, the subject who is constituted as subject—who is 'subjected'—is he who obeys."[28]

Here is one influential contemporary version of Shelley's insight. Of Blake, McGann writes,

> That his ideas and goals were partly mystified in themselves seems quite clear[;] crucial to th[is] historical meaning of Blake's work was his conviction, which he shared with every major poet of his age, that art is a nonideological agency. Of course Blake understood very well that imagination and poetry are human acts embedded in their times of conflicting vision and contested human interests. But he also, and contradictorily, believed that there could be—had to be—an originary Prophet of such Losses who would not be subject to those losses. . . . This idea—the Romantic Ideology of the Poet as Genius—is one of the last infirmities of those noble Romantic minds.
>
> It was, in addition, a mental infirmity which they themselves recognized— in others.[29]

We can agree with McGann and others that Genius, like other words, historically has been used for ideological purposes. This does not inevitably mean, however, that Genius is essentially or only an ideological concept, and our only authentic critical response to expose it as such. The important questions raised by McGann's argument, after that of whether belief in Genius is such an infirmity, are those we have been considering throughout this chapter: Did Blake believe wholeheartedly that he was an "originary Prophet" not subject to "conflicting vision and contested human interests"? Should we interpret his poetry as if he or his speakers—those not obviously ironized—were such prophets? (Also, should we assume that by doing so we become mirror-images of such prophets? What is our status as masterful interpreters of such masters?) In asking these questions again, we find ourselves encountering again the belief, shared by McGann and Frye in spite of their seemingly fundamental differences, in Blake as a systematizer. To Frye, Blake's system constitutes a profound understanding of the human condition, but to McGann, a profound misunderstanding. Neither takes seriously the possibility we have been exploring, that Blake's attitude toward his own system was complex (see Rajan, *Supplement of Reading* 197–274 for the best extended consideration of this complex attitude). For all the recent critical emphasis on Blake as a creation of his age, there is as striking an absence of emphasis on the complexity of subjectivity, and Blake's understanding of its relations to subjection, as there is absence of emphasis on the complexity of prophetic identity.

Probably we remember here Los's often-cited words, "I must Create a System, or be enslav'd by another Mans"; we should also remember, however, that shortly thereafter Los is described as "Striving with Systems to deliver Individuals from those Systems" (*J* 10.20, 11.5; *E* 153, 154). Larrissy initially argues that in these passages Blake means that "The 'system' must be a creation of the individual. Inherited systems are deadly, for by virtue of being inherited they represent 'imposition' without energy—deadly 'bound or outward circumference.'" "But," he continues, "Blake's texts reveal an uneasy awareness that such a notion is untenable. Their constant use of quotation, parody and derived terms lays bare their indebtedness and undermines the 'firm perswasion' of originality" (107–8).

Larrissy's continuation here suggests how we can read Blake in a critical relation to his own system (not only, as Frye shows us, to other systems). But Blake's use of inherited forms and conventions, cultural and specifically literary, does not seem to me "uneasy" or "anxious" (23), particularly when those forms are popular or somehow marginal—for example, ballad or nursery-song. It may be more anxious when he associates them with dominating cultural representations—for example, *Paradise Lost* or the Bible. (It is equally true, I suspect, that the anxiety may be ours; in either case, I do not know what would count as evidence here.) Viscomi has demonstrated the extent to which Blake's graphic practice too is inherited. "When Blake's innovations are defined technically and placed historically," he argues, "illuminated printing can be seen to share many of the aesthetic aims of techniques that were then becoming established precisely because they were meeting the demands of a commercial bourgeoisie. In other words, Blake was joining an argument—and endorsing, reinterpreting, and rejecting the ideological positions underlying that argument—rather than starting one" (172; see esp. 168–76).

Just as Blake is not, and does not see himself as, outside form—graphic, literary, cultural—or outside its potential duality of originality and inheritance, he is not, and does not see himself as, outside opposing readings. Clearly he believes in Christ-as-human and believes that God-as-father-priest-king is an oppressive mystification, but he does not achieve permanent freedom from the latter. That he understands aesthetic prejudices against his art in ideological terms—"The Mocker of Art is the Mocker of Jesus" (*E* 767)—does not free him from their effects, as his unhappy poem and comment to Thomas Butts attest:

O why was I born with a different face
Why was I not born like the rest of my race
When I look each one starts! when I speak I offend
Then I'm silent & passive & lose every Friend

> Then my verse I dishonour. My pictures despise
> My person degrade & my temper chastise
> And the pen is my terror. the pencil my shame
> All my Talents I bury, and Dead is my Fame
>
> I am either too low or too highly priz'd
> When Elate I am Envy'd, When Meek I'm despised
>
> This is but too just a Picture of my Present state I pray God to keep you
> & all men from it & to deliver me in his own good time. (*E* 733–34)[30]

Even more relevant is that his most heroic poetic character, Los, so frequently is in danger of becoming what he struggles against.[31]

So far, discussing the "Introduction" to the *Songs of Experience* has led us to see the ambiguity central to how we understand the Bard and to appreciate more deeply Blake's understanding of his audience as well as the relation of his artistic theory to his practice in this poem. How far has this analysis taken us in understanding the Bard's relation to Blake? I believe we can find a suggestion in Mark Reed's recommendation on how to read Wordsworth's central poem.

> *The Prelude* is not best read, as a poem, as presenting a speaker who claims secure possession of a redemptive imaginative vision, but who nonetheless undermines and gives a desperate look to his assertions by concurrent admissions of doubts and personal limitations. It is more properly read as an expression of the vision of a single, plainly not perfect, human mind that has been enabled to affirm its "Genius, Power, / Creation and Divinity" because of its firm knowledge of what the "mighty Mind" . . . that constantly possesses such a vision is. The speaker's conviction, in other words, is that his mind's growth has expressed and participated in the characteristic qualities of the self-realization of such a mind—not that it was identical with it.[32]

Only by understanding that there are limits to such participation, *for both speaker and poet*, can we see how readings—whether formalist, mythic, or historicist—of Blake's "Introduction" or of any Romantic poem can relate adequately to authorial intention, and vice versa. Without such understanding, we have only two ways of talking about the coming and going of irony, and both are inadequate. One, we build external contexts for its likely presence or absence—

for example, the Bard is deluded because his vision does not match Blake's system, or he is prophetic because it does match. Two, we assume either total control of the poet over that irony (the poet is aesthetically deified) or total lack of such control (the poet is exclusively subjected to forces of history, culture, desire). The first case is undermined if we do not accept a systematic Blake. The alternatives in the second case are disturbingly incompatible: one makes the poet omniscient and omnipotent; the other simply omits distinctions between poet and narrator-speaker, and so far it has been essentially incapable of incorporating formalist readings. (I omit here the unprincipled locating of irony, as for example when we identify Los with Blake until Los clearly does something wrong, at which point we say that Blake is ironizing Los.)

The deepest sort of irony, setting aside the irony that manifests its author or speaker's superior understanding, originates elsewhere, in the kind of intention implied in Reed's characterization of *The Prelude*'s speaker as poet, and poet as speaker. I mean an irony resulting from the author's awareness that his or her subjectivity inevitably includes both mastery and its limits, an awareness that "All individuals attain their subjectivity by mastering cultural and symbolic codes—and by being mastered in turn by the codes they acquire."[33] Understanding this reciprocal mastery leads to irony, since part of what we understand is that we are never fully in control of our meanings.[34]

Even if we attain such understanding, it is still more or less local. We may understand, for example, what I have just claimed about irony in the previous paragraph without understanding its implications for our reading of other texts, or for other parts of our lives. Likewise, Blake may understand that his own subjectivity, and that of his poems' speakers, is complex without responding adequately to complex subjectivity in other texts. His reading of the *Canterbury Tales*, for example, exhibits exactly the kind of simplification of character against which I have been arguing: the knight "is a true Hero, a good, great, and wise man"; the prioress "has certain peculiarities and little delicate affectations, not unbecoming in her, being accompanied with what is truly grand and really polite"; the monk "is a leader of the age, with certain humourous accompaniments in his character, that do not degrade, but render him an object of dignified mirth"; Chaucer observes others "as a master, as a father, and superior, who looks down on their little follies" (*E* 533–34). (Such simplification has its own history in Chaucer criticism, as in Romantic criticism; Blake's reading of Chaucer's characters is not unusual in that history.) Similarly, Blake may understand that the "mind-forg'd manacles" (*E* 27) of church, state, and art academy master and oppress their subjects, even though he may not always recognize all forms of such mastery. This is suggested by the tone of his description, in a letter to William Hayley, of the economic struggle between "Journeyman Printers" and "their Masters" in 1805: "The Journeyman Printers throughout London are at War with their Masters & are likely to get the better Each Party meet to consult against the other, nothing can be greater than the Violence on both sides Printing is suspended in London Except at private Presses. I hope this will become a source of Advantage to our Friend Seagrave" (*E* 764).[35]

I am suggesting, though, that Blake understands better than most of us the human condition as one of reciprocal, and therefore partial, mastery, and that such understanding does not transcend that condition to become itself a form of mastery. Blake provides an explicit example of what I mean in his comment on how he represents Time in his painting of the Last Judgment.

> The Greeks represent Chronos or Time as a very Aged Man this is Fable but the Real Vision of Time is in Eternal Youth I have however somewhat acco- modated my Figure of Time to the Common opinion as I myself am also infected with it & my Vision is also infected & I see Time Aged alas too much so (*E* 563)

Time as "Eternal Youth" is time as creative possibility: "Every Time less than a pulsation of the artery / Is equal in its period & value to Six Thousand Years. / For in this Period the Poets Work is Done" (*M* 28.62–29.1; *E* 127). But Blake is not asserting that he has permanent residence in such an eternity; *Milton* makes this explicit in presenting complex relations among Blake, Milton, and Los, "by mortals nam'd Time . . . / But they depict him bald & aged who is in eternal youth / All powerful . . . / He is the Spirit of Prophecy" (*M* 24.68–71; *E* 121). Blake is expressing his conceptual and creative disagreement with the "Com- mon opinion," and his partial subjection to the manacles of time as inexorable aging, *and* his clear awareness of that subjection—an awareness, we might notice, that permeates his letters (see for example *E* 706, 719–20, 756–57, 767, 775). Such awareness enables him to gain some psychic and aesthetic control of time, as his use of the verb "accommodate" implies. Although that control is limited, as Blake is painfully aware, applying it to the "Introduction" to *Experience* never- theless enables us to understand that the Bard not only can represent in his confusion and complexity the poet's own similar confusion and complexity but can also, at the same time, be a character created by the poet and whom the poet partly controls.

Evading this complexity is a temptation—and one to which we have often succumbed. When Hartman asks, "What is the status of Blake's system?" he suggests that perhaps we and not Blake are the origin of that system: "There is a remarkable surface to Blake. We are unable to grapple with that surface lest we drown or get lost in its dark and dangerous forest. We have therefore projected ourselves out of it, like Frye, and constructed a total form. Might it be better to do for a while without the idea of total form?"[36] This chapter implicitly has argued that the idea of total form is not necessarily a transcendental projection out of Blake's "surface," that total form, or system, is for Blake (and ought to be for us) not such a myth but a fiction, in Frank Kermode's sense: "Fictions can degenerate into myths whenever they are not consciously held to be fictive."[37] We should notice that Kermode's distinction depends on how we respond to what Hartman calls "form," not to its presence or absence or its particular shape. Even "total form," then, can be mythic or fictive. For Blake it is both necessary and fictive, and we can come to understand this, I have been suggesting, through encounters with his text that lead to a kind of impasse. That is, we come to understand that we cannot master the Bard's complex subjectivity, or Blake's— by attempting but failing to account for every textual detail, in the service of a masterful interpretive structure, our own "total form." We build that structure out of the textual details, but beyond a certain (unpredictable) point, it begins to break down; we reach an impasse when the details no longer fit even an ingeniously adapted structure. This formalist impasse is, I am arguing, a necessary one; bypassing it also bypasses, as I am trying to show in specific instances throughout this book, and as de Man has asserted on a more general level, "the existence and nature of the constitutive subject" ("Form and Intent" 32–33).

Similarly, the Bard attempts but fails to account for every textual detail in the Bible: he cannot fully merge the conflicting images of God the father-priest-king and God the forgiving Christ, and his syntactic confusion is one mark of their uneasy coexistence. Finally, while it is true that Blake deliberately presents the Bard struggling to master his conflicting cultural texts, that presentation does not free Blake from the same struggle; it only makes him more aware than his protagonist of what both are doing. The similarity can perhaps best be seen if we recall these two texts in juxtaposition:

The Greeks represent Chronos or Time as a very Aged Man this is Fable but the Real Vision of Time is in Eternal Youth I have however somewhat accomodated my Figure of Time to the Common opinion as I myself am also infected with it & my Vision is also infected & I see Time Aged alas too much so

Hear the voice of the Bard!
Who Present, Past, & Future sees

Whose ears have heard,
The Holy Word,
That walk'd among the ancient trees.

It is a struggle for many of us as readers of Blake's text not to envisage the Holy Word as God the Father, "a very Aged Man" walking in the Garden, so "infected" is our Vision with that Old Testament stereotype. It is a struggle for the Bard and for Blake as readers of their central cultural text. He *and* his visions, as he says, are similarly "infected."

2 *The Rime of the Ancient Mariner*

Distinguishing the Certain from the Uncertain

The issue of narrative point of view in Coleridge's *The Rime of the Ancient Mariner* has until fairly recently surfaced only intermittently as a problem for, rather than a solution to, reading the poem. This might seem odd, since although the poem's narrator is almost invisible, the gloss in the 1817 poem embodies the problem openly. It might seem even odder given formalism's sustained and principled interest in point of view. The most likely immediate cause is the influence of Robert Penn Warren's New Critical reading, which emphasized not point of view but unity in the poem, which unity Warren described in terms of Coleridge's philosophy of sacramental vision and his theory of the imagination.[1] This terminology invites an ideological analysis showing how Warren's Christian reading of the poem dominated other formalist responses in that it shared with much New Criticism the commitment to a unity that was a sometimes covertly displaced theological belief; the invitation has been taken up by Homer Brown and McGann, who in this way have explained persuasively Warren's importance and influence.[2]

But I want to emphasize for a theoretical purpose a remark Brown makes for an ideological one, that "Warren's explication of the poem consists of elucidation of the text by reference to Coleridge's critical and philosophical prose" (239). In effect, Brown's remark implies, Warren's reading was ideologically influential not so much because of its formalism but in spite of it. Warren stopped short of a rigorously formalist reading, in favor of one that sought to justify itself in terms of Coleridge's "own view of the world, his own values," which, despite Warren's disclaimer ("without regard to the question of the degree of self-consciousness on the part of the poet at any given moment of composition" [203–4]), remains not only an intentionalist reading but one that constructs Coleridge's intentions as unambiguous.

Unsurprisingly, Warren says the gloss is "a device for pointing at a central fact of the poem . . . that there is a spiritual order of universal love, the sacramental vision, and of imagination" (266). Equally unsurprisingly, deconstructive and historicist readers have denied Warren's "central fact," and in doing so they have suggested that any adequate reading of the gloss can derive only from deconstructive or historicist premises. I want to show instead that neither a formalist nor an intentionalist reading of the gloss in particular inevitably binds us to Warren's reading—a reading that amounts to saying of the poem what New Criticism tended to believe of all poetry, that, as Brooks put it, its poetic unity "lies in the unification of attitudes into a hierarchy subordinated to a total and governing attitude. In the unified poem, the poet has 'come to terms' with his experience" (*Well Wrought Urn* 207). Instead, a formalist reading shorn of Warren's (and Coleridge's) theology leads to what in the first chapter I called a formalist impasse, de Man's "unitarian criticism [that] finally becomes a criticism of ambiguity, an ironic reflection on the absence of the unity it had postulated" ("Form and Intent" 28), and in becoming so complements a more complex sense of intention than New Criticism ever articulated.

Contemporary readers of Coleridge's poem had no such need to justify its unity in quasi-theological terms, and they found, to their frequent dismay, little unity in any terms. Charles Lamb's remark that the poem is "fertile in unmeaning miracles" may well have represented their interpretive frustration. Later formalist readers often have tried to master such frustration by finding meaning in those miracles, but nevertheless they have remained generally ill at ease with the Neoplatonic beings and events attributable to them discussed most frequently in the gloss to Parts 5 and 6 of the poem, in which the Mariner loses consciousness and his ship returns mysteriously home. W. J. Bate comments that "while as a whole [the poem] is so open in what it includes and even more suggests, much of what the classical critic would call its 'machinery' seems deceptively closed and specific, virtually crying out for allegorical interpretation."[3] Humphrey House is troubled by the relationship between this machinery and the poem's "framework of ordinary Catholic theology," finding it "one of the hardest points in the poem to be clear or confident about"; he remarks that most of Parts 5 and 6 "do not seem at first sight to have quite the same coherence and point" as the other parts of the poem, because they contain apparently "'unmeaning marvels' and an elaborated supernatural machinery which dissipates concentration"—in other words, because they contain the Neoplatonic machinery that invites allegorical interpretation.[4]

It seems to me that in terms of both intention and poetic form this invitation is both deliberate and deceptive: that is, there are unmeaning miracles in the poem (for example, Parts 5 and 6 especially are resistant to interpretive mastery), and such miracles deceptively invite allegorical interpretation.[5] Nonetheless, as will be seen, certain modern readings of the poem (mistakenly) accept this invitation, albeit on another level, a psychoanalytic one, than that on which the invitation is offered. Careful consideration of psychoanalytic theory's relation to the poem highlights the illusory nature of the interpretive mastery that such allegorizing promises, and it results in a critique of the current claim that historicist method alone can free us from this illusion.

These conclusions can be reached only indirectly. Let us first return to Lamb's remark. I quoted him out of context: he was not characterizing the whole poem but rather one part—and by implication other parts—of the poem as first published in 1798. He was responding to Robert Southey's criticism that "Many of the stanzas are laboriously beautiful; but in connection they are absurd or unintelligible," specifically five stanzas early in Part 5.[6] Lamb wrote, "You have selected a passage fertile in unmeaning miracles, but have passed by fifty passages as miraculous as the miracles they celebrate."[7] In his thorough study of Coleridge's revisions of the poem, B. R. McElderry shows that this charge of unintelligibility was most frequently leveled against Parts 5 and 6 of the 1798 version of the poem and that most of the revisions between 1798 and 1800 were in response to this charge and were made in Parts 5 and 6.[8]

We have then a long history, which I have sketched out of sequence, of critical perplexity over Parts 5 and 6 of the poem and over the importance to the rest of the poem of the Neoplatonic machinery invoked in the gloss to those parts and elsewhere. Readers often have either remained perplexed or have concluded that the machinery, and much of Parts 5 and 6, are aesthetic flaws in the poem.[9] Coleridge himself tacitly admitted them to be flaws, so the argument goes, by adding the gloss between 1800 and 1817—the gloss being therefore his way of clarifying the poem's true meaning, unclearly realized in the earlier versions of the poem.

This argument is fundamentally wrong, on both intentionalist and formalist grounds. Only in the gloss are the Spirit and the two voices placed in a specifically Neoplatonic context and the Mariner's experience interpreted as, in part, a Neoplatonic allegory. Therefore, if we assume that the gloss clarifies the poem by interpreting correctly, we must suppose the poem's meaning to be at least partly Neoplatonic in a systematic, allegorical sense. This supposition cannot be justified. To understand why, we must begin by distinguishing between beliefs fundamental but not exclusive to Neoplatonism, and specifically Neoplatonic doctrine. By the first I mean especially its vision of the unity of all being and its sense of an invisible transcendent world, and by the second its esoteric tradition, especially dæmonology—specific and schematic knowledge of the invisible world. Coleridge himself consistently made the same distinction, throughout both the composition and subsequent revisions of *The Ancient Mariner*.

The well-known letter to John Thelwall asking him to buy various Neoplatonic works for Coleridge is often quoted as evidence of Coleridge's early Neoplatonic beliefs: "Metaphysics, & Poetry, & 'Facts of mind'—(i.e. Accounts of all the strange phantasms that ever possessed your philosophy-dreamers from Tauth [Thoth], the Egyptian to Taylor, the English Pagan,) are my darling Studies."[10] But "strange phantasms," "possess[ion]," "philosophy-dreamers," and "darling Studies" all imply a conscious exploitation of useful fictions, not an intellectual adherence to philosophical doctrine. I do not mean "exploitation" disparagingly; the point is that Coleridge consistently regarded such "strange phantasms" as affectively valuable rather than referentially true.[11] Even in the notebooks, where he was most willing to speculate and to "Try all things,"[12] he was usually careful to distinguish what he found valuable in such esoteric thought: that such thought "instead of lulling the Soul into an indolence of mere attention . . . rouses it to acts and energies of creative thought" (3:3935), thus "rendering the mind lofty and generous & *abile* by splendid Imaginations" (3:3820). He valued any philosophy that affected rightly human feelings. Consequently for him, in 1810 as well as in 1796, "One excellence of the Doctrine of Plato, or of the Plotino-platonic Philosophy, is that it never suffers, much less causes or even occasions, its Disciples to forget themselves, lost and scattered in sensible Objects disjoined or *as* disjoined from themselves." He opposed to this "the modern Philosophy" that "calls the mere understanding into exertion without exciting or wakening any interest, any tremulous feeling of the heart" (3:3935).

Coleridge thus continued to value Neoplatonism not for its referential knowledge but for its passages "that relate to the moral claims of our Nature," because they give to man "an inward opening, of a system congruous with his nature, & thence attracting it" (3:3935). This congruity of human nature with the nature of the invisible world, dear to Coleridge as well as the Neoplatonists, was however to him an affective congruity, as "opening" suggests, not one known to the human intellect. He was skeptical of such ability on the part of the intellect (3:3825), and he faulted Neoplatonism, ultimately, for its reliance on that ability: "Is it not true what has just suggested itself to me, that Pagan-plotinic Religion differs from the Christian, to the infinite advantage of the latter, *essentially*, in proceeding from the Intellect as from the Apex, downward to the *moral* Being—from the speculative to the practical Reason? Whereas Christianity . . . begins with the moral will, & ends with it, and regards the intellect altogether as *means* and aidences?" (3:3918). When Coleridge seems to have advocated Neoplatonism's claims to systematic knowledge of the invisible world, he characteristically presented such alleged knowledge as accessible only in such highly qualified, usually extraterrestrial contexts as the sun (2:2541), other planets (2:1555), or the state of impending death (1:186). This suggests in turn that such knowledge cannot be systematized accurately but instead will appear only as Coleridge described its appearance to "Enthusiast[s]," as "twilight Glimpses of awful Truths misapprehended by the unequal Intellect of the Beholder, & strangely mixed with the shapings of his own fancy" (3:3847). While Coleridge affirmed of this visible world both the existence of an underlying and ascending unity of being culminating in man and its accessibility to scientific understanding,[13] he remained carefully speculative concerning such a hierarchy above man in other visible worlds (2:2555) or in the invisible counterpart to our visible world (1:1000H).

Coleridge maintained consistently his attitude toward Neoplatonic dæmonology as a useful fiction. Therefore we cannot assert him to be a Neoplatonic true believer at the time either of the composition of *The Ancient Mariner* or of the addition of its gloss. To assert either alternative ignores not only this characteristic attitude but also the nature of Coleridge's revisions to, and later remarks about, the poem.

If we suppose such an unlikely doctrinal adherence on Coleridge's part at the time of the poem's composition, why did he fail to make such beliefs explicit in the 1800 version, in all revisions of which he seems to have responded to the charge of unintelligibility? Instead, he even omitted a long passage from Part 6 containing two stanzas supposed by one advocate of the poem's Neoplatonism to contain a crucial allusion to Taylor, the English Neoplatonist:

I turn'd my head in fear and dread,
And by the holy rood,
The bodies had advanc'd, and now
Before the mast they stood.

They lifted up their stiff right arms,
They held them strait and tight;
And each right-arm burnt like a torch,
A torch that's borne upright.
Their stony eye-balls glitter'd on
In the red and smoky light.[14]

J. B. Beer comments that "in Thomas Taylor's writings, the torch-bearer is identified as the interpreter of the mysteries. The Mariner has been initiated into the meaning of the central mystery of the universe," namely the "Platonic ideal," in which "all human beings are in communion with God and therefore in harmony with one another" (*Coleridge the Visionary* 163, 162). But such an ideal is not confined to Neoplatonism, and Coleridge's omission of these two stanzas suggests that he did not regard the passage as initiation into a central mystery.

If we suppose instead that Coleridge became aware of a specific Neoplatonic system in his poem only some time after writing it and revising it once, we also have to suppose of him an astonishing lack of understanding of his own poetry—a lack hardly likely, given the depth of his understanding of poetry in general and given his well-known remarks in the *Biographia Literaria*, contemporaneous with the final version of *The Ancient Mariner*, that in the poem "the incidents and agents were to be, in part at least, supernatural; and the excellence aimed at was to consist in the interesting of the affections by the dramatic truth of such emotions, as would naturally accompany such situations, supposing them real," thus "transfer[ring] from our inward nature a human interest and a semblance of truth sufficient to procure for these shadows of imagination that willing suspension of disbelief for the moment, which constitutes poetic faith."[15] Dramatic truth is not truth, and suspension of disbelief is not belief, in the systematic sense of the words that concerns us here. Finally, excepting the gloss, Coleridge's major revision of the poem between 1800 and 1817 is the dramatic context of the Mariner's storytelling, and as McElderry shows it "secure[s] in the final form a beautiful adjustment of the part of the Wedding Guest to the Mariner's recital of his tale" (86). The remarks in the *Biographia* and the late revisions of the verse text that accompany the addition of the gloss have in common a concern for affective value rather than for clarification of any Neoplatonic doctrinal message in the poem. Indeed the epigraph, one of these revisions, is explicitly skeptical of such doctrine.

Now, the Neoplatonic machinery in the gloss may seem intended to clarify the poem's meaning, since it appeals to the intellect, encouraging it to schematize the Mariner's world into what James Twitchell has called a "logically and rigorously organized system": "(God)—'My kind saint'—Seraphim—Undifferentiated angels—Ethereal dæmons—Polar Spirit—Albatross/Ancient Mariner" (114, 115). (Twitchell asserts Coleridge is "using this apparatus not for philosophical but for psychological reasons"—that is, "reverse [the scheme] and you have psychological layers" [115], which, however, he does not describe.) But we have found no evidence in Coleridge's comments either about Neoplatonism or about the poem, at any time, whether that of the initial composition of the poem or that of the addition of the gloss, to indicate that he had in mind a specific Neoplatonic message to be conveyed by the poem.

For this reason, and, even more importantly, for reasons internal to the final poem, we should look to the gloss as only one part of *The Ancient Mariner* rather than as a privileged, extra-poetic commentary on its meaning. First, if the gloss exists to clarify in Neoplatonic terms otherwise obscure passages, it does not do its job satisfactorily: we still do not know how the machinery introduced in the gloss fits into the poem. For example, in Part 5 the gloss reads, "The bodies of the ship's crew are inspired, and the ship moves on; But not by the souls of the men, nor by demons of earth or middle air, but by a blessed troop of angelic spirits, sent down by the invocation of the guardian saint." This passage introduces Neoplatonic lore but only gratuitously, denying its relevance. Instead, the gloss simply elaborates on the Mariner's own explanation, that "'Twas not those souls that fled in pain, / Which to their corses came again, / But a troop of spirits blest[.]" Second, as has often been observed and as the previous example shows, the gloss most often does not clarify obscure passages but only makes explicit what is at least clearly implicit in the verse text. Without it we might be forced to study the text carefully before concluding that the shipmates' morality is pragmatic or that the ship is at the equator when becalmed, for example, but it is not necessary for such conclusions.[16]

The gloss consistently makes explicit two levels of meaning, moral and geographical, examples of which I have just given. It also makes explicit a third, philosophical level of meaning when the verse text appears to invite it—and here we return to the Neoplatonic machinery. It is, granted, only at obscure points in the poem that this machinery is invoked as having explanatory power. But the verse text itself deliberately hints that such obscurity is intentional precisely where the gloss invokes Neoplatonic philosophy in greatest detail— at the end of Part 2 and at the end of Part 5.

In Part 2 the gloss confidently asserts that "A spirit had followed them; one of the invisible inhabitants of this planet, neither departed souls nor angels; concerning whom the learned Jew, Josephus, and the Platonic Constantinopolitan, Michael Psellus, may be consulted. They are very numerous, and there is no climate or element without one or more." The verse text gives little warrant for such confidence, however. The Mariner's experience itself is dreamlike in important ways, which makes the verse text at this point a kind of dream-within-a-dream, with a consequently enigmatic relationship to truth:

> And some in dreams assured were
> Of the spirit that plagued us so;
> Nine fathom deep he had followed us
> From the land of mist and snow.

The shipmates' interpretation of their dreams occurs almost immediately after their disastrous misinterpretation of waking experience—that is, their pragmatic justification of the Mariner's crime—which is hardly a context to inspire confidence in their interpretive abilities.

Both the gloss and the Mariner have such confidence, however, one result being that in Part 5 the Mariner is certain not only that it was this same Spirit "That made the ship to go," but that the Spirit was again "nine fathom deep." But Part 5, in which the Spirit is mentioned more frequently by the Mariner and the gloss than in any other part of the poem, opens with the Mariner uncertain about whether he is awake or asleep, and closes with the Mariner in a trance, a more explicit and elaborate dream-within-a-dream than in Part 2:

> How long in that same fit I lay,
> I have not to declare;
> But ere my living life returned,
> I heard, and in my soul discerned
> Two voices in the air.

The gloss confidently identifies the two voices as "The Polar Spirit's fellow demons, the invisible inhabitants of the element"; however, there is no evidence in the verse text for this identification—the Mariner is unconscious—and further, the identification does not clarify other difficult parts of the poem.

In short, the Neoplatonic machinery in the poem occurs in the glosses to those places in the verse text that appear most inexplicable; even more important, it is especially those places that call into question the validity of any allegorical interpretation, Neoplatonic or otherwise, of the Mariner's experience, by their insistence on the problematic relationship between dreaming and waking experience. This relationship is reflected in the equally uncertain relationship between the world of the Mariner's experience and the frame-world of hermits and wedding guests and weddings. Interpretive uncertainty thus not only includes the Neoplatonic elements in the poem but extends to the Catholic elements as well. We, as well as the Mariner and the gloss, have no more justification for concluding that "Mary Queen . . . sen[ds] the gentle sleep from Heaven, / That slid into [the Mariner's] soul," that the rain is sent "By grace of the holy Mother," that "a blessed troop of angelic spirits [is] sent down by the invocation of the guardian saint," or that the Spirit acts "in obedience to the angelic troop" than we do that there is a Neoplatonic Spirit or that the two voices are "The Polar Spirit's fellow demons." Although the poem does not question the reality of guilt and suffering, it does question the accessibility of such mysteries to systematic human understanding. The question becomes one of the relationship not between Neoplatonic and Catholic hierarchies but between felt reality and rational, allegorical interpretations of that reality, which within the poem take the form of Neoplatonic and Catholic hierarchies.

The addition of the gloss doubles and therefore obviously foregrounds this problem of interpretation, but the problem is central to all versions of the poem. Martin Wallen's deconstructive claim that Coleridge's revisions mean that the text "ceases to be a stable field of signification and instead becomes a restlessly wavering confluence of counter-references and cross-hatchings" seems, then, a false opposition: none of the versions is such a "stable field," since all of them embody interpretation as a problem rather than a solution; on the other hand, they have this problem in common and thus are not "restlessly wavering."[17] Jack Stillinger's more detailed and comprehensive description of the poem's "separate versions," of which there are "at least eighteen," stops short of Wallen's deconstruction, recognizing that "a dozen of these contain only minor distinctive differences." But he does conclude that "the earliest version," without the gloss, "is a relatively simple story of crime, punishment, and partial redemption; the latest version is an elaborate, multilayered narrative (or set of narratives) saturated with historical, social, moral, and theological significance, involving themes like the unity and sanctity of nature, original sin, social alienation and communion, fatalism, and the creative imagination" (60).[18] All these significances and themes seem present in all versions of the poem, if more complexly in the late versions. That is, Neoplatonic and Catholic hierarchies exist together only in versions with the gloss, from 1817 on. But even without the Neoplatonic gloss, the earlier versions of the poem, from 1798 until 1817, embody—

although not yet in the "doubled" form of 1817—the same problematic relationship between felt reality and allegorical mastery of that reality.

Rather than assuming that Coleridge carefully added a gloss that clarifies what is already clear and fails to clarify what is unclear, we can see the gloss as the record of the responses to the verse text of a character within the poem as a whole—that character being by definition the glossator. I do not intend to reconstruct his personality and cultural milieu, a task that has already been done,[19] but want to show briefly how attributing the gloss to the glossator rather than to Coleridge reflects the poem's essential concerns, which persist through its early and late versions.

One of these is the incommensurability of the Mariner's moral to his tale; it results from the incomplete success of the Mariner's attempt to understand his own experience. This gap between experience and understanding is emphasized when Coleridge presents a second character struggling with the same problem vicariously, namely the glossator, struggling to understand the Mariner's experience. The struggle is shown in part by the variety in the glossator's explanations: sometimes he is able to make geographical sense of the experience, sometimes moral sense; sometimes he attempts a Neoplatonic explanation. Once, in the most famous of the glosses, he responds by identifying unconsciously with the Mariner in the Mariner's awakening perception of beauty in nature: "In his loneliness and fixedness he yearneth toward the journeying Moon, and the stars that still sojourn, yet still move onward; and every where the blue sky belongs to them, and is their appointed rest, and their native country and their own natural homes, which they enter unannounced, as lords that are certainly expected and yet there is a silent joy at their arrival." This gloss, beautiful as it is, does not, and clearly is not intended to, explain obscurities and therefore can hardly be attributed to Coleridge's desire to make his poem more intelligible.

It is here especially that the gloss may be overdetermined, reflecting not only the character of the glossator but Coleridge's as well. Echoing the gloss, Lawrence Lipking makes the biographical parallel: "By the time that Coleridge wrote the gloss, his own early dream of presiding over a happy home had long been dead; his sojourns did not end with silent joy. Yet no one loves his native country so much as an exile. The serene distance of olden times, like the distance of the moon and stars, invests the gloss with an aura of unproblematical faith, of certain knowledge, that can pierce the heart of a reader less sure where he belongs." He adds, "Coleridge himself was such a reader" (618–19). But such a reader *is* "less sure" and thus reflects not only Coleridge's but the glossator's and our own unsatisfied desire for mastery—for "unproblematical faith," "certain knowledge."

With the partial exception of this more complicated gloss, the glossator's responses mirror—in kind if not always in the specific solutions offered—our own attempts to understand intellectually the Mariner's experience, just as the Wedding-Guest's responses mirror our own initial affective responses to the tale. The poem deliberately invites us, just as the Mariner's tale invited the glossator, to interpret it, especially its "unmeaning miracles." It is no sleight of hand, done to make the problem disappear, to say that the meaning of such miracles is that they are unmeaning—or, more precisely, that whatever meaning they have is inaccessible to the human mind.[20] This inaccessibility is emphasized by the many perspectives on the action in the poem: the Mariner's while he undergoes and retells the experience, the Mariner's retrospectively when "left . . . free" from the compulsion, the Wedding-Guest's, the glossator's. None of these figures interprets authoritatively. The only figure in the poem who might be supposed to have such authority is the narrator, and he is reticent, indeed mute on the subject.[21]

To conclude that the poem's miracles are unmeaning is not to conclude that the poem is unmeaning or that the miracles are anomalous flaws in an otherwise interpretable poem. The inaccessibility of their meaning to human understanding is presented in and by the poem, and it therefore rather than being anomalous is an integral part of its meaning.

This conclusion, that a fundamental mystery at the heart of human existence as it is presented in the poem "explains" the inexplicability of its machinery, is in fact explicit in the epigraph from Burnet that Coleridge added to the 1817 version. In translation, the epigraph begins: "I readily believe that there are more invisible than visible beings in the universe. But who will explain to us the family of all these? and the ranks and relationships and differences and functions of each one? What do they do? What regions do they inhabit? Human intelligence has always circled round knowledge of these matters, but has never attained it." *The Ancient Mariner* presents us with such circling on the part of the Mariner, and especially in its final version, by the example of the glossator, it deliberately invites us also to circle.

Up to now I have deliberately avoided McGann's reading of *The Ancient Mariner*, in spite of the fact that it is now widely regarded as the most significant contribution to our understanding of the poem since the formalist readings begun by Warren and best exemplified by House and Bate. Indeed, McGann's claim about *The Ancient Mariner* has become an article of faith for historicist study of all literary texts: "meaning, in a literary event, is a function not of 'the poem itself" but of the poem's historical relations with its readers and interpreters" (*Beauty of Inflections* 137–38). Elsewhere McGann puts his thesis less strongly: for example, "the preparation of a finished close reading [is] *not incompatible with an historical procedure*" (5; emphasis added). My argument here will corroborate this weaker thesis but will contest the binary opposition in the stronger one.

I have omitted any consideration until now of this stronger claim precisely because I want to have shown that the poem's meaning is not *exclusively* a function of the poem's historical relations with its readers, relations themselves not transparent but subject to the same desire for interpretive mastery I discuss throughout this book. McGann argues that an "analytic summary of the poem's interpretive tradition is necessary if we are to come to grips with the problem of the 'Rime' and its meaning" ("Ancient Mariner" 137); however, careful study of at least its modern tradition, beginning with Warren's reading in 1946, reveals a spectrum of more or less adequate readings, adequacy affected as much by this desire for mastery in particular readers as by their specific cultural influences or critical school.

Parenthetically, it is worth noticing here that there are differences within historicism as significant as those within New Criticism. The latter may, from our time's viewpoint, take on the uniform appearance of formalism, but as Warren among others objected at the time, "the 'New Critics,' who are so often referred to as a group, and at least are corralled together with the barbed wire of a label, are more remarkable for differences in fundamental principles than for anything they have in common."[22] Such differences among new historicists can be exemplified in the study of *The Ancient Mariner* by comparing McGann's historicism with those of Daniel Watkins and Patrick Keane.

For Watkins, "the poem's horror elements" must be "contextualize[d] (or historicize[d]) . . . in the same way that social and historical criticism has begun to explain the Gothic imagination, that is, as a displacement of the pressures and fears arising from the rapidly shifting social ground during the Romantic period." Watkins does not specify in Coleridge's poem the "very real and very accurate depictions of family life, religion, social class, political power, and so on" that he and others have located in Gothic fiction but makes only the more general claim that the poem's psychological power "is the *effect* of disintegrating social relations" as embodied in "religion . . . family and community."[23] It is hard to find what is historically specific about this claim; the poem seems instead evidence for a transhistorical (though not transcendent) truth, that "*All* social reality is precarious. *All* societies are constructions in the face of chaos. The constant possibility of anomic terror is actualized whenever the legitimations that obscure the precariousness are threatened or collapse."[24] What differentiates Watkins's historicism from McGann's here is the former's emphasis,

neither new nor exclusively historicist, that despite Coleridge's "desire for a ben-
evolent God who directed man in society toward universal goodness" (33), the
poem embodies "a view of society grounded in individual desire[,] . . . potentially vicious, for it promotes the private consumption of the world"; the disjunction is possible because "the poem is finally larger than Coleridge himself,
emerging from an array of historical and cultural crosscurrents that cannot be
reduced to authorial intention" (32).

Keane sees his own historicism as tentative, qualified by his "borderline bal-
ancing on the question of conscious authorial intent" and his rejection of "re-
ducing" the poem "to a proof-text for a predetermined . . . neohistoricist view
of textuality." He nevertheless follows Watkins's crosscurrents: "Given the chaotic universe of the poem, which seems rather more terrible than merciful, does
the saint-inspired blessing, as opposed to the initial aesthetic response, reflect
less love than fear—fear of the consequences of *not* blessing the snakes and then
seeking an orthodox imprimatur? If so, the blessing is the thematic prelude to
the poem's end, where, in the Mariner's fond vision of communal prayer, 'each
to his great Father bends.'"[25]

Keane shows that "The crucial images—of dungeon-grate, slave, underwater
convulsion, and spiritual or quietist benediction—are recurrent emblems in Coleridge's political lexicon, both in prose and in his millennial-apocalyptic poems
referring to international and domestic political events from 1789 to 1798" (7). To
this point, Keane's careful study of word-meanings amounts to exemplifying
W. K. Wimsatt Jr.'s observation in "The Intentional Fallacy," that "the meaning
of words is the history of words, and the biography of an author, his use of a
word, and the associations which the word had for *him,* are part of the word's
history and meaning."[26] There is no theoretical conflict here between Keane's
historicism and an adequately formalist or intentionalist reading of the poem—or
with a deconstructive one: "If an aporia *is* revealed by the Mariner's 'dungeon-
grate,' or by the simile of the 'slave' stilled 'before his lord,' it is the subversive gap
or slippage between the free and spiritually coherent cosmos Coleridge longs
for and the penitential nightmare world he fears" (210). Along with Frances Ferguson and Raimonda Modiano, I have shown earlier in this chapter that both a
careful formalist reading of the poem, and an adequately complex understanding
of intention, can and do admit such a gap; it remains "subversive" only of interpretations that find the Mariner's moral—and the glossator's espousal of that
moral —adequate to his experience. I have argued that neither the poem itself
nor the poet—nor, I shall argue later, the Mariner—finds it adequate. It may
well be true, then, for adequately formalist, intentionalist, deconstructive, and
historicist readings alike that "In blessing the snakes, the Mariner unconsciously
seeks reintegration into what he and Coleridge would like to believe is a benign

and coherent universe" (202). What Coleridge "would *like* to believe," however, is not an informing principle of interpretation for any of these readings. From this viewpoint, Keane's subsequent argument becomes no more than a possible biographical parallel, that "Political Coleridge—equally 'unaware' of his poetry of displacement and repressing his fear that the world may not be providential—may be seeking in the snake-blessing a 'loyalist' and 'quietist' accommodation with the local branch of the cosmic tyranny: the arbitrary and repressive Pitt government of 1798" (202–3). This would be a parallel, as Keane's own careful biographical study in effect implies elsewhere, that does not take into account the complexity of "the Coleridge of the 1790s, a man . . . capable of skepticism . . . about the 'one Life' and 'harmony' as well" (239). This Coleridge Keane contrasts with the later Coleridge "who, as harmonizing glossist in 1817, reconciles his own inner divisions by explaining, and occasionally explaining away, the jarrings and conflicts *un*reconciled in the 1798–1800 text of *The Rime of the Ancient Mariner*" (236). I have argued for the essential continuity of the poem's texts; if anything, the later texts foreground interpretive jarrings and conflicts.

To return to the question of the poem's critical history, for its study we might begin even earlier than Warren, with John Livingston Lowes, whose source-study has been as ignored as it has been admired, and whose interpretation of the poem has been equally ignored. Both eventually seemed irrelevant to later readers for whom, in Warren's response to Lowes, "in so far as the poem is truly the poet's, in so far as it ultimately expresses him, it involves his own view of the world, his own values" (Warren 203). But a rigorously poststructuralist reading of the poem, having marginalized "the poet," would thereby find itself closer to Lowes than to the poem's later New Critical readers, because in its detailed exposition of Coleridge's memory as associative, Lowes's source-study implies an authorial subject who is no more than an intertextual site and who consequently cannot master "his" poem in Warren's sense. Having split off the poem from the poet as a controller of its meanings, Lowes in effect has no reason to attempt the connection crucial for Warren, that "the statement that the poem does ultimately embody is thoroughly consistent with Coleridge's basic theological ["One Life"] and philosophical ["imagination"] views as given to us in sober prose" (Warren 203). Lowes is thus free to argue what Warren explicitly rejects but what returns as central to later psychoanalytic readings, that "the 'moral' of the poem" is irrelevant to its events, because "consequence and cause, *in terms of the world of reality*, are ridiculously incommensurable" and the Mariner's "punishment . . . palpably does not fit the crime."[27]

For Warren, and according to McGann for most of the poem's subsequent readers, this lack of fit is to be ignored because it is covered over by Coleridge himself in the gloss, "which," McGann asserts, "to this day most readers"—

"nearly all contemporary interpretations" ("Ancient Mariner" 140)—"take to represent at least one level of Coleridge's own interpretation of his poem" (138).[28] Coleridge's own intention, McGann continues, has been a controlling one. Even "Before we can take up the hermeneutical problem" of understanding the gloss and its relation to the verse text properly, argues McGann, "we must elucidate more clearly the historical significance of the textual events . . . the sorts of continuities which exist between the 'radical' Coleridge of the 1790s and the Sage of Highgate" (142–43). In other words, we cannot understand the poem without understanding how "the multiple points of view which are embedded in the total work" include, especially, "Coleridge's, or the contemporary author's— who operates in a determining way, controlling all the others" (142), and which McGann argues "represents Coleridge's special religious/symbolic theory of interpretation founded upon his own understanding of the Higher Critical analytic" (152), "his great theme of the One Life" (153). Without a proper historical understanding of Coleridge's own theory of interpretation, McGann concludes, we cannot understand the gloss.

But the misunderstanding of the gloss cited by McGann, whether or not it characterizes most modern readers, is not formalist. In seeking to locate the author's intentions by privileging one point of view within the poem, it is, as I have shown in the first part of this chapter, neither formalist nor even adequately intentionalist. At this point, then, McGann's theoretical argument would seem to be against a naive intentionalism rather than against limitations inherent in formalism.

I am not questioning McGann's claim that Coleridge's biblical scholarship significantly affected his creation of the poem's gloss; building on the work of E. S. Shaffer, McGann makes that connection persuasively.[29] I am questioning the theoretical consequence he draws from the connection, that ignorance of it—and of the poem's historical contexts more generally—inevitably works to coopt formalist readers into readings that are no more than "vehicles for recapitulating and objectifying the reader's particular ideological commitments" (157), commitments that McGann argues amount to Coleridge's own controlling religious intentions. While a "close reading," as I have intended the first part of this chapter to be, is in McGann's own words "not incompatible with an historical procedure" (*Beauty of Inflections* 5), such a procedure is not a necessary precondition for a close reading.[30]

The next part of this chapter agrees up to a point with McGann's assessment that a "general uniformity of approach to the poem's formal and thematic aspects is illustrated quite clearly in the various contemporary handbooks and student guides" (138, n. 10), which find the poem as a whole to be structurally and thematically coherent. But even as of the first publication of this assertion in 1981, those guides were not strictly speaking "contemporary," dating as they did from 1966 and 1969, and the subsequent readings McGann cites as representative and coopted by their neglect of the poem's history date from 1971 and 1973. By 1981, formalist and deconstructive readers alike—Sarah Dyck (1973), Ferguson (1977), Modiano (1977), and the complexly intentionalist Lipking (1977) —already had been denying to the gloss this privileged interpretive authority. To take into account such readings dramatically alters McGann's version of the critical history of the poem; it forces us to see that his claim—that any reading finding structural and thematic coherence in the poem is ultimately and necessarily coopted by "Coleridge's special religious/symbolic theory of interpretation," "his great theme of the One Life"—is yet another manifestation of our desire for mastery, in this case mastery over the poem's critical history.

Other readings within the poem's critical history that would complicate McGann's version of it are specifically psychoanalytic, and they generally ignore or deny the poem's structural and thematic coherence in favor of the apparent similarity of the Mariner's central experience—the telling of which takes up most of the poem—to dream experience, a similarity assumed as well by nonpsychoanalytic readings. But neither group has directed itself to the prior and investigable question of the precise relationship between poem and dream.[31] If we pay closer attention to this question, I believe we shall come to understand that psychoanalytic readers of the poem, in their desire for interpretive mastery, have succumbed—like McGann's formalists, albeit in a very different way, since they implicitly reject Coleridge's own "One Life" ideology—to its deceptive invitation to be allegorized. We shall also come to understand that McGann's reading of the poem is compatible with, but not a necessary historicist corrective to, a properly formalist or psychoanalytic reading. Finally, we shall be able better to understand the Mariner himself, especially the relationship between his moral and his experience.

Let me begin by recalling part of the poem's epigraph: "Human intelligence has always circled round knowledge of these matters, but has never attained it." Circling, however, for all its appropriateness to Freud's own relation to psychic truths, has not been congenial to interpreters who read this poem in his name, who find textual truth susceptible to being mastered. Instead of exploring what Freud himself finds problematic, the relationship between the latent and manifest content of dreams—which he calls the "dream-work" or "primary process," a relationship that in this chapter will turn out to be directly relevant to *The Ancient Mariner*—psychoanalytic readers of the poem mistakenly move straightforwardly through the *poem*'s "manifest content" to its "latent content."

To explain adequately how mistaken is this movement, I must here rehearse some basic psychoanalytic theory that for some time now interpreters have been taking for granted. The manifest content of *dreams* is made up of scraps of memories, both imagined and real: specifically, infantile fantasies and what Freud calls the "day's residues"—"indifferent refuse left over from the previous day." These scraps in turn make up the language of the manifest content, which Freud likens to a rebus or picture-puzzle. It cannot be overemphasized for our purposes that this puzzle, while meaningful, is rationally incoherent; before it makes sense it must be translated into the latent content, which is "entirely rational." But this latent content, the dream's "meaning," is accessible only through the dreamer's associations and the analyst's knowledge of dream symbolism and of the dreamer's personal life; "dream-interpretation . . . without reference to the dreamer's associations, would in the most favourable case remain a piece of unscientific virtuosity of very doubtful value."[32]

Apparent coherence in the manifest content is misleading: "for carrying out the work of interpretation . . . we should disregard the apparent coherence between a dream's constituents as an unessential illusion, and . . . we should trace back the origin of each of its elements on its own account." This apparent coherence is the result of "secondary revision," which "produces a complete misunderstanding" of the dream; "it remains an essential rule invariably to leave out of account the ostensible continuity of a dream as being of suspect origin, and to follow the same path back to the material of the dream-thoughts, no matter whether the dream itself is clear or confused" (*SE* 5:449, 500).

Now the "ostensible continuity" of the Mariner's experience is exactly what does make sense to all major nonpsychoanalytic interpreters of the poem, including those who regard the experience as dreamlike. They see this sense as moral in nature: James Boulger's comment that "the theme of wandering, punishment, and salvation [is] agreed upon by all major commentators on the poem" is accurate, so long as we realize that they do not all agree on the extent of the Mariner's salvation.[33] Even the reader whose interpretation is most at odds with Warren's classic formulation of this theme, Edward E. Bostetter—arguing that "the Mariner's pious moral becomes inescapably ironic" and accuses Warren of "imposing the moral laws of what Coleridge called the reflective faculty upon a universe of pure imagination" (71, 77)—finds the world of the poem to be a moral one. Bostetter argues that the poem "is not morally meaningful beyond our fears and desires," but he does not thereby conclude that it is morally meaningless: while the dice game "knocks out any attempt to impose a systematic philosophical or religious interpretation," there still exists a "primitive and savage . . . Old Testament morality of the avenging Jehovah" (77, 68, 69).

If the Mariner's account of his experience were truly dreamlike in its content, we should find in it at most an illusion of coherence, concealing only thinly the fact that the experience is composed of fragments of infantile fantasies and the day's residues. But the coherence that Lowes, Warren, and House find in the poem is demonstrably not the sort of surface coherence created by secondary revision in dreams. For example, Warren shows in the poem "the stages of the [Mariner's] redeeming process: first, the recognition of happiness and beauty; second, love; third, the blessing of the creatures; fourth, freedom from the spell. The sequence is important," because in it the two basic themes of the poem, "the theme of the sacramental vision and the theme of imagination[,] are fused" (244, 213). This sort of coherence permeates the poem and makes it intelligible not only narratively but thematically. The "apparent coherence" of a dream, however, leads dream interpretation to a dead end; the dream therefore "must be broken up into fragments" by "leav[ing] out of account [its] ostensible continuity," because that continuity is only ostensible. In this fundamental respect, then, the poem is not like a dream.

Existing psychoanalytic interpretation of the poem does not even consider this problem, however, but takes for granted the poem as a "conglomerate" of infantile fantasies and the day's residues. It seems difficult to ascribe such memories to the Mariner, a fictional character, with the result that such interpretation tends to ascribe them to Coleridge. There is an immediate, practical objection to this ascription: namely, the inaccessibility of either the day's residues or the infantile fantasies of the poet Coleridge. Both sorts of information are methodologically necessary to dream interpretation. In the case of most poems, this argument would be effective, since we rarely have the kind of day-to-day biographical record needed for such analysis. But in Coleridge's case the argument is weaker, since we have the extraordinary notebooks, which might serve as a kind of written record of a day's residues. Our knowledge of Coleridge's infantile fantasies would then be provided by the notebooks, by the existence of psychological problems in Coleridge's adult life that clearly are rooted in his early life, and by the attribution of the Mariner's experience to Coleridge's fantasy life (on the basis of Freud's assertion that such fantasies are universal).

But the universality of such fantasies does not make people alike in all other respects, and there is no compelling reason to believe the situation is different with respect to literary characters, assuming that we can endow them with infantile fantasies. It thus does not follow, even if the Mariner manifests characteristics of his creator, that Coleridge becomes the Mariner and that therefore the Mariner's experience is a fantasy in which Coleridge is the protagonist. Examples of this identification nonetheless abound. Mary Jane Lupton argues that since the Mariner desires sleep and since Coleridge suffered from insomnia, whatever else is true psychologically of one can be applied to the other: for example, "The pitcher, the buckets, the basin, the bowl, the sieve—these metaphors suggest the emptiness or fullness of the mother's breast, the success or failure of Coleridge's quest for oral gratification."[34] David Beres argues that since in the poem "the image of the mother appears as the Avenger, the Spectre-Woman, Life-in-Death, and as the forgiving 'Holy Mother' who brings rain and sleep," and since Coleridge's life reveals "His deep conflict [ambivalent hate-love] about his mother," the conjunction of the Mariner's killing of the albatross and Coleridge's "murderous wishes" against his mother means that in the poem "the Albatross is the symbol of the mother." The guilt of the Mariner is thus Coleridge's guilt, "his aggressive, murderous impulses against an object associated with food and protection."[35]

There have been several arguments against this interpretation in particular, and against psychoanalytic interpretation in general. But none of these arguments identify the fundamental problem in the kind of interpretation just cited, and as a result they are subject to psychoanalytic counterarguments. Lupton suggests that since Beres finds the albatross to be symbolic of Coleridge's mother, and since other psychoanalytic interpreters find it to be symbolic of his father or his sexual ambiguity, "the psychoanalytic interpretations begin to give the impression of so much inconclusive, 'unscientific bickering'" (150).[36] But the variety and number of symbolic substitutions for the albatross in these psychoanalytic readings of the poem do not invalidate a psychoanalytic approach, because in dreams they do not cancel each other out, since according to Freud dreams are "over-determined": "Associative paths lead from one element of the dream to several dream-thoughts [latent content], and from one dream-thought to several elements of the dream" (*SE* 4:284). This means that if the Mariner's experience were equivalent to a dream, the albatross might well be symbolic of the dreamer's mother and father, for example, so long as both the mother and father played intelligible roles in the fantasies constituting the latent content of the Mariner's experience. This also means that a single element of the latent content, the mother for example, might be present in the Mariner's experience in more than one form—the albatross, Life-in-Death, the water-snakes, "Mary Queen" of heaven.

The argument usually advanced against existing psychoanalytic interpretations of the poem is not that they differ from one another, however; it is, in

D. W. Harding's words, that "psychological doctrines [are] imported into the interpretation, the facts of the poem being racked to make them fit." Harding's argument against Beres is representative: he accuses Beres of ignoring the facts that, for example, the albatross "was a receiver, not a giver of food" (as the mother would be), that "the Albatross is referred to as 'him,'" and that "Coleridge's Albatross—as distinct from Beres's—is given a role much more like that of a child than a mother."[37] But if the Mariner's experience were essentially like a dream, the interpreter would be justified in ignoring its apparent meaning, so long as he thereby found meaningful latent content, since any meaning overtly present in the manifest content is, according to Freud, an "unessential illusion." Indeed, Freud specifically takes into account diametrically opposed manifest and latent content: "reversal, or turning a thing into its opposite, is one of the means of representation most favoured by the dream-work and one which is capable of employment in the most diverse direction" (*SE* 4:327).

Harding's conclusion is that "the dangers of the psychological approach . . . arise from a failure to give close enough attention to what precisely the poem says." Precision here "precludes the drawing out of remote meanings from one fragment of the poem without regard to the control exercised over it by the rest" (64). But such control, according to Freudian theory, is illusory on the level of the manifest content; it exists as a determinant of "remote meanings" only on the level of the latent content (whose relationship to the manifest content may not be at all apparent) and is itself determined only by the interpreter's knowledge of the dreamer's personal life, specifically the day's residues, and by his knowledge of dream symbolism. If the poem, like the manifest content of a dream, were not in itself meaningful, the interpreter would be fully justified in deconstructing the text as it appears, in order to reveal its underlying, perhaps multiple, meanings.

The weakness in the existing arguments against psychoanalytic interpretations of the poem, of which Harding's argument against Beres is the best example, is that—in spite of their reiterated accusation of reductionism—they do not lay bare the underlying assumption of such interpretations: that the poem, or the Mariner's experience within the poem, can be treated as a dream (whether the Mariner's or Coleridge's). This assumption is one, imprecise version of what de Man has called the essence of post-formalist interpretation: "a methodologically motivated attack on the notion that a literary or poetic consciousness is *in any way* a privileged consciousness, whose use of language can pretend to escape, *to some degree*, from the duplicity, the confusion, the untruth that we take for granted in the everyday use of language" ("Criticism and Crisis" 8–9). Emphasis added here underscores what de Man parenthesizes, and it is intended to highlight how de Man's own generalization gives rise to the kind of imprecision present in the psychoanalytic readings I have been discussing, by its implicit indiscriminate mingling of *all* language use as "everyday" and characterized by "duplicity," "confusion," and "untruth." Most existing psychoanalytic studies of poems take for granted the success of such an attack or are not even aware of the need for the attack. In the case of *The Ancient Mariner*, at least, the result is a consistent disregard of coherent meaning that exists in the poem. Warren and Bostetter, whatever their disagreements, accept coherence in the Mariner's experience as he tells it (of course not necessarily equivalent to whatever coherence the Mariner might see in it).

To reject the sort of psychoanalytic interpretation we have considered might be taken as a denial of the poem's psychological affect. Beres believes that the poem's affective appeal is due to its embodiment of Coleridge's fantasy life, whose appeal is explained by its universality: "it can only be because his conflicts and fears and hopes are not basically different from those of other men that the poem has for more than a century and a half continued to fascinate generations of readers" (97). But to reject the Mariner's experience as literally a dream, thereby rejecting the albatross-mother equation, for example, does not deprive the poem of its psychic verisimilitude or affect. Harding shows the way to an understanding of how the sort of psychic conflict Beres describes can be present in the poem without being present in the form of an infantile fantasy: "In that very general sense [the albatross] does possess an essential characteristic of the mother, in being a safeguard against the threat of loneliness, but it shares this characteristic with innumerable other forms of life, including children and pets who are really at the mercy of one's aggressive impulses in a way that the mother in reality is not. No doubt the value the Albatross represents is a value first experienced in the mother-child relation" (61).[38] Harding implies here what seems quite true—that the sort of spiritual isolation so powerfully felt by the Mariner stems genetically from the infant's sense of isolation from the mother (imago). The nature and meaning of Coleridge's sense of isolation early in life undoubtedly played a part in his creation of the isolated figure of the Mariner, but that early sense of isolation explains neither the isolation of the Mariner (which has philosophical and moral, as well as psychic, significance) nor even the meaning (though of course it may be a cause) of Coleridge's own "search for a unity with an all-powerful, all-good Being," which Beres equates with "the unconscious wish to be devoured" (115). Here, and in his analysis of the poem generally, Beres is replacing the isolation found in the poem, with its overtones of philosophical and religious import, with the closest analogue to it in the experience of the infant. Such a substitution would be justified only if adult experience were not only rooted in, but equivalent in meaning to, infantile experience, or if the poem were a dream. Neither equation is valid.

The best argument for equating poem and dream has not been used by psychoanalytic interpretation. It is that both the Mariner's account of his experience and dreams are similar in form and therefore must be similar in content. Although the conclusion to this argument is not true—and, we shall see, in any case does not follow logically from its reason—there remains the question of the extent to which the form of the Mariner's experience is truly dreamlike.

To answer it we must return to Freud's "dream-work" or "primary process." Freud hypothesizes that thinking is divisible into "primary" and "secondary" processes. The second is conscious and preconscious, and it corresponds to what is commonly called logical thinking. Its function in dreams is peripheral, being confined to "secondary revision." Primary process thinking, characteristic of dreams and of all fantasy, is unconscious and is characterized by "condensation," "displacement," "considerations of representability," "symbolism," and "over-determination." In condensation, a single idea becomes the focus of a number of unconscious meanings, or, conversely, a single unconscious meaning attaches itself to more than one idea. Displacement means the transference of psychic meaning from one idea to another that itself has no "logical" relationship to the first. Symbolism, as it occurs in dreams and fantasy, has in effect been the subject of our earlier discussion of dream content. Overdetermination here is a corollary to condensation.[39] Considerations of representability mean that "of the various subsidiary thoughts attached to the essential dream-thoughts, those will be preferred which admit of visual representation" and that can be "transformed into pictorial language" (SE 5:601, 344, 340).

Lowes's book throughout testifies to the omnipresence of such "pictorial language" in Coleridge's poem, but all these formal dream features are characteristic of the Mariner's account of his experience, and they have been dealt with by classic formalist studies of the poem—though not in psychoanalytic terms. For psychoanalytic interpretations, the form of the Mariner's account has been, by implication (for there is no explicit consideration of the subject), taken as no more than evidence that its content is fundamentally infantile; hence their continual genetic reduction of all experience in the poem to its closest infantile analogue.

It is true that Freud does seem to justify such reduction, because he explicitly links formal qualities of dreaming (the operations of the primary process) with the content of dreaming (infantile experience, "real" or fantasied): "dreaming is on the whole an example of regression to the dreamer's earliest condition, a revival of his childhood, of the instinctual impulses which dominated it and of the methods of expression which were then available to him." But Freud then makes a crucial distinction that psychoanalytic interpretations of *The Ancient Mariner* ignore, between "*temporal* regression, in so far as what is in question is a harking back to older psychical structures," and "*formal* regression, where primitive methods of expression and representation take the place of the usual ones" (*SE* 5:548; an additional form of regression, "*topographical*," is not directly relevant to my argument here, although it helps to understand the importance of pictorial language to considerations of representability). While Freud does not maintain the distinction he has just made — "All these three kinds of regression are, however, one at bottom and occur together as a rule; for what is older in time is more primitive in form and in psychical topography lies nearer to the perceptual end" — Pinchas Noy, in a comprehensive review and extension of primary process theory, argues convincingly for reestablishing it: "The fact that primary-process expression is always combined with a regression in many other aspects . . . is related only to the pathological situations of regression"; in "'normal' phenomena of regression, we are confronted with an isolated expression of primary processes in the formal sphere without any signs of regression in other aspects, such as infantile behaviour"; therefore, "we are really not justified in drawing inferences from clinical evidence and stating that any expression of primary processes constitutes a regression."[40]

If the primary process is indeed fundamentally different from and potentially independent of regressive content (Freud's "formal" and "temporal" regression), the best argument psychoanalytic critics have for disregarding coherence in the poem is wrong — that argument being that the regressive manner in which the Mariner describes his experience inevitably signals the exclusive presence of regressive content, and that therefore the philosophical, moral, and aesthetic coherence in the Mariner's account is illusory. Instead, the dreamlike qualities of the Mariner's account can be admitted as evidence of, and can be understood in terms of, the primary process, without thereby making the content of the experience identical with the latent content of dreams.

Existing psychoanalytic interpretation of *The Ancient Mariner* thus makes two causally related mistakes. First, it either ignores or regards as illusory the coherence of the poem, in spite of the fact that almost all important nonpsychoanalytic interpretation of the poem finds that coherence to be significant. Second, it assumes that the symbolic content of the poem, the existence of which much nonpsychoanalytic interpretation also admits, is infantile in nature, presumably on the basis that primary process thinking — characteristic both of dreams and of the Mariner's account of his experience — is regressive both in form and content (that is, the infantile content to which it is supposedly bound necessarily).

It makes this assumption in spite of the evidence both within and outside psy-choanalytic theory—namely, the existence of all cultural achievement that has primary process characteristics—that the primary process does not necessarily signal the presence of infantile, immature thinking or content of that thought but is "primitive" or "regressive" only in the sense that it is ontogenetically prior to the secondary process.

So far my examination has yielded explicitly only negative results, but im-portant positive results are implicit in its conclusions. First, at least some recent psychoanalytic theory itself corroborates much in the nonpsychoanalytic studies of Warren and House, for example, as well as in the psychological study of Harding, which is not specifically psychoanalytic: what psychoanalysis calls pri-mary process thinking can in art be nonregressively significant and evidence of mature mental functioning—a conclusion implicit in every interpretation of *The Ancient Mariner* that finds the Mariner's experience to be more than an elab-oration of infantile fantasy.

Second, a greater understanding of the functioning of the primary process in relation to the secondary process gives us insight into the character of the Mariner himself. Noy conjoins the two processes in the following way: "reality adaptation [the function of the secondary process] is dependent on maintain-ing self-continuity and sameness [the function of the primary process], while the healthy self has to be experienced as a part of the real world. Any disinte-gration between those two groups of processes disrupts normal activity and existence, and expresses itself in various pathological forms" (175).[41] We do not have to accept Noy's implied absolute distinction between "normal" and "pathological" here, because it assumes a mythical split between a perfectly stable and centered self in complete mastery of its world, and a wholly unstable and decentered self overwhelmed by its world. But we can see how far apart are the two processes in the Mariner, whose disintegration takes its most important form in the disjunction between his moral and his retelling of his experience, a disjunction reflected in Modiano's description of his "two modes of language," which "remain relatively distinct": a "language of the self" or "sensory lan-guage," "based on concrete perceptions of individual objects," and a "language of social discourse," based "on more abstract and conceptual interpretations of events" (51, 52, 53).

To anyone who is drawn into the Mariner's account of his experience, in-cluding the Mariner himself, the moral at the poem's end is at least insufficient. It seems insufficient to the Wedding-Guest and by implication to the narrator, who ends his story not with the moral but with the reaction of the Wedding-Guest:

He went like one that hath been stunned,
And is of sense forlorn:
A sadder and a wiser man,
He rose the morrow morn.

Especially given the emphasis on the uncertainty of human knowledge in the epigraph from Burnet, we must conclude that the ending of the poem contains similar uncertainty, even ambiguity, about the nature of the truth attained by the Wedding-Guest. He is now "sadder," suggesting not only a deprivation of "sense" (itself ambiguous) but a deprivation of consciousness—in part what has happened to the Mariner—because of a blow, the source of the blow more likely being the whole account than the moral.

But it does not follow from this insufficiency that, as Bostetter and others conclude, "In the lurid light of his tale the Mariner's pious moral becomes inescapably ironic" (70–71; see also Beverly Fields 84, 91, and Lupton 142). Among nonpsychoanalytic interpretations antedating deconstructive and new historicist readings, Bostetter's is one of two poles —Warren's being the other—around which other significant interpretations (of the verse text, not the gloss) have gathered: for example, A. M. Buchan and Paul Magnuson around Bostetter, House and Bate around Warren. A careful study of the Mariner's psychological state moves these two closer together, because it enables us to recognize the importance both of the Mariner's terror and his sense of the irrational, which Bostetter emphasizes, and of the Mariner's moral and its relevance to his sense (however unclear) of the existence of crime and punishment (if not salvation) in the central experience, which Warren emphasizes. The two are not incompatible, although most studies of the poem—and all the psychoanalytic ones except Leon Waldoff's—seem to regard them so. (In this respect House and Bate are notable exceptions.) Waldoff argues that the poem's "Oedipal fantasy" is "the psychological key" to the moral ("Quest for Father" 439), which is "an appropriate summation of the Mariner's experience" because "submissive love and reverence will enable a man to pray, see the will of his Father, and feel certain of his place in the universe. To defy the father is to be unwittingly cut off from one's identification with him; to love him and identify with him is to gain an identity" (450–51). But the Mariner does not gain an identity or feel certain of his place in the universe.

The moral is the Mariner's, not necessarily Coleridge's, the narrator's, the Wedding-Guest's, or ours—unless we choose to see it as an adequate, even perhaps mastering, interpretation of the experience. (The glossator does choose to do so, his gloss on the Mariner at this point in the poem reading "to teach, by his own example, love and reverence to all things that God made and loveth.")

The moral results from the Mariner's—and our—genuine attempt to un-derstand the moral implications of his experience. That this attempt is not wholly successful does not make it self-deceptive, unless we and the Mariner regard it as wholly successful, and unless we believe the frame-world of the poem to be less real than the world of the central experience. Bostetter—followed here by Magnuson and by the psychoanalytic studies considered earlier—believes this to be so, thus the title of his essay, "The Nightmare World of *The Ancient Mari-ner*," which implicitly equates the world of the Mariner's experience with the total world of the poem. "Nightmare" is in some respects well chosen, but just as the sensory and psychic intensity of a nightmare does not make that experi-ence more real than other psychic experience, including waking experience, so the nightmarish qualities of the Mariner's experience do not make that experi-ence totally supplant the world of the Wedding-Guest, or our world.[42]

Obviously our reactions, and the degrees of our self-deception, vary. It is less obvious that the Mariner's own reaction is equally complicated, inasmuch as he responds in significantly different ways to his own experience. This observation returns us to the insufficiency of the Mariner's moral: it is an insufficiency that he too feels deeply, although he does not understand his own feeling. The dis-junction between his experience and the moral he draws from it is a direct reflection of his psychic disintegration. In psychoanalytic terms, his primary and secondary processes are functioning not synthetically but in isolation from one another; in terms of Noy's formulation of the psychic significance of the two modes of thinking, the processes of self-integration and of encountering reality are split off from one another, a split resulting from the Mariner's genu-inely terrifying psychic experience.[43]

The Mariner attempts to heal this split and to restore his sense of self by assimilating that experience into the self. The degree to which he is successful is measured by the adequacy of his moral to that experience. Those readers who argue the moral's lack of integration in the poem on the basis of its inadequacy seem not to realize that the Mariner himself is unable to integrate his tale and his moral and that this inability is portrayed by and in the poem and is thus an essential part of it, rather than being a flaw of the poem—a flaw that such readers usually attribute to Coleridge's own psychological problems.[44]

The Mariner is partly successful: the moral is not wholly inadequate to the experience. It speaks directly to the crime that he committed and indicates his increased understanding of the nature of that crime. In addition, his general formulation of a moral truth that connects praying and loving and that con-nects apparently dissimilar realms of being—man, bird, and beast—indicates that he is now capable of seeing meaning below the immediate surface of life. He sees his isolation as spiritual as well as physical:

> this soul hath been
> Alone on a wide wide sea:
> So lonely 'twas, that God himself
> Scarce seemed there to be.

He is also now capable of comparative moral insight:

> O sweeter than the marriage-feast,
> 'Tis sweeter far to me,
> To walk together to the kirk
> With a goodly company!—

> To walk together to the kirk,
> And all together pray. . . .

It has been noticed that this moral comparison, along with the Mariner's tale itself, implies a spiritual wedding celebration supplanting the one to which the Wedding-Guest was going: "the closing lines of the poem focus upon the Guest who chooses not to attend the wedding feast after all. . . . We are left to surmise that the guest . . . has had a vision of the higher marriage of man to God's world. In rising a 'wiser' man, he comes to acquire something of the knowledge that the Mariner has gained."[45] But the Mariner is unaware of why he is choosing one over another. Nor is it clear that the Wedding-Guest "chooses" not to attend the marriage feast; instead, he is "like one that hath been stunned, / And is of sense forlorn"—that is, he has been affected powerfully in such a way that "turn[ing] from the bridegroom's door" seems an action not wholly under his conscious control. Watkins concludes that "the Wedding Guest's turning from the marriage celebration" constitutes a culmination of the "change" charted by the poem "from a view of society grounded in public exchange and sharing," exemplified by "the picture of happiness and strength in social solidarity . . . at the poem's beginning," "to a view of society grounded in individual desire," exemplified by "the Mariner and the Wedding Guest parting ways, each left to his own private existence" ("History as Demon" 32). The Mariner "is no longer an integral part of his community" but represents "individualism at its most vicious: it professes community and sharing while in reality pursuing only individual power" (31). But it is not at all clear that the Mariner *pursues* such power; it seems rather a by-product of his compulsive reenactment of his experience. The most prominent acts of "social solidarity" early in the poem appear to be the shipmates' self-serving interpretations of the albatross and their subsequent scapegoating of the Mariner. A benign social solidarity seems in this poem edenic, not historical.

The view of the Mariner's tale as a sacramental and universal analogue to the wedding celebration that the Guest misses has been criticized strongly by many readers—their central objection being that the Guest after all does miss it.[46] It is true that neither the Mariner nor the Guest can now enjoy the wedding. This does not mean, however, that they misunderstand everything about the Mariner's experience and its relevance to ordinary life. Such a complete misunderstanding would indeed make the moral irrelevant. But instead, their apparent inability to perceive "not . . . contrast between marriage and sacramental love, but one as image of the other" (Warren 255) reflects the incompleteness of their understanding. That the Mariner cannot enjoy the wedding celebration implies that he cannot see it as an analogue of his own "marriage" to the natural world, which in turn indicates that his marriage is incomplete, for he is still alienated from others (even though he sees himself as a teacher).

His social alienation in turn mirrors his own internal alienation. This psychic fragmentation is evident in his compulsive behavior with respect to the experience; he feels it to be something outside himself that takes possession of him:

Forthwith this frame of mine was wrenched
With a woeful agony,
Which forced me to begin my tale;
And then it left me free.

Since then, at an uncertain hour,
That agony returns:
And till my ghastly tale is told,
This heart within me burns.

He has no conscious or rational control over either the manner of his telling or the matter of which he tells; the Mariner as narrator is almost indistinguishable from the Mariner as participant. He seems to relive his experience with each telling; the "agony" remains unchanged. After the reliving, he feels himself left "free," and only then can he look retrospectively and rationally at the experience, draw a moral from it, and regard it as something he "teach[es]" to others. Were the moral a fully adequate representation to the Mariner himself of the value and meaning of his experience, it would indicate his assimilation of that experience. That assimilation has not occurred: the experience remains baffling, enigmatic, and most of all terrifying to him, although he may not always realize it. The best he has been able to do is the moral; but that moral and the tale itself result from separate states of mind, or two ways of looking at the experience, which remain, as does the Mariner's psyche, fragmented.

My argument here is closest to that of Boulger, who tries to adjudicate between Bostetter and Warren by arguing that a serious consideration of the nature of dreams is necessary to such a judgment and to understanding the poem: "Dream is not nightmare, nor is it sacramental vision."[47] But his identification of "dream" with the "primary imagination" prejudges the issue ontologically in favor of Warren. The identification only *seems* Coleridgean. The imagination "reveals itself in the balance or reconciliation of opposite or discordant qualities . . . a more than usual state of emotion, with more than usual order; judgement ever awake and steady self-possession, with enthusiasm and feeling profound or vehement" (*Biographia* 1:12). Therefore it cannot be understood as a faculty of the mind, as Bate, for example, rightly emphasizes (*Coleridge* 157–69), and it cannot be compared to such other faculties of mind as logical reasoning—a comparison at the center of Boulger's interpretation as well as Warren's. It seems to me that the mode of perception characteristic of the Mariner during his experience and its reliving is accurately described as "a more than usual state of emotion" *without* "more than usual order." This is not the Coleridgean imagination but the Freudian primary process.

Nevertheless, the poem implies value in alienation from self and others. The Mariner is made aware of a spiritual depth in life of which he was previously unaware, and the Guest too is "sadder and wiser." Warren attributes the source of this alienation to the imagination: "The imagination does not only bless, for even as it blesses it lays on a curse. Though the Mariner brings the word which is salvation, he cannot quite save himself. . . . The very gifts, the hypnotic eye, the 'strange power of speech,' set the Mariner apart" (257). But the hypnotic eye and power of speech seem more attributable to the compulsive manner in which the Mariner reenacts his experience than to the imagination. Also, the compulsive nature of this reenactment stems not from the imagination but, as we have seen, from the Mariner's inability to assimilate the experience, which in turn results from the fundamental shock to his sense of self brought about by his apparently motiveless malignity—and, more precisely, by his growing consciousness of the self that has been so overwhelmed. Forest Pyle argues that "Coleridge finds in the imagination both the condition of perception and social being *and* the principle of an *eventual* cohesion" but that imagination "does not *presume* the unity of either subject or [society]," and that in the former case, with Coleridge as the subject represented in his *Biographia Literaria,* "the imagination promises the coherence between the two subjects of narration (he who writes, he who gets written)"; "The imagination is what would allow Coleridge to make his life story, so full of the words and thoughts of others, his own."[48] We might find this equally true of the Mariner, who has yet to achieve such coherence in his own story and life; we might say that the Mariner is, both at the poem's end and its beginning, only at the beginning of that process, individually and socially.

It is thus self-consciousness, an important element in the workings of the imagination but not identical with it, that is both a blessing and a curse. This link between consciousness and sin is of course at least as old as Genesis, and its presence there is evidence that, as has been often noted, Coleridge's intent to write "an Epic Poem" on "The Origin of Evil" was partly realized in *The Ancient Mariner* (see *Notebooks* 1:161; Lamb, *Letters* 1:97). Here we are brought full circle, back to the critique of the psychoanalytic studies of the poem with which I began this section: the consciousness and guilt we see in the Mariner are not reducible ontogenetically to their analogues or ancestors in the infant, just as the isolation of the Mariner is not so reducible to the isolation experienced by the infant. The essential difference is not in the roles played by self-consciousness: in both the infant and the Mariner it is rudimentary (indeed a knowledgeable self-consciousness might have precluded his slaying of the albatross), and in both the growing into self-consciousness is painful but illuminating. What makes the two different is the nature of the self and world, and of their interaction, on which consciousness begins to work. The infant's self is embryonic, defined largely in terms of a very limited (to the mature adult) world of parents and "others." In the Mariner, however "immature" his sense of himself, that self possesses a greater complexity, because it exists and seeks to understand itself in terms of a more complex world, which still includes the world of the child but also includes "all things both great and small," as well as private and interpersonal acts of the self—prayer, killing an albatross, marriage, explaining one's life.

The preceding paragraph may seem pointless: few would argue that self-consciousness is regressive. But my argument applies equally to the role of primary process thinking as to self-consciousness in the poem: neither indicates regressive modes of behavior in the Mariner, and therefore neither justifies the search for infantile fantasy as the exclusive determiner of meaning in the poem. (The almost exclusive presence of primary process thinking in the Mariner while he tells and relives his experience shows, I have argued, his psychic fragmentation; still, such disintegration is not always regressive in its nature or infantile in its causes, as I have also argued.) In essence what we have learned in this examination of psychoanalytic theory and its relation to *The Ancient Mariner* is that such theory itself does not justify this sort of ontogenetic reduction, because the Mariner's account of his experience is demonstrably and significantly different from dream accounts, whose latent meaning is invariably an infantile fantasy. The similarity between the two lies in the presence of primary process thinking and in the fact that such thinking is concerned with the affective significance of the world as it impinges upon the self. But the contents of the Mariner's world, with which his primary process—and, at the end, his secondary process—is working, includes but goes beyond the world of the infant to become the world of irreducibly complex human meaning, a world with philosophical, religious, ethical, social, and aesthetic dimensions—as well as psychological.

3 *The Prelude*

Still Something to Pursue

Readers of Wordsworth's *Prelude* who interpret the Snowdon episode at
the poem's end generally agree that the narrator now believes he has
mastered what was earlier mysterious; they differ radically, however,
about whether that belief indicates the narrator's understanding or his
self-deception relative to his responses to earlier similar experiences, the
Stolen Boat episode in Book 1 and the Simplon Pass episode in Book 6.
Some readers find a mature, fully self-conscious and self-understanding
ego: Melvin Rader, for example, concludes that Wordsworth's "long
struggle to achieve psychic integration had culminated in a majestic but
precarious synthesis" ("precarious" here referring not to the synthesis
within the poem but to Wordsworth's later years). Others, including
those influenced by Hartman, find an ego in self-deceptive triumph over
a discontinuous and fragmented true subject: Thomas Weiskel, for example, claims that "The discontinuities that erupt in the central (but un-
characteristic) Simplon Pass passage are here almost programmatically
elided," in "the subsequent editorializing in which he turns experience
into emblem and takes possession." In a sustained critique of Hartman,
Charles Altieri argues that "Recurrence," as in the repeated mountain
scenes, "creates a center which gives meaning and purpose to the play
of differences. One still can not say who he is, but he can become secure
in the process that is his intellectual and emotional growth."[1]

I shall argue for such an essential continuity between the Stolen Boat and Snowdon episodes, a continuity that obviously also includes the Simplon Pass episode; I shall argue also that while the narrator does understand more fully at *The Prelude*'s end, like the poet he reaches limits to that understanding, limits that he acknowledges consciously. ("Wordsworth" and "the narrator" become one here for all readers, explicitly or implicitly, since whatever their disagreements they agree that the narrator's understanding—or misunderstanding—at the poem's end, if not at its beginning, matches the poet's. Reed, in his rigorous separation of the two, puts it this way: "The point of view from which the speaker's mind recounts its own growth is the condition of imaginative vision toward which his mind's growth was tending"—namely, that of "the poet" ["Speaker of *The Prelude*" 280; see esp. 289, 291–92].)

As we have seen already, in reading Blake's "Introduction" to *Songs of Experience*, this fundamental disagreement about understanding versus self-deception is not confined to recent Wordsworthian interpretation alone. How we understand all Romantic poetry on this issue depends on where we locate the Romantic subject in relation to the ego. M. H. Abrams has masterfully presented a view that until poststructuralist criticism was a consensus, one that conflated the two by identifying the mature subject with consciousness: for the Romantics, he argues, "The mind of man . . . develops through successive stages of division, conflict, and reconciliation, toward the culminating stage at which *all* opposites having been overcome, it will achieve a *full* and *triumphant* awareness of its identity" (*Natural Supernaturalism* 188; emphasis added). Abrams's recognition that this final "self-unity . . . can never be completely attained" (215) rarely affects his central argument, which, with a confidence akin to that of its manifesto, Wordsworth's own Prospectus to *The Recluse*, in effect subsumes the fundamental anxieties of Coleridge's "Frost at Midnight," the elegiac tone of "Tintern Abbey," and the uncertainties of *The Prelude*, to an "exemplary lyric form" in which "the interchange between [the] mind and nature constitutes the entire poem, which usually poses and *resolves* a spiritual crisis" (92; emphasis added). This virtual identification of subject and ego has been challenged more recently by critics like McGann, for whom "The idea that poetry, or even consciousness, can set one free of the ruins of history and culture in general is the grand illusion of every Romantic poet."[2] McGann may be right when he goes on to claim that "This idea continues as one of the most important shibboleths of our culture," but he mislocates its origins in the Romantic poets, who more often than some of their critics see and present this illusion as a fantasy.

The Prelude specifically considers the fully self-knowing and fully imaginative subject an attractive fantasy of omnipotence. It is ironic, then, that readers' interpretive rhetoric so often has assumed mastery of this text when they have

stopped short of its truth and Wordsworth's own understanding of that truth—
especially in the central scenes about mastery, the Stolen Boat episode in Book
I and the Snowdon episode in Book 13.

In this century, psychoanalysis appears more able than any previous interpretive theory to articulate subjectivity; it is thus supposed to be more advanced
than a nontheoretical text such as *The Prelude* that shares the same explicit interest in subjectivity. I hope to show plainly just how far such theory does and does
not go down the text's own path toward the origin of meaning and interpretation. This is a reservation about psychoanalytic interpretation I share with
Catherine Belsey, who remarks critically that in actual practice "this criticism
which repudiates the possibility of a metalanguage, psychoanalysis[,] tends to
be introduced precisely as if it were such a metalanguage, a 'discovery' which
enables us to define the essential structures of subjectivity across history." She
briefly considers *The Prelude,* and the Stolen Boat episode in particular, in terms
of a psychoanalysis that "offers a model of subjectivity which radically undermines [both] the concept of consciousness as the origin and determinant of meaning and of history [and] the concept of the author or reader as the origin and
determinant of the meaning of the text"; nonetheless, our readings take us to
very different conclusions about human subjectivity, as I shall discuss later.[3]

Psychoanalytic readers of *The Prelude,* and of the Stolen Boat episode in particular, like Hartman and McGann, distinguish sharply between Wordsworth's
conscious ego and his real subjectivity. Richard Onorato, in the best example
of such interpretation based on classical psychoanalytic theory, argues that in
that episode, "Despite his explanation of Nature's intentions, Wordsworth has
unconsciously recollected and characterized a striking Oedipal experience."
"Guilt in this kind of symbolically enacted sexual fantasy derives from . . . a
psychic confrontation with the paternal Presence," of which "The 'huge cliff'
that stands towering over the boy is . . . an unconscious projection. . . . The boy,
his pride in manliness cast down, is a guilty child; he meekly renounces his . . .
desire to possess . . . what belongs to another man."[4] Onorato's subtle remark
that "surely I was led by her"[5] implies that "as in the Oedipus complex, Nature,
like the permissive mother who has 'led' him, has also seemed to summon the
absent father" (273)—an absence suggested by Wordsworth's presentation of
the "huge and mighty Forms" as "*not* liv[ing] / Like living men" (1.426–27;
emphasis added).

Onorato's argument seems to explain elements in the episode that had
not been explicable by historical interpretations, whether constructed from

Wordsworth's own remarks about the imagination or from eighteenth-century discussions of the aesthetics of the sublime. The "stealth and troubled pleasure" and the boy's pride are anomalous emotions, and there are details—the repeated "struck the oars and struck again" (386, 409), the "huge Cliff" that "like a living thing, / Strode after me" (410, 412–13)—that in different ways disconnect the scene from both. The first detail suggests aggression; the second goes beyond metaphor as a component of the imagination, and beyond fear or terror as a component of the sublime, to the boy's obscure sense of impending punishment.

Onorato's reading of the scene thus claims greater explanatory power than readings based on eighteenth-century theories of the sublime, and greater than those based on what we might suppose to be Wordsworth's own understanding of the scene—a claim evidenced in the persistent tendency of psychoanalytic readings to insist on how unaware Wordsworth is of what they find: "If the frightening confrontation in the climax of the Oedipus complex is a psychic ritual of growth necessary to manhood and to man's likeness to other men, then in his poetic intention to seek the latent meaning of his life, Wordsworth was *unconsciously* seeking to free himself from his *obsession* with the mother and from the very bondage to Nature he was celebrating" (Onorato 274–75; emphasis added). But what is explained when we reach terms such as "paternal Presence," "the absent father," "the permissive mother," "psychic ritual of growth," and "manhood"? This question applies also to subsequent psychoanalytic readings of the Stolen Boat episode, the most detailed being that of David Collings. Despite his subtitle, "The Poetics of Cultural Dismemberment," text and cultural analysis seem subordinate to psychoanalysis throughout his argument, just as "poetics" and "cultural dismemberment" are distinctly subordinated to "masochistic fantasy" in his reading of the Stolen Boat episode: an "act [that] has less to do with genital sexuality than with an anxious, masochistic fantasy." In that fantasy "Wordsworth conflates murder and sex, oedipal violence and anal intercourse, as if being stabbed, castrated, and penetrated are versions of the same event that demonstrates beyond doubt the father's vengeful love."[6]

I shall argue here that Onorato's and Collings's terminology, like the eighteenth-century terminology of the "sublime" and the "beautiful," does not provide an interpretive mastery of Wordsworth's poem and does not represent limits beyond which interpretation cannot go. Timothy Bahti likewise argues that the metaphoric or figurative language of that episode—and his complex reading of the Stolen Boat episode demonstrates convincingly the omnipresence of figuration there—is not finally reducible to or mastered by psychoanalytic language.[7] But in arguing for the primacy of figuration itself and against the primacy of any other level of interpretation, he denies "a *self* whose consciousness would then be found in some relation to figural language; rather, structures of language would be the condition of possibility—if that—for the self and its faculties of consciousness" (99).[8] Although we agree that the Wordsworthian self is not independent of figurative language (and cannot master that language), I do not believe it necessarily follows that "Wordsworth" cannot be located in some nonderivative relation to figurative language, an argument made later in this chapter in relation to Miller.

Here my argument depends first on seeing how psychoanalytic theory itself does and does not warrant taking its own terms as absolutes. The classical description of the Oedipus complex depends on a vocabulary drawn from adult experience: in Freud's words, it is "Being in love with the one parent and hating the other," "direct[ing] our first sexual impulse toward our mother and our first hatred and our first murderous wish against our father" (SE 4:260, 262). However, words like "being in love with," "hating," "sexual impulse," and "murderous wish" do not have identical meanings for the child and the adult. Parricide and incest are what Oedipus commits; they are not what the infant desires, except figuratively. Aggression toward the father and desire for his absence, to have the mother to itself, are truer ways of putting this desire. The infant has no adult concept of parricide or incest; it has some notion (not conceptual, not articulate) of absence and presence, and of sensual satisfaction. As Freud elsewhere is careful to argue, "a child's idea of being 'dead' has nothing much in common with ours apart from the word"; "the child has learnt [only] one thing by experience [so far]—namely that 'dead' people . . . are always away and never come back" (SE 4:254, 258).

What the infant desires can be understood only when we recognize the metaphoric or figurative role of "mother" and "father"; this is why psychoanalysis sometimes speaks of mother and father "figures" or "imagos": human figures who play cultural as well as natural, biological roles for that infant. In moving from nature to culture, we are not transcending body and nature, since the infant's bodily experience of the "imago" and of itself are central to the infant; we are moving away from body and nature as givens of meaning. Rather than taking the words naturally or absolutely, as origins of meaning, we must look at psychoanalytic descriptions of the mother and father "figures" to see what they mean to the infant. (We speak of "figure" instead of "imago" because the latter suggests that the infant's internal world is filled with images only and does not suggest that world's metaphoric depth, for which I shall argue later.) We find "mother" used for the human context that is not only nurturing (hence the usual connection with the biological mother) but symbiotic—to the extent that the "mother"-infant relation seems sufficient to both, a dyadic relation that for the infant constitutes an uninterrupted cycle of need and gratification of need (to be fed, to be held, to be warm). We find "father" used for the third term that interrupts this cycle, "the world out there" personified, outside the symbiosis, to which the "mother" turns and in which "she" by definition lives when not satisfying the infant's needs (though the infant is nevertheless experiencing those needs). Consequently, Lacan identifies the "father" with the Law, as something outside the self of the infant (or child, or adult) that cannot be shaped by the self's desire but remains unalterable. Also, he identifies this "father" with "the Name of the Father," because this "father" is a name, a metaphor that stands for something in the nature of the world that the infant does not have but wants—the power to be at one with its world symbiotically.[9]

"Mother" is also metaphoric, in the same sense I have allegorized "father," as well as in a different sense—in that the infant does not need metaphoric capability to experience the "mother's" presence, since by definition such presence consists in gratification of need. The infant is not forced to make metaphors, to make sense of a world that does not frustrate it. There is no cause for interpretation.[10] The metaphoric character of both terms here helps to explain why Wordsworth can imagine nature as alternately masculine and feminine (in eighteenth-century aesthetics, the sublime and the beautiful). I would argue that the reverse is equally true: Wordsworth's shifting imagery helps to explain the terms' masculine/feminine metaphoric character. It is this metaphoric character, it seems to me, that enables Mary Jacobus to read the Snowdon episode in terms of a "maternal Sublime" rather than Weiskel's Oedipal Sublime, but with similar conclusions about Wordsworthian subjectivity. "The view from Mount Snowdon images the source of all signification, all images; Wordsworth terms it nature, but Kristeva would call it the pre-Oedipal, the soul that nature lodges in the abyss, corresponding to the earliest, most fragile sense of self." "Her account of the Oedipal as the overlay of an already triangulated pre-Oedipal elaborates a structure which might be called not simply the natural Sublime, but (doubly naturalized) the maternal Sublime."[11]

Lacan has gone farther than Onorato, in that he is aware that "father" is itself metaphorical and therefore subject to further interpretation. Like classical psychoanalysts, however, Lacan elsewhere stops short of this metaphoric awareness, and in doing so he implies prematurely both a mastery of his subject and an end to its interpretation.

To see this similarity, and to understand sufficiently what psychoanalysis does and does not contribute to our understanding of subjectivity here, we must study in some detail Freud's well-known account and interpretation of the child's "fort-da" game, and Lacan's own subsequent interpretation of the game as well. For both of them, as for Wordsworth in the Stolen Boat episode, the child's meta-phoric power and mastery of its own subjectivity are the central issues. To deal with the frustrating absence of his mother, says Freud, the child throws a spool out of sight and then retrieves it, while uttering the sounds "fort" (gone) and "da" (there) to indicate its absence and then presence. To Freud the game is overdeter-mined, in that it suggests a compulsion to repeat a frustrating experience as well as an attempt to master it (*SE* 18:14–16). Lacan proposes an additional signifi-cance: "the moment in which desire becomes human is also that in which the child is born into language" (*Ecrits* 103). "Desire becomes human." That is, for the child the spool now symbolizes the mother, and the mother is therefore no longer present, so "the symbol manifests itself first of all in the murder of the thing [mother, in this case]." Further, "this death [absence] constitutes in the subject [the child] the eternalization of his desire" (104), because that desire, now focused on symbols, can never be fulfilled.[12] "The child is born into lan-guage." That is, the child in "mastering his privation" begins to use words met-aphorically (fort/absence); in so doing, the child also becomes used by language, that is, subjected to (while, in his pleasure at his game, apparently making use of) the endless metaphoricity of language. "Confronted by a power that is law, the subject who is constituted as subject—who is 'subjected'—is he who obeys."[13]

But in the fort-da game, we do not see what its representations by Freud and Lacan imply: the origin of meaning, a progression from passivity to activity, from literal to metaphoric capability. Instead we see the child already capable of metaphor—perhaps most importantly in what Freud's and Lacan's accounts seem to take for granted, that the child is playing what is already a game for him. (They also seem uninterested in how the child learned the game, and in how he got the spool.) He takes pleasure in the metaphoricity of his activity, its status as game, and his pleasure is not derived from merely one part of it, the symbol-ized return of the mother. To go even farther: it is hard to see why the child's use of language marks his entry into metaphoric capability, since the child's vocalizing of fort-da is only one of two metaphoric acts he manifests, the other being his "staging the disappearance and return of the objects within his reach." The child is indeed staging, rather than being an obsessive role-player, just as the child is not controlled by the spool-as-mother: "If, for the child, the spool is a signifier of the mother's body, it does not cease, for all that, to be what it was: a spool."[14] In his creation of the game, the child manifests, not only to others but to himself, desire as a fact of his life, with which he tries to cope in the game. To "cope with" does not mean to master. The child does not master need-frustration by his game. He does gain some control over it, but only temporarily. The impor-tant point is that the child can imagine power over frustration, and he can take pleasure in such imagining because he does not literalize his game.

To interpret the fort-da game, then, solely as the child's attempt to master, however overdetermined the mastery, is to suppose the subject acts only out of its fantasy of omnipotence, of being in control (of its own hands, of its mother's absence, of its own anxiety). But the child's pleasure in his game can derive from his self-awareness as an active being without equating activity with attempted mastery, as Freud and Lacan seem to suggest in their interpretations. The more the subject grows up and comes to terms with its own desire, the more it comes to see and accept that achieving such mastery is, in the nature of the self and the world, impossible, except in fantasy.

Lacan sees this fantasy reflected more clearly and earlier than in the fort-da game, in the mirror stage: the infant's jubilation at its own image (whether in a literal mirror or a metaphoric one—the face of another, especially the "mother") implies both its prematurity and its desire for a whole body-image. To Lacan this image is inevitable but also negative, a "lure," a trap for the subject, in that the subject progressively identifies itself with this "ego." It becomes, perhaps forever, hostage to its image of itself as an "ideal unity": organized, coherent, and hence in control—a "statue" (*Ecrits* 1–4, 18–19, 43). Thus we might suppose that Lacan has outflanked the argument that the child's metaphoric ability antedates the fort-da game, by locating it earlier, in the mirror stage, and making it a matter solely of a deluded imagistic identification. Yet even there we must suppose that there is already present in the infant a reflective power, one at least proto-metaphoric in capability—as Freud's footnote to the fort-da suggests (*SE* 4:15). In Freud's note the child plays fort-da with his own mirror image, knowing that his image relates to himself like the spool to his mother: the mirror image signifies the infant but is not confused with the infant by the infant. Otherwise, how could the infant be aware of any relationship between itself—experienced (says Lacan) as a fragmented body (prematurity)—and its unified image, seen as a wished-for entity?

Embedded even in Freud's and Lacan's central accounts of the subject's earliest, most critical experiences there is a primary metaphoric ability or power. This helps us see a third alternative to the deluded subject-ego identification Lacan rejects and to the virtual banishing of the subject into, as Lacan's best commentators, John Muller and William Richardson dispiritedly put it, a "sheerly linguistic role," caught in the incessant sliding of signifiers. I believe one exemplary alternative to be the Wordsworthian subject. I need now only, first, emphasize that we are finding it in Freud's and Lacan's own texts, and second, describe briefly the interpretive consequences for a Lacanian reading of *The Prelude* that does not find this alternative.

One general consequence is the same as for Onorato—that Wordsworth is radically self-deceived. Robert Young begins his Lacanian reading with the axiomatic claims that "art becomes an exemplary fiction which 'the (imaginary) self tells itself in order to defend its (illusory) sense of autonomy' [the deluded subject-ego identification Lacan rejects]," and that "Wordsworth's own fiction (which he calls truth) is the concept of the imagination," which is "the represencer of a lost totality [and] the fantasmatic goal of Wordsworth's quest." It follows necessarily for Young that "the true subject of *The Prelude* behind its veil of representation is the indeterminacy of its subject." One specific consequence is that Wordsworth's "description of the mind at Snowdon . . . hark[s] back to this primal myth, the poem's original seduction and deceit," "the child['s] wholeness and totality that the adult can only enviously desire, or fantasize as still possessing himself."[15] Wordsworth's terms for his subjectivity are then for Young (like, apparently, all artistic terms) escapist. When we come shortly to look closely at the Snowdon episode, we shall see how unfounded these claims are. Now let us to return to the problem of the subject in Lacan, with the sense I have adumbrated here of what is at stake for how we understand *The Prelude*.

The consequence of Lacan's "radical depersonalization of the subject," Muller and Richardson suggest, is that by the end of the *Ecrits* "the most we can say is that the 'I' has [this] sheerly linguistic role, the function of shifter, not signifying but simply designating the speaker." If this speaker is the "subject," then "This subject, like the 'I' that fades from discourse, appears to be not a perduring, substantial entity but rather a kind of intermittent presence caught between desire and discourse, subject to the laws of language and their impersonal processes" (416, 417).

If we think instead of the subject as neither static being (ego) nor incessant flux (linguistic shifter) but as always in the act and process of becoming, as in the act of appropriating and creating its own (hi)story, we see a subject that is originally and essentially (not peripherally) imaginative or metaphorically capable, a subject that while "decentered" from the ego is not lost in the interstices of the signifying chain, even though not fully master of that chain.[16] In the non-Lacanian terms used for Blake in chapter 1, the subject is defined by its presence in this reciprocal, partial mastery.

The subject is not lost, because it has a sense of having a — its own — (hi)story.[17] Having one's own story begins an answer to Richardson's question, "how the subject can say 'I' independently of his fascination with his own imaginary ego" (58). Specifically, for example, although we cannot recapture the "original" mirror stage as part of our histories, since it is a metaphor anyway, we can appropriate it as a specular relationship in our personal histories, to the extent that we recognize any such final self-definition as a lure.[18] Our answer to Richardson's question goes beyond the "sheerly linguistic role" he and Muller ascribed to the subject. I believe it is the same answer suggested in his paraphrase of Lacan's rewriting of Freud's *"Wo es war, soll ich werden"*: not "Where id was, there shall ego be" but "Where it [i.e., the network of signifiers] was, I-as-articulator . . . must come to be—that is, must realize my relation to, place within, that network" (63). Richardson goes on to cite Lacan's own further comment: "there is only one method of learning that one is there, namely, to map the network. And how is a network mapped? One goes back and forth over one's ground, one crosses one's path" (*Four Concepts* 45).

This analysis indirectly but powerfully helps us articulate subjectivity in Romantic poetry generally, as well as in *The Prelude*. What is Lacan's critique of the ego but a recognition that the subject beyond time and change is a fantasy? In later eighteenth-century and Romantic poetry, this fantasy appears as a lyric self transcending time through sublime experience. Not that such transcendence is achieved—in the sublime, as Martin Price persuasively argues,[19] unself-consciousness is never achieved—but it remains the goal for later eighteenth-century poetry. In Romantic poetry, we have only to recall how Keats, in the "Ode on a Grecian Urn," for example, wrestles with this fantasy and eventually rejects it to see how far beyond Lacan's statue, Keats's "marble men and maidens," the major Romantic poets take the subject. Wordsworth's narrator is defined, or characterized, by his life story. The narrator is not a static self, always the same, whose essence remains for the most part hidden from him except for a few, central, sublime moments of lyric inspiration and insight; he is not even such a lyric self as that whose essence is revealed progressively in the poem's narrative. Nor does the narrator vanish in discontinuity and division, like the "sheerly linguistic" Lacanian subject of Muller and Richardson, and of Young. His subjectivity is his own story, "going back and forth over one's ground," anxiously as well as joyfully. His story happens over time and narrative in two senses: chronological time from youth to adulthood, and compositional time in the poem's own terms, from Book 1 to Book 13—"the narrator himself, in the very telling, is seeking an adequate poetic structure. . . . The two developments, the young man's growth and the narrator's quest, often seem to run in parallel courses."[20]

Furthermore, the subject in *The Prelude* is marked from the beginning by metaphoric capability and the power of imaginative reexperience in time. The child's ability to create metaphor permeates his experience and is not confined to what is obviously "Oedipal"; he imagines not only the cliff as "a living thing" but just as significantly the boat as an "elfin Pinnace." This ability is not derivative from or bound to Oedipal experience; it is primary, and not exclusively poetic, but constitutive of human subjectivity. For Wordsworth, the poet "is a man speaking to men," and "nothing differ[s] in kind from other men, but only in degree." He continues, "The pleasure which the mind derives from the perception of similitude in dissimilitude"—the metaphoric power of the human subject—"is the great spring of activity of our minds," and the "origin . . . of the sexual appetite, and all the passions connected with it. . . . It" is "the life of our ordinary conversation," and of "our taste and our moral feelings."[21] This metaphoric power, then, is not childish, as evidenced also by Wordsworth's climactic, self-conscious use of it at the poem's end: "the scene . . . appear'd to me / The perfect image of a mighty Mind" (13.67–69). It is also an adult power, upon which the whole poem is built.

The poem is also built upon the interplay between past and present. Just as metaphoric capability is not the child's prerogative, so is imaginative reexperience not the adult's: the child too subsequently reexperiences the scene. I do not mean here that the boy or the narrator masters the experience. It is evident the boy does not, both in the mountain's perceived overcoming of his sense of limitless power and of understanding within the experience, and in the troubling quality of his subsequent dreams:

> after I had seen
> That spectacle, for many days my brain
> Work'd with a dim and undetermin'd sense
> Of unknown modes of being. . . .
> (1.418–21)

The narrator does not achieve mastery either, because his own reflections bear the stamp of the same enigmatic features—and, as James Chandler points out, "these obscure feelings" described in 1.418–21 *themselves* "are responsible for the reconstruction of the experience that impressed Wordsworth's mind with the image of huge and mighty forms. The passage is thus simultaneously a narrative of a past experience and an enactment of a present experience, the present experience of recalling and recounting the earlier one through the medium of these surviving feelings."[22] Even at the poem's end, when the protagonist, now grown and virtually identified with the narrator and the poet, ascends a mountain instead of being towered over by it, that ascent does not mean his mastery of it or of his experience. It is true he is able to meditate more articulately than he was able years before, just after stealing the boat. But the initial experience itself of Book 13 is not one he controls: like other central mountain experiences in the poem, it is unpredictable. He climbs a mountain to see the sun rise, but he sees instead, still on his way up, the moon.

In addition, even his mature, rational, metaphoric meditation consciously and deliberately contains within itself not the origin of meaning and interpretation, but an original mystery, a mystery so powerful that it is present not only in the meditation but in the scene itself:

> a blue chasm, a fracture in the vapour,
> A deep and gloomy breathing-place . . .
>   in that breach
> Through which the homeless voice of waters rose,
> That dark deep thorough-fare had Nature lodg'd
> The Soul, the Imagination of the whole.
> (13.56–57, 62–65)

In the meditative metaphor and the narrator's subsequent musings, the moon, "naked in the Heavens, at height / Immense" and "look[ing] down upon this shew / In single glory" (41–42, 52–53), at first seems identifiable allegorically with "Imagination," inasmuch as that "Is but another name for absolute strength / And clearest insight" (167–69). This identification would make the imagination master over all it sees, like the moon above the sea and mist and chasm. However, Wordsworth radically complicates this identification by immediately identifying the imagination with "the stream" that "we have traced . . . / From darkness, and the very place of birth / In its blind cavern, whence is faintly heard / The sound of waters" (172–75), and that, after we "follow'd it to light / And open day," "lastly" suggests to us "The feeling of life endless, the one thought / By which we live, Infinity and God" (13.175–76, 182–84). The "mighty Mind" as the moon, then "is exalted by an under-presence, / The sense of God, *or whatso'er is dim / Or vast* in its own being" (13.69, 71–73; emphasis added) which is the chasm, or "abyss" (14[1850].72).[23]

I cite both the 1805 and 1850 texts here, partly to make the point that my larger argument about Wordsworth's awareness of the mysterious origins of the imaginative self is one that characterizes both texts. Wolfson argues the point specifically and in detail of the Drowned Man episode in Book 5: "throughout, the poem's most powerful moments of imagination, *from earliest drafts to late revisions,* are triggered by recollections that defeat control by imagination and containment by poetic form: moments of shock, mischance, chance, and surprise" (*Formal Charges* 118; emphasis added). In relation to this argument, it is (parenthetically but importantly) increasingly difficult to accept Young's claim that the poem's "true subject . . . the indeterminacy of its subject" is hidden "*behind* its *veil* of representation" (emphasis added).

Thus, the initially clear interpretive "meditation" (or "calm thought" in 1850), which began by seeing "the scene" as a "perfect image" (or the "Vision" as a "type" in 1850), ends not with an origin but with a mystery; that is, it ends with a mysterious origin, rather than a clear one by which the narrator (and the reader) comprehends all experience. Such an ending can be said to represent what Miller finds everywhere in Wordsworth's poetry, and most clearly in the Arab Dream episode of Book 5: "The theme of the dream is language or the sign-making power. The essence of this power in the dream is the naming of one thing by the name of another which puts in question the possibility of literal naming. All names, it may be, are metaphors, moved aside from any direct correspondence to the thing named by their reference to other names that precede and follow them in an endless chain" (*Linguistic Moment* 93–94). Miller demonstrates repeatedly and persuasively the "pervasive shimmering play of figure" throughout Wordsworth's poetry; it is not so clear, however, that "*The* source of the [concomitant] irresolvable ambiguities of Wordsworth's verse is the originally figurative nature of language" (47; emphasis added). Such ambiguities and uncertainties, we have seen, characterize Wordsworth's "imagination" in the Snowdon vision; the imagination becomes both the subject of that vision and the interpretive agent of the vision's elaboration in the narrator's meditation. But we have seen something else, at least equally important to our understanding of poetic subjectivity here: the imagination is experienced by the narrator, and articulated consciously by him, as finally mysterious.

While the principal vision is spatial and visual, the central metaphor of imagination as river or stream is temporal. This means time is not just the necessary, fallen-world medium in which imagination must operate but seeks to transcend, to attain a lyric self; it is also an essential part of imaginative activity. The self in *The Prelude* is not separable from "this *Record* of myself"; the poet's mind is not separable from "the *history* of a Poet's mind" (13.389, 408; emphasis added). At the same time, the self and the poet's mind are the sources of the record and history. The subject objectifies itself in its history; in *The Prelude*, however, the narrator explicitly does not fully comprehend his own subjectivity, does not find or create a perfect narrative that illustrates a comprehensible subject-become-object:

> Where is the favoured Being who hath held
> That course, unchecked, unerring, and untired,
> In one perpetual progress smooth and bright?
> —A humbler destiny have we retraced,
> And told of lapse and hesitating choice,
> And backward wanderings along thorny ways. . . .
> (14[1850].133–38)

Wordsworth recognizes the desire, but does not finally seek, to master his experience with a timeless moral, as the Ancient Mariner tries to do. Here imaginative reexperience needs to be distinguished carefully from compulsive reliving. The second characterizes Coleridge's Mariner: he relives the experience essentially without change and without imaginative perspective—during the retelling he rarely interprets, presenting events sequentially, not causally (except ll. 286–87, 294–96—1817 ed.). Although he often creates metaphors, there is no apparent self-consciousness in his doing so, suggesting he has been dominated by the experience while retelling (and reliving) it. It is the form he gives, or does not give, to his account as much as his description of his experience's bodily effect on him ("this frame of mine was wrenched / With a woeful agony, / Which forced me to begin my tale") that convinces us of his obsessive relation to his story. Unlike the Mariner, then, Wordsworth tells a story that includes time and admits meaning as becoming, and he does not surrender to the dream of meaning as being—Lacan's reified ego.

My emphasis here on "the narrator" and on "Wordsworth" contrasts sharply with most poststructuralist avoidance of the human subject in *The Prelude*—except as a figure projected out of Lacan's unending signifying chain, a figure with a "sheerly linguistic role, the function of shifter, not signifying but simply designating the speaker" (Muller and Richardson 416). As one example of this avoidance and its consequences, let us consider what happens to narrator and poet in Belsey's Lacanian reading of *The Prelude*.

Belsey observes that "*The Prelude* is composed of two distinct discourses which coexist uneasily, frustrating the reader's impulse to reduce the text to a single, coherent meaning, and thus withholding from the reader the mastery which is also denied to the child" ("Romantic Unconscious" 71). Other readers have made a similar distinction, although they call it a difference in voice or rhetoric rather than "distinct discourses," and by doing so tend to retain as the origin for whatever rhetorical shifts they find a subject conscious of its rhetoric.[24] Part of my argument throughout this book is that such a subject, with such a consciousness, does not necessarily "identif[y] with the unitary self of imaginary misrecognition" (62) that for this poststructuralist reading seems the only possible conscious self.

Belsey's second, participial observation, that these shifts or discourses frustrate our attempts to master the text, does not accord with all recent critical emphasis on such frustration; for some reader-response critics, that frustration exists only to be overcome. For Belsey it exists permanently, and at this point our arguments converge. But notice the consequences of conceptualizing the issue as two separate and essentially unrelated—"the two bear little relation to each other" (71)—*discourses* alternating throughout the poem: "the discursive organization of the text presents an oscillation of sense and nonsense as each episode is contained by passages of 'philosophy' which constantly strive to master its meaning" (69). Belsey's formulation collapses both "narrator" and "poet" into (a quasi-personified) "discourse," leaving no critical vocabulary that might enable any further questions about where either subject might be positioned in relation to the two discourses she identifies. Other readers have attributed these discourses, or rhetorical shifts, to Wordsworth's attempts both to represent and to understand his experience. What to them is representation is for this Lacanian reading "signifying nonsense" (69), tacitly equated with the "dramas of subjectivity"; what to them is an attempt to understand is here a delusion. Implicitly, then, the subject is caught within the drama. It has no other position, even temporary or shifting, from which to view that drama except for the false one revealed (or created) by the surrounding "explanatory discourse[,] which so signally fails to explain" (71).

Likewise, to Collings the Wordsworthian subject is always caught in this drama, and any position outside it seems inauthentic and even deluded: in the Snowdon episode, "No longer within the landscape, no longer subject to a nameless, hostile gaze, Wordsworth can now gaze around upon the creation like a latter-day Noah to see what else has escaped inundation"; "it is as if he can watch and listen to the deluge from a safe distance and contemplate from above the 'hollow rent' in nature through which he once journeyed"; "No longer overmastered by imagination, he masters it" (203, 204). But if, as Collings argues throughout, "*imagination*—that deep, resonant innerness beloved of humanist criticism—is an alibi for the erotics of disorientation, the pleasures of the wound" (13), which, as his book's subtitle ("The Poetics of Cultural Dismemberment") suggests, constitute and define Wordsworth as a poet, the position Wordsworth claims here must be illusory. (Collings does not discuss the relationship between such a self-deceived Wordsworth and a Wordsworth who "*recognizes* that [significant cultural] opposites are identical, that he is implicated in what he attacks, and that finally there is no escape from cultural dismemberment," whose origins "as a poet of hyperbole" Collings locates in "neither a historical occasion (e.g., the war with France) nor a largely biographical response to it (a crisis) but an *interpretive act*, a *decision* to read culture as the scene of its own undoing" [7, 35–36; emphasis added].)

For such poststructuralist reading, understanding is always an attempt at mastery and therefore always not only failed but deluded. My argument throughout this chapter has been that Wordsworth and eventually his narrator both evidence understanding without mastery and that both recognize such mastery as a dream. I do not mean that Wordsworth always understands his own limits adequately or that he and his readers all agree or should agree on where to place them; I mean only that a careful reading of his poem shows that he (implicitly) and his narrator (explicitly) acknowledge limits to understanding there and that both recognize mastery, a complete understanding, to be a fantasy.

Belsey, Young, and Collings are not of course the only poststructuralist readers of *The Prelude,* although perhaps they bring into sharpest relief a common poststructuralist critique of the humanist subject as, in Belsey's words, the deluded "unitary self of imaginary misrecognition" (62), whose understanding of its own intentions must be equally deluded. Miller's influential reading of the Arab Dream episode in Book 5, which I have mentioned earlier in this chapter, in particular does not find the poet Wordsworth to be such a deluded subject; indeed, his readings characteristically do not claim such delusion on the part of the poet: "any cultural expression in our tradition, such as a literary text, is undecidable in meaning, though the choices the text offers . . . may be precisely defined. This plurality, in my examples at least, does not result from any confusion on the part of the author, his inability to get his thoughts straight or to say what he means" (*Linguistic Moment* 54). But Miller then skirts the issue of intentionality, by making the poem's "plurality of meanings" *exclusively,* on the theoretical level at least, a function of "an intrinsic necessity of language" (54), thus in effect dissolving the author into language — "The linguistic moment in Wordsworth is this transfer of the poet himself into language" (112).

On a less theoretical level, Miller himself accepts from time to time a separation between poet and poem, and a correspondence between intention and meaning. For example, "The pervasive figure in 'Composed upon Westminster Bridge' is the personification of the city as a sleeping human figure who wears only the transparent garment of the morning," and in a note on the same page, "Wordsworth intended the beautiful oxymoron of a garment that yet leaves its wearer 'bare,' as is indicated in the letters cited by De Selincourt in a note" (73). That we tend not to be troubled by, perhaps even not to notice, such inconsistency between practice and theory may exemplify in such cases not the reputed blindness of common sense but rather Miller's own claim that "The intersection of a theory of criticism with an actual poem to be criticized is always unique and always bends the presupposed theory" (xxi).

Elsewhere Miller repeatedly blurs poem and poet, by enacting the same metonymy he locates in Book 5 of *The Prelude* — "A book — a 'Shakespeare,' a 'Milton,' a 'Wordsworth,' as we call such volumes by a familiar metonymy" (104) — enabling him to move back and forth between the two, his theoretical justification implicitly being that dissolution of poet into poem. But I am interested here in situations where that metonymy does not provide such ease of movement. They include, for example: "Wordsworth's use of the sonnet and his theory of its use must be understood in the context of this theme of poetic impotence" (65); "Rarely has the sovereignty of the mind over things been more extravagantly asserted than by Wordsworth, both in theory and in practice" (72); "Some passages by Wordsworth seem to affirm this view, but in fact Wordsworth's thinking on this matter is more complicated" (79); and, "Wordsworth's concern for this question is indicated by his fascination with all kinds of written language" (80). Perhaps most tellingly, what Miller asserts to be "one of those patterns of thought inherent in the metaphorical tissue of our languages," namely a "reversal" in which the book in the Arab Dream "is part of a double metaphor in which the secondary is used as the figurative expression of the primary, of that from which it is derived or on which it is modeled" (83), he derives on the previous page from "Wordsworth['s] fascinat[ion] by stones in themselves"; the poet was "impelled, when he found on an island or on a mountain top a stone he especially admired, to scratch a poem on it" (82). At the very least, then, this "pattern of thought" must be seen as somehow "Wordsworth's" and not just an intrinsic feature of language.

I mentioned earlier the surrender of eighteenth-century poets of the sublime to the dream of Lacan's reified ego, of Belsey's "unitary self of imaginary misrecognition," of Miller's "false idea of the unity, simplicity, and identity of the self" (277), of meaning as being. If we look more closely at an example of such a poet's version of narrative, we can see even more clearly Wordsworth's advanced understanding of subjectivity as necessarily interwoven with, and not master of, temporal experience, and we see by contrast how inadequate are eighteenth-century conceptions of sublimity for such an understanding. Beattie's *The Minstrel* is especially appropriate here, not only because it once made a strong impression on Wordsworth (Dorothy Wordsworth wrote in 1793 that "the whole character of Edwin resembles much what William was when I first knew him after my leaving Halifax" in 1787, and in a 1795 letter Wordsworth quotes from the stanza I quote below) but also because it parallels *The Prelude* in its intent to accommodate subjective growth and therefore time, as suggested by Beattie's subtitle "the Progress of Genius" and Wordsworth's description of *The Prelude* as a poem on "the growth of my own mind."[25]

Notice how in the following stanza from *The Minstrel* Beattie is unable to go beyond correlatives in nature for his protagonist's subjective mood, in which Beattie is primarily interested:

Thence musing onward to the sounding shore,
    The lone enthusiast oft would take his way,

Listening, with pleasing dread to the deep roar
Of the wide-weltering waves. In black array,
When sulphurous clouds roll'd on th' autumnal day,
Even then he hasten'd from the haunt of man,
Along the trembling wilderness to stray,
What time the lightning's fierce career began,
And o'er heaven's rending arch the rattling thunder ran.
(1.478–86)

Edwin the minstrel only appears to find "pleasing dread" in the "roar / Of the wide-weltering waves." Since he deliberately seeks "the sounding shore" and "the trembling wilderness," the real catalyst is internal; he unconsciously seeks objective correlatives for his feelings.

When T. S. Eliot invented the phrase "objective correlative," he did so to argue that *Hamlet*'s aesthetic problem is Hamlet's psychological problem: "the absence of objective equivalent to his feelings." Eighteenth-century poetic versions of the sublime, as exemplified in *The Minstrel*, leave us unmoved for the same reason *Hamlet* left Eliot dissatisfied: like Hamlet, their poetic protagonists are "dominated by an emotion which is inexpressible, because it is in excess of the facts as they appear."[26] A storm or seashore is not sufficient to originate Edwin's emotion. Although Beattie's poem implies that the minstrel's emotion exceeds the natural facts, since Edwin continually seeks new ones, neither Edwin nor Beattie seems able to recognize this excess. We might say then that *The Minstrel*'s aesthetic problem is Edwin's psychological problem (a more justifiable criticism of Beattie than Eliot's of Shakespeare, which is based solely on the fact of such excess).

The most serious weakness in Beattie's poem may be this inability to deepen our understanding of subjectivity, as opposed to cataloguing its sublime proximate causes and psychological effects. Wordsworth too links sublimity with obscurity, but he does so consciously, aware that origins of complex subjective feelings are unrecoverable:[27]

I deem not profitless those fleeting moods
Of shadowy exultation: not for this,
That they are kindred to our purer mind
And intellectual life; but that the soul,
Remembering how she felt, but *what she felt*
Remembering not, retains an obscure sense
Of possible sublimity, to which,
With growing faculties she doth aspire,

With faculties still growing, feeling still
That, whatsoever point they gain, they still
Have something to pursue.
(2.331–41; emphasis added)

When we recognize that "sublimity" was for the eighteenth century not only an aesthetic term but a psychological one, reflecting the period's interest in subjectivity, we can see the importance to my argument of Wordsworthian sublimity: it differs from Beattie's not only because its link with obscurity is deliberate but because it is subjectively more profound, encompassing more complex feelings than Beattie's "pleasing dread," and because it is not static but dynamic, associated with a sense of growth. Josephine Miles has shown that "the sublime poem" has a "vocabulary of cosmic passion and sense impression."[28] Its ontological context, the Cartesian split of subject and object and the empiricist emphasis on the latter and on being rather than becoming, helps explain why poetry like Beattie's presents subjects whose inner life is objectified in sense impressions and cosmic, not complex, passion. Obviously the inner life of *The Prelude*'s protagonist is both richer and more expansively presented, and so is Wordsworth's vocabulary for that life.

To consider time provides one way of seeing how far Wordsworth has come from Beattie, and indeed from his earlier poetic presentation of Snowdon,[29] in his understanding of subjectivity. In *The Minstrel* there are no real distinctions between sublime experiences at the beginning and at the end of the poem, notwithstanding Beattie's professed claim "to give an account" not only of the "birth" and "adventures" of a bard but of his "education."[30] There is no education in the poem. Edwin ends as he begins, experiencing an unchanged sublimity—or rather, experiencing the same emotions in response to the natural and the rhetorical sublime (landscape and literature). His "education" consists only of (1) taking "walks of wider circuit" to see "vales more wild, and mountains more sublime" (2.48, 49); (2) adding Vergil and Homer to his landscape: "sweet delirium o'er his bosom stole, / When the great shepherd of the Mantuan plains / His deep majestic melody 'gan roll," and "what transport storm'd his soul, / How the red current throbb'd his veins along. / When . . . / Homer rais'd high to Heaven the loud, th'impetuous song" (2.533–40); and (3) adding the pathos of history, or History, since Edwin never engages real history but only hears an aestheticized version secondhand—"to Edwin's ardent gaze / The Muse of history unrolls her page" (2.290–91)—and his response consists in being "Enraptur'd by the hermit's strain" (2.496). It is striking to find all this after Book 2 opens with the narrator intending to confront "time and change" (2.12). In a third book Beattie intended "to have introduced a foreign enemy as invading [Edwin's] country, in consequence of which the Minstrel was to employ himself in rousing his countrymen to arms" (Beattie, *Poetical Works* lxxv–vi). Given the absence of real history in Edwin's education in the second book, it is not surprising that Beattie never wrote the third. Theresa Kelley argues that in *The Prelude* Wordsworth associates the kind of single-minded preoccupation with sublimity we have seen in Beattie's "lone enthusiast" with a dangerous ahistoricality in revolutionary consciousness, and that his decision to expand "the two-part *Prelude* of 1798–99" was prompted by his desire for a specifically narrative "poetic texture that frames or subdues" that text's sublime experiences: "the sublime or visionary encounters gathered together in the 1798–99 poem had to be scattered in the expanded poem, where they are joined by troubling figures of *revolutionary* sublimity."[31]

Kelley's reading of the Snowdon episode, which "recapitulates the revisionary aesthetics of *The Prelude*" (128) by "secur[ing] the ascendancy of values that belong to the beautiful over those of the sublime" (130), might make what I would argue to be a crucial distinction between "frames" and "subdues," corresponding to the difference I am asserting throughout this book between "understands" and "masters." But inasmuch as she claims that Wordsworth's sense of the relation of sublime experience to the rest of his life is *un*deceived, our arguments complement one another: "Critics who prefer the two-part *Prelude* (where sublime outcroppings do dominate the argument) and those who emphasize sublime, visionary moments in later versions tend to neglect the rhetorical (and aesthetic) occasion that prompted Wordworth's decision to expand the poem on his life—his experience in revolutionary France" (92; see also 1–7). Howard Erskine-Hill argues in effect that Wordsworth's historical consciousness antedated this decision and was present from the poem's inception: probably the opening question "'Was it for this . . . ?' in the 1799 *Prelude* referred rather to political dismay than poetic unfulfillment"; even in the 1805 *Prelude*, "the broad poetic projects concerning nationalism and liberty just invoked [prior to the same, displaced question] hardly allow the claim that the poet's desire to develop his talent was an a-political matter." Further, the "early episodes" in both versions, including the Stolen Boat episode, while "not political (nor a-political)," "concern the primal awareness of the untaught human being ('the naked savage'), the earliest predatory impulses, conscious guilt, enterprise, and rebuff, free enjoyment both social and solitary. They contain the germs of political ideas capable of being experienced later in practice, in specific historical situations, later still of being meditated upon and generalized."[32]

Whatever their differences, Kelley and Erskine-Hill both argue, as I have done, against the primacy of an ahistorical or antihistorical sublimity in the poem. From seemingly very different perspectives, all these arguments are akin to de Man's argument against Hartman, that even the most visionary of moments in the poem, in Book 6, "is not the result of 'unmediated vision' but of another mediation, in which the consciousness does not relate itself any longer to nature but to a temporal entity [that] could, with proper qualifications, be called history, and it is indeed in connection with historical events (the French Revolution) that the apostrophe to Imagination comes to be written. But if we call this history," de Man continues, in a passage that understands history quite differently from the most influential recent historicist critics, "then we must be careful to understand that it is the kind of history that [is] the retrospective recording of man's failure to overcome the power of time . . . , a common temporal predicament that finds its expression in the individual and historical destinies that strike the poet as exemplary." This predicament is "always a negative one for us, for the relationship between the self and time is necessarily mediated by death; it is the experience of mortality that awakens within us a consciousness of time that is more than merely natural."[33] Here de Man's argument shows implicitly that a deconstructive reading of Wordsworth's poem does not inevitably find the poet more deluded than the reader—whether about the subject's relation to nature, to language and figuration, or to history.

Potts suggests that Beattie's poem cannot cope with such a "consciousness of time," that it "breaks off in heart-consuming grief . . . over the loss of his friend John Gregory." She continues, "Such literary behavior is not characteristic of Wordsworth, even in the loss of his brother John" (76). This biographical difference confirms the differing abilities of the two poets to confront "time and change," and their differing attitudes to narrative. John Sitter argues convincingly that "one of the fundamental [literary] movements [of] the mid-eighteenth century is a lyric flight from immediate history and a visionary approach toward History" and that such flight means the longer narrative poetic forms are "at odds with the poets' desire for intensity or momentary sublimity."[34] We have seen this lyric flight in Beattie concurrent with his desire for intensity; we have seen in Wordsworth a consistent and deliberate contextualizing of such desire in narrative. Indeed Peter Brooks suggests that such contextualizing characterizes nineteenth-century discourse, whether historical, philosophical, or literary, and that narrative constituted for its contemporaries "a prime, irreducible act of understanding how human life acquires meaning."[35]

If genuine narrative cannot be reduced to an origin in theoretical law, whether that law be aesthetic or psychoanalytic, it cannot be dispensed with in favor of its own end. (The Snowdon episode does not make superfluous the Stolen Boat experience; Book 13 does not render irrelevant the preceding twelve.) In Lacan's words, there is no end to the signifying chain. Nevertheless, it is important to situate ourselves in it, to come to see something of its power over us and by doing so to have some power within it—a condition of reciprocal, partial mastery. The meaning is in the search, and narration, not in the end or origin toward which we are always arriving. This is perhaps as true of interpreting a narrative as it is of creating one.

Wordsworth writes of subjectivity as essentially, not peripherally, coming-to-be in time. This emphasis on the subject as coming-to-be in time illuminates Terry Eagleton's suggestion that the fort-da game "can also be read as the first glimmerings of narrative. *Fort-da* is perhaps the shortest story we can imagine: an object is lost, and then recovered."[36] But the same object is not recovered. The child does not recover the real mother, he creates the spool/mother. We have seen the double significance in the child's game and his pleasure: the child is both actor in a drama (attempted mastery of his mother's absence) and creator of a narrative that is self-referential but also metaphorical. Where biographical-historical truth is located in such a narrative becomes perhaps unanswerably complex, as Freud saw in his last paper on the subject: "often we do not succeed in bringing the patient to recollect what has been repressed. Instead of that, if the analysis is carried out correctly, we produce in him an assured conviction of the truth of the construction which achieves the same therapeutic result as a recaptured memory" (*SE* 23:265–66). Wordsworth saw as much in *The Prelude:*

> I cannot say what portion is in truth
> The naked recollection of that time,
> And what may rather have been call'd to life
> By after meditation.
> (3.646–49)

The recognition that origins are mysterious, that the original object or event is recoverable only in fantasy, that we never reach the end of desire, is what makes *The Prelude* in Kermode's sense a "modern classic," not "a repository of certain, unchanging truths," "a closed book."[37] Beattie lacks this recognition; Freud and Lacan share it with Wordsworth. As we have seen, however, their theoretical interpretations—and the uses to which psychoanalytic readers of *The Prelude* often put them—sometimes obscure the truths about subjectivity embedded in their central narrative of the fort-da game. Wordsworth certainly is not immune to the lure of interpretive mastery in his narrative, but characteristically he subsumes it in that narrative.

Why does the recognition that mastery is impossible and its origins are mysterious provide to Wordsworth and his narrator less a source of anxiety than "Impediments . . . *more sweet*" (4.261; emphasis added)? Why does it, or does it not, raise in us the suspicion that the narrative is self-deceptive? These are questions pointing to the mysterious origins of belief itself.

4 The Intimations Ode

An Infinite Complexity

Like Wordsworth's meditation after climbing Snowdon in the last book of *The Prelude*, the ending of the Intimations Ode has encouraged readers to look for a generic closure that, in Barbara Herrnstein Smith's characterization of what she aptly calls the "narrative lyric," is achieved "through the poet's more or less clear statement, at the end, of the significance of the events so reported."[1] The Ode's position at the end of the collected poetry doubles that expectation. But for many readers the final statement of interpretive mastery is not very clear, and the closure seems forced: "the solution is asserted rather than dramatized"; "the central achievement of the *Ode*, the glorious child, seems betrayed . . . by [Wordsworth's] shift in emphasis to transcendent divinity"; "the ode dims to a noble conclusion, where the poet assuages his banishment from life eternal by vague intuition that in some sense the pilgrimage into mortality is necessary and just"; and, "the poem becomes dishonest . . . the philosophic mind has not mastered the grief but rather come to live side by side with it."[2]

I shall argue that Wordsworth deliberately suggests and then refuses such mastery, that while the odic tradition warrants the attempt at closure and mastery, the Intimations Ode's deliberate refusal is generically unique. In doing so I shall depend on Rosalie Colie's argument that genre, or literary kind, reflects not only "connections between topic and treatment within the literary system" but also "connection . . . with *kinds* of knowledge and experience. . . . The kinds honor aspects of and elements of culture and in their conjunctions help make up culture as a whole."[3] The connections Colie here asserts will enable us to understand better both the ending of Wordsworth's poem and his reason for placing it at the end of his collected poetry.

Since my argument will not always be straightforward, I should perhaps begin with the difficulties of relating the Intimations Ode to a generic "odic tradition." The first is the extent to which Wordsworth's theoretical statements about his poetry do not admit Colie's "literary system" of recognizable, and therefore conventional, genres. Wordsworth writes to another poet, "You feel strongly; trust to those feelings, and your Poem will take its shape and proportions as a tree does from the vital principle that actuates it. I do not think that great poems can be cast in a mould" (*WL* 5:352). In the 1815 Preface, even when he does carefully set out the "divers forms" or "various moulds" of all poetry, Wordsworth subsumes such a division of his collected poems in a set of co-existing orders "with reference to the powers of mind *predominant* in the production of them" (e.g., "Poems of the Imagination"), "to the subjects to which they relate" (e.g., "Poems Referring to the Period of Childhood"), and "to the mould in which they are cast" (e.g., "Miscellaneous Sonnets"). These three orders he subordinates in turn to two more: the first, "according to an order of time, commencing with Childhood, and terminating with Old Age, Death, and Immortality," thus "the small pieces . . . might be regarded . . . as composing an entire work within themselves"; and the second, "as adjuncts to the philosophical poem, 'The Recluse'" (*Prose* 3:27, 28). Any conception of genre as significantly formal or conventional gets short shrift here, obscured by the multiple substantive conceptions. The same emphasis on subject governs his retrospective sense of how the Intimations Ode in particular should be read:

This poem rests entirely upon two recollections of childhood, one that of a splendour in the objects of sense which is passed away, and the other an indisposition to bend to the law of death as applying to our particular case. A Reader who has not a vivid recollection of these feelings having existed in his mind in childhood cannot understand that poem. (*WL* 5:189)

Wordsworth's emphasis is a commonplace in Romantic discussions of form, its best-known version being Coleridge's preference (after Schlegel) for "organic form" over "mechanic" or "predetermined form."[4] Following this lead, most important generalizations about Romantic lyrics ignore or deny "predetermined form" in favor of a substantive conception. For example, to Abrams "the greater

Romantic lyric," which "displaced . . . 'the greater ode'—the elevated Pindaric," is a "descriptive-meditative poem" characterized by a "process, in which mind confronts nature and their interplay constitutes the poem."[5] To Irene Chayes it is necessary to "go beyond the older exclusive and now inadequate concern with prosody, stanzaic structure, and conformity to classical models." Building on Norman Maclean's thesis that the ode moved from neoclassical narrative action to pre-Romantic lyric image, she characterizes "the Romantic ode" by a "dramatic Plot . . . develop[ing] within a lyric frame, with the speaker playing the role of a protagonist whose 'actions' are contained in his words and who is brought to a Reversal or Discovery by what he himself says."[6] Such generalizations imply that the Romantic ode is generically independent of earlier odes, in that its form is determined by a different essence, its "process" or "Plot."[7]

This point brings up a second difficulty: understanding what "ode" meant in Wordsworth's time. Well before that time, the word had become a terminological dumping ground. Reading through the relevant volumes of Robert Anderson's *The Works of the British Poets*, Wordsworth's main text for reading earlier poetry, we might agree with Eric Rothstein that eighteenth-century writers "seized on irregular odes for so many purposes that the genre lost its specific force and meaning."[8] Worse, the irregular Pindaric, "like any loose form," remarks Maclean, "attracted scores of writers who aspired to the heights of poetry because of the difficulties of prose" (424).

We may suspect that, however imprecise the terminology of second-rate poets, Wordsworth did not use the word carelessly. But his use does seem confusing at first. He employs the same verse form (essentially tetrameter stanza, rhyming *ababccdd*) not only for the Horatian "Ode to Duty" but for "Incident, Characteristic of a Favourite Dog" and "Fidelity," written about the same time (1804–1806)—one about a dog that mourns its companion, drowned chasing a hare across a barely frozen river, the other about a dog that stays by its dead master for three months. Such regular odic verse forms characterize a number of poems that Wordsworth does not call odes. Conversely, in a note added in 1800 to "Tintern Abbey," he comes close to calling that poem an (irregular) ode though it is quite without any odic verse form: "I have not ventured to call this Poem an Ode; but it was written with a hope that in the transitions, and the impassioned music of the versification, would be found the principal requisites of that species of composition" (*Poetical Works* 2:517). His note suggests, as does the occurrence of regular odic verse forms in poems he does not call odes, that he reserves the word for elevated subject matter and therefore that he defines the genre substantively.

But his emphasis on "transitions" and "versification" as generic characteristics and his final refusal to call "Tintern Abbey" an ode show that he is also aware of the formal dimension of the irregular ode. This awareness is implicit in his later concern about the example he might be setting by his 1816 Thanksgiving Day Ode:

> I threw off a sort of irregular Ode upon this subject, which spread to nearly 350 lines. . . . [U]pon the correction of Style I have bestowed, as I always do, great Labour. I hope that my pains in this particular have not been thrown away. . . . But I do not like to appear as giving encouragement to a lax species of writing except where the occasion is so great as to justify an aspiration after a state of freedom beyond what a succession of regular Stanzas will allow. (*WL* 5:284)

This "aspiration after a state of freedom" is presumably what modern readers, following Coleridge, seize on as the Intimations Ode's most important odic characteristic—the aspiration here, as Wordsworth said about the 1800 *Lyrical Ballads*, being to reflect "the fluxes and refluxes of the mind when agitated . . . " (*Prose* 1:126).[9] Such readers then turn to the poem's other generic modes, pointing out important elements of pastoral and elegy and finding relevant antecedents for its verbal allusions, ideas, and structure, in Wordsworth's own "Tintern Abbey," Vergil's fourth eclogue, and Milton's "Lycidas" or *Paradise Lost*, but rarely Milton's Nativity Ode—or any other ode, for that matter.[10] I do not mean to disparage these findings. They may imply the extent to which Wordsworth defines the genre substantively, thus including in his ode elements characteristic of other forms, or the extent to which the genre is changing at the turn of the century, thus enabling him to include in his ode elements formerly associated with other genres.

But I think this inclusiveness suggests more. First, it has a generic model in the Nativity Ode. Milton's work is both mixed and inclusive, containing elements of pastoral—"shepherds" and "sheep"; song—the angels' and spheres' "holy song"; elegy—nature's "weeping" and "lament" for the "parting Genius," "nymphs . . . mourn[ing]"; and prophecy—the "Earth . . . / Shall from the surface to the centre shake; / . . . at the world's last cession" (Anderson 5:163–64). Later in the seventeenth century, Thomas Sprat remarked on this mixture as a generic characteristic of Cowley's pseudo-Pindaric odes: "the irregularity of the number . . . makes that kind of Poesie fit for all manner of subjects: For the Pleasant, the Grave, the Amorous, the Heroic, the Philosophical, the Moral, the Divine."[11]

In addition, there is a more indirect argument for the inclusiveness of Wordsworth's ode. From its beginning, the English irregular ode was compared to the epic—for example, by Drayton in his prefatory remarks to his own odes: "Some [odes are] transcendently lofty, and far more high than the epic (commonly called the heroic poem) witness those of the inimitable Pindar" (Anderson 3: 577). This sort of comparison persisted into the eighteenth century: "the first two lyric kinds—the divine and the heroic [odes—were] near the top of the poetical hierarchy (along with epic and tragedy) and the minor lyric near the bottom" (Maclean 410). Ralph Cohen has shown that for eighteenth-century critics and poets each kind "was, either in terms of its parts or as a whole, inter-related with other forms" and that this hierarchy "can be seen in terms of the inclusion of lower forms into higher."[12] Since the epic traditionally included all lower genres, the irregular ode too was at least poetically inclusive, a kind of highly compressed epic.[13] Certainly eighteenth-century epideictic odes reflected an awareness of their possible epic status:

> Of arms and war my muse aspires to sing,
> And strike the lyre upon an untry'd string:
> New fire informs my soul, unfelt before;
> And, on new wings, to heights unknown I soar.
> . . . .
> Say, sacred nymph, whence this great change proceeds,
> Why scorns the lowly swain his oaten reeds,
> Daring aloud to strike the sounding lyre,
>   And sing heroic deeds;
> Neglecting flames of love for martial fire?
> (Congreve, "To the King, on the Taking of Namur. Irregular Ode,"
> Anderson 7:536)

> Not Pindar's theme with mine compares
>   As far surpast, as useful cares
> Transcend diversion light and glory vain:
>   The wreath fantastic, and shouting throng,
>   And panting steed, to him belong
> The charioteer's, not empire's golden rein.
> (Young, "Imperium Pelagi. A Naval Lyric: Written in Imitation of Pin-
> dar's Spirit," Anderson 10:182)

Although Wordsworth's ode makes no explicit epic claims, their absence does not make its relation to epic irrelevant. For his epic purposes in *The Prelude*'s early books, on which he was probably working at the same time that he composed stanzas 5–11 of the Intimations Ode, Wordsworth rejects—or at least apparently finds wanting—martial subjects in favor of private experience (1.158–272,

3.168–94).[14] We can surmise, then, that for his own ode he saw in epideictic odes not just the impossibility of praise for epic "outward things / Done visibly for other minds" (*Prelude* 3.174–75) but the possibility of something like epic inclusiveness. I am not quite suggesting that he incorporated as many generic modes as possible so that his ode would be recognized as aspiring to epic status. The initial epigraph for the ode is, after all, "*Paulo* majora canamus," "let us sing of matters greater *by a little*" (emphasis added).[15] Yet while this line does not make an epic claim, it puts the possibility into our minds, much as Wordsworth suggests that we think of "Tintern Abbey" as an ode when he tells us that he has not ventured to call it one.

From the beginning, then, the English irregular ode intentionally was or sought to be a mixed and inclusive genre, in both theory and practice. Wordsworth's ode therefore is not generically idiosyncratic in including other generic modes. The most apparent of these are pastoral—"young Lambs bound[ing]," "happy Shepherd Boy . . . shout[ing]," "Children . . . pulling . . . Fresh flowers" (sts. 3 and 4); and elegy—"soon thy Soul shall have her earthly freight, / And custom lie upon thee with a weight, / Heavy as frost, and deep almost as life!" (st. 8). But there are also song, or at least a report of it—"the Birds . . . sing[ing] a joyous song" (st. 3)—in the service of epithalamium; satire at the expense of "The little Actor [who] cons another part" (st. 7); and allegorical romance (sts. 5–8).[16] All these, as in epic poetry, are subordinated to the narrative of a single life that is somehow exemplary: the poem moves consistently from "I" in stanzas 1–4, to the "Child" separated from "us" in stanzas 5–8, to "We" and "I" together in stanzas 9–11 (see Anne Williams 6, 8). The subordination of the various modes implies that any single one of them would be inadequate to the complexity of that life, and here Colie's connection between kinds of literature and kinds of experience begins to emerge: "everything utterable has its genre, and . . . a complex, large, inclusive utterance may require mixture of the kinds" (28).[17]

The Intimations Ode's unusual generic comprehensiveness reflects the substantive comprehensiveness that Wordsworth implies by consistently placing the work at the end of his collected poetry, usually unsubsumed by any category.[18] He placed it at the end of the 1807 *Poems* before he had conceived of his temporal scheme from childhood to immortality. He seems to have modified his original scheme in order to keep the ode last, since in the earliest version of his plan, in an 1809 letter to Coleridge, the ode was to be last only within the first class of poems, those "relating to childhood, and such feelings as rise in the mind in after life in direct contemplation of that state" (*WL* 2:334). William Knight moved the ode from its proper position in his 1889 chronological edition to place it last in his 1896 chronological edition, because "Mr. Aubrey de Vere has urged me to take it out of its chronological place, and let it conclude the whole series of Wordsworth's poems, as the greatest, and that to which all others lead up. Mr. De Vere's wish is based on conversation which he had with the poet himself."[19]

It is worth noting that the Intimations Ode is not the only prominently placed ode in Wordsworth's collected poems. To see why its positioning is significant, we must look briefly at the placement of other major poems in his publications, which I believe establishes a pattern into which his odes fit. Frequently he places an important poem at the end of a group.[20] This practice begins as early as *Lyrical Ballads*. In 1798, "Tintern Abbey," distinctly not a ballad, is the final poem. In 1800, despite much rearranging of other poems, "Tintern Abbey," now akin to an ode, is still last in the first volume; "Michael, A Pastoral" concludes the second volume. In the 1807 *Poems, in Two Volumes*, the first, untitled group ends with "Ode to Duty"; the second, headed "Poems, Composed during a Tour, Chiefly on Foot," ends with "Resolution and Independence"; the final, untitled group ends with the Intimations Ode, here titled simply "Ode." In the 1815 *Poems,* the first collected edition, the last three poems in the group "Poems Founded on the Affections" are "The Idiot Boy," "Michael," and "Laodamia"; the last poem in "Poems of the Imagination" is "Tintern Abbey"; the last poem in "Poems Proceeding from Sentiment and Reflection" is "Ode to Duty"; the last poem in the collection, and the only one not part of a larger group, is the Intimations Ode, now including for the first time the longer title and the epigraph, the last three lines from the first poem in the collection, "My heart leaps up." Similarly, in the 1849–50 *Poetical Works,* the last collected edition during Wordsworth's life, the public odes on Napoleon's fall close the group "Poems Dedicated to National Independence and Liberty." Despite some changing of final poems throughout the various collected editions, the concluding poems are now also significant ones. "The Waggoner" ends "Poems of the Fancy"; in "Poems of the Imagination," the 1828 ode "On the Power of Sound" and "Peter Bell" displace "Tintern Abbey" at the end; and, as always, the Intimations Ode is last of all.

Perhaps, as other critics have remarked, the Intimations Ode implicitly encapsulates the whole, much as the Mount Snowdon revelation recapitulates earlier crucial scenes from *The Prelude* and helps make the poem, as Abrams comments, "about its own genesis—a prelude to itself" (*Natural Supernaturalism* 79). At this point, however, I want to press this notion of recapitulation only far enough to suggest that Wordsworth implies a comprehensiveness in the poem he places last in his collected poetry.

Clearly Wordsworth did not put his great ode at the end because he despaired of classifying it. Its position might have seemed obvious, since its ostensible subject, immortality, accords with the overall temporal organization of his poems, and since the epigraph, added in 1815, links it with the beginning of the collected poems. Every edition from 1827 on includes immediately after the epigraph an explicit reference to the opening poem—for example, "See Vol. I. page 3" (1827). In addition, as we have now seen, odes and narratives end significant groups with a frequency out of proportion to their frequency in the collected poetry. This fact suggests that the ode's final position also may have to do with its generic comprehensiveness and that such comprehensiveness for Wordsworth characteristically entails going beyond the lyric mode to the narrative.

What I mean by this movement beyond lyric to narrative is sufficiently important to my argument to justify an illustration from *The Prelude*. Wordsworth does not habitually find Pindaric ecstasy congenial; he opens *The Prelude* with the failure of "mak[ing] / A present joy the matter of my Song":

> the harp
> Was soon defrauded, and the banded host
> Of harmony dispers'd in straggling sounds
> And, lastly, utter silence.
> (1.55–56, 105–8)

In the same work he even follows his lyric flights by analysis or narrative, often prosaic in tone.[21] Let us take the chasm after the Simplon Pass. The overwhelming natural details that

> Were all like . . .
> Characters of the great Apocalyps,
> The types and symbols of Eternity,
> Of first and last, and midst, and without end

are followed by apparently mundane narrative interpolation:

> That night our lodging was an Alpine House,
> An Inn or Hospital, as they are named,
> Standing in that same valley by itself
> And close upon the confluence of two streams,
> A dreary Mansion, large beyond all need,
> With high and spacious rooms, deafen'd and stunn'd

> By noise of waters, making innocent Sleep
> Lie melancholy among weary bones. (6.568–72, 573–80)

But my phrase "narrative interpolation" is only a half-truth. Although this passage is certainly narrative, it is not an interpolation—in composition or in substance. (There is no evidence that Wordsworth wrote it and the immediately preceding passage at different times; see Reed, *Wordsworth* 12–13, 641–42.) Its neglect by most of the excellent readers who have looked carefully at the Simplon Pass section may reflect a tacit assumption that it is an interpolation; in any case, their neglect seriously, if only implicitly, undervalues Wordsworth's reservation about the lyric moment. Here this reservation takes the form of apparently prosaic narrative. But Reed convincingly shows that "the richness of symbolic overtone in the poet's language is hardly less [here] than in the preceding lines" and concludes that the two passages share "a demonstration that both experience and acknowledgement of experience of limits of understanding and action may become vital parts of creation" ("Speaker of *The Prelude*" 287, 289).[22] I would add only emphasis: the two parts *put together* especially emphasize the narrator's awareness that such limits permeate experience, that they are not reserved only for dramatic events such as stealing a boat, climbing a mountain, or composing a poem. If we were to take a narrative addition (like the lines about confused sleep) as mere interpolation, required either to keep the story going or to avoid confrontation with apocalypse,[23] we would be forced to see *The Prelude* and its poet as centered, intentionally or not, on the lyric moment, which excludes narrative and the creative mind's acknowledgment of limits. But all through his poetry, Wordsworth took pains to show the inadequacy of this moment: even a poem like "I wandered lonely as a cloud" is implicitly narrative; at the other extreme, the dominant order of his collected poems ("according to an order of time") may be narrative as well.

Thus even where *The Prelude* is generally considered to be at its greatest lyric intensity, Wordsworth's concern is also narrative. By this I mean not that such moments are wholly subsumed in and mastered by narrative, only that they are habitually conjoined. To some extent, as Jonathan Bishop puts it, "the feelings embodied in the original mysterious event remain attached to the structure of the event itself."[24] But as Chandler has argued in some detail, "From its very outset . . . the poem admonishes its reader *not* to focus on the spots of time to exclusion of the temporal field behind them" (187).

This narrative concern gives birth to Wordsworth's temporal scheme for ordering his shorter poems; it also becomes, as I am trying to show, an informing source of—if it does not give birth to—the odic form of the Intimations Ode. Wordsworth may not have conceived his ode's generic comprehensiveness when he began it, presumably with stanzas 1–4. But he never saw these four stanzas, mostly pastoral and implicitly elegiac, as a complete poem—because, I believe, they did not answer their question. That is, for Wordsworth the poem was not yet narrative. In this context it is significant to note again that he probably was writing the final seven stanzas of the ode, which make the poem essentially a narrative, during the first months of 1804—a time when most of his other composition was also narrative. He was then working on *The Prelude* and *The Ruined Cottage* and "carefully considering the project of a long narrative poem" (Reed, *Wordsworth* 246; see also 11–12, 22, 27, 36, 246–54).

In this respect the Intimations Ode differs radically from the characteristic eighteenth-century irregular ode, for which narrative "plot" was subsidiary. Narrative was "not what held a poem together, but stirring incident that could serve as the occasion for lofty utterance" (Maclean 414). The loftiness of this utterance derived precisely from a sometimes fictive lyric inspiration, as the cliché "Pindaric ecstasy" might imply. The irregular ode—itself often believed to be, in Edward Young's words, "the eldest kind of poetry" ("On Lyric Poetry," in Anderson 10:41)—imitated primitive poetry, whose apparent or real lack of order was attributed to unself-conscious inspiration. Hugh Blair, writing in 1783, is representative: "Poetry . . . in its ancient original condition, was perhaps more vigorous than it is in its modern state. It included then, the whole burst of the human mind. . . . It spoke then the language of passion, and no other. . . . [T]he early Bard . . . sung indeed in wild and disorderly strains; but they were the native effusions of his heart. . . ."[25] This "original condition," however, was in an important sense fictional, even in the English ode's beginnings. Cowley and at least some later poet-critics knew that Pindar's odes were carefully formed; yet they established the pseudo-Pindaric form as representing a kind of formlessness—one suggested, paradoxically, by Pindar himself.[26] We have already seen a late version of this attitude in Wordsworth's characterization of the irregular ode as a "lax species of writing," with its "impassioned music of versification" reflecting "a state of freedom."

The fiction that the ode is formless, whatever the reasons for it, was useful to the eighteenth-century poet, because it seemed to reflect unself-consciousness, an escape from time that is as manifest to the poet in the "rich and intimidating legacy of the past" as it is to the man in the "crushing presence of history."[27] Akenside's "On the Absence of the Poetical Inclination," Collins's "Ode on the Poetical Character," Gray's "Progress of Poesy," for example, are not all really epideictic, as was the neoclassical ode, but elegiac or invocatory, lamenting lost or absent unself-conscious power. This fantasy of absorption into lost power, this sought-for moment of unself-consciousness, is a central attribute of the eighteenth-century sublime. This link between the sublime and timeless ecstasy is explicit in, for example, Gray's description of Milton as "he, that rode sublime / Upon the seraph-wings of ecstasy" ("The Progress of Poesy. A Pindaric Ode," Anderson 10:220). It is central also to Edmund Burke's argument: "Whatever is fitted in any sort to excite the ideas of pain, and danger, that is to say, whatever is in any sort terrible, or is conversant about terrible objects, or operates in a manner analogous to terror, is a source of the *sublime;* that is, it is productive of the strongest emotion which the mind is capable of feeling." This "terror is in all cases whatsoever, either more openly or latently the ruling principle of the sublime." Notice that timelessness, and implicitly unself-consciousness, are central to this mind possessed by sublime emotion: "all its motions are suspended. . . . [T]he mind is so entirely filled with its object, that it cannot entertain any other, nor by consequence reason on that object which employs it."[28]

Throughout the eighteenth century the irregular ode was, as Maclean tells us, "everywhere identified with sublimity," to the point that it was most often called "the sublime ode" (420). But Wordsworth does not trust the sublime, lyric moment to be definitive of the ode, or of poetry in general. Consistently and deliberately he includes lyric in a larger, narrative "plot." We have seen this inclusion in Book 6 of *The Prelude* and in the arrangement of his collected poems— both in their overall temporal sequence and in the frequency with which narratives and odes end groups of poems. The same temporal sequence appears in miniature in the Intimations Ode's epigraph, which signals not only the plot, child to man, but an anxiety to explore that plot—"I *could wish* my days to be / Bound each to each" (emphasis added)—rather than elegize or eulogize it. This ode, then, confronts time, and for Wordsworth the confrontation is necessarily narrative. That narrative is, in the collected poems as well as in the Intimations Ode itself, as comprehensive as possible—with comprehensiveness sanctioned in the collection by the traditional pattern of the major poet, who moves from less to more inclusive genres, and in the poem by seventeenth- and eighteenth-century theory about the odic form and by the example of Milton's Nativity Ode.

The characteristic sublime odes of the mid-eighteenth century, in contrast, seek neither narrative nor comprehensiveness. Instead the odes of Akenside, Collins, and Gray reveal their speakers' common desire for the sublime lyric moment, their invocations to various passions arising from a desire for unself-conscious absorption in such passions, from a fantasy of oneness. Not only the subjective odes but the epideictic odes of the eighteenth century that aspire to epic share this fantasy, seeking to immerse the praising self in the "deeds sublime" of public figures (Congreve, "A Pindaric Ode, Humbly Offer'd to the Queen, on the Victorious Progress of Her Majesty's Arms under the Conduct of the Duke of Marlborough," Anderson 7:571), whose actions become more sublime than any art, because they rouse even greater, unself-conscious passions than art does:

> The poet's name
> He best shall prove,
> Whose lays the soul with noblest passions move.
> But thee, O progeny of heroes old,
> Thee to severer toils thy fate requires:
> The fate which form'd thee in a chosen mould,
> The grateful country of thy sires,
> Thee to sublimer paths demand;
> Sublimer than thy sires could trace,
> Or thine own Edward teach his race,
> Though Gaul's proud genius sank beneath his hand.
> (Akenside, "Ode XVIII. To the Right Honorable Francis Earl of Hunting-
> don. 1747," Anderson 9:786)

This absorption in otherness is what the speaker in Wordsworth's ode has already lost in stanzas 1–4, the loss taking the form of both a perceptual change ("The things which I have seen I now can see no more") and a psychological separation from the pastoral scene ("To me alone there came a thought of grief"). Perception and psyche come together in the persistent dream imagery of this first part of the poem, the word "dream" implying that this absorption was always a fantasy. It remains a powerful fantasy, and the sometimes strained rhetoric and rhythm of stanzas 3 and 4 show that the speaker is attracted back to it. The strange lines "Oh evil day! if I were sullen / While the Earth herself is adorning" provide further evidence. They are strange because they deny sullenness even while tacitly admitting the sense of self-consciousness and therefore psychological isolation from the scene that presumably causes sullenness. They suggest that the speaker is trying to talk himself into unself-conscious identification with the pastoral scene; they do not describe it as already achieved. However powerful the natural longing for such unself-consciousness, Wordsworth's speaker does not spend the entire poem in that longing, whether hopeful or despairing. Even in the first four stanzas he rigorously counterbalances his longing by his recurrent, explicit recognition of felt reality: "The sunshine is a glorious birth; / *But yet* I know . . . ," "Now, while the Birds thus sing . . . / . . . *To me alone* there came a thought of grief," "with joy I hear! / —*But* there's a Tree" (emphasis added).[29] It is a felt reality: the tree and field "speak of something that is gone"; neither they nor he can explain what it is. But he is able to articulate the question at the end of stanza 4, and in doing so—and in trying in the rest of the poem to understand his loss rather than invoking the return of a state before loss—he leaves behind the subjective odes of the mideighteenth century.

Wordsworth thus makes opposite use of a genre that the previous poetic generation had often used to seek freedom from time consciousness through the lyric intensity of the sublime. This radical difference may help explain why Wordsworth's ode has few generic allusions: earlier odes, at least those immediately preceding it, provide the wrong sort of model for a poet whose conception of "greater things" (majora) includes intellectual and emotional understanding, not just sublime feelings. This conception animates all the poetry of this writer, who "wish[ed] either to be considered as a Teacher, or as nothing" (WL 2:195). It perhaps illuminates a larger reason for his general lack of allusiveness when compared with earlier major poets: Wordsworth sought a wider but less educated audience, which would become broader the more his poetry, even his great ode, diverged from Gray's palimpsest-like poems, whose audience was defined by its education. (Wordsworth sharply criticized Gray for such allusiveness: "He wrote English Verses, as he and other Eton school-Boys wrote Latin; filching a phrase now from one author, and now from another. I do not profess to be a person of very various reading; nevertheless if I were to pluck out of Grays tail all the feathers which, I know, belong to other Birds he would be left very bare indeed" [WL 5:301].) We recall here Wordsworth's acute concern for the audience that habitually read "half-penny Ballads, and penny and two-penny histories"; "of these straggling papers," he writes:

> I have so much felt the[ir] influence, . . . that I have many a time wished that I had talents to produce songs, poems, and little histories, that might circulate among other good things in this way, supplanting partly the bad; flowers and useful herbs to take the place of weeds. Indeed, some of the Poems which I have published were composed not without a hope that at some time or other they might answer this purpose. (WL 2:248)

We are reaching a paradox, in my argument at least, for I am contending both that Wordsworth's ode is significantly indebted to the odic tradition and that it rarely reflects that indebtedness with overt allusion. If I am right, then his engagement with earlier odes is fundamentally solitary. In fact the one ode to which Wordsworth unequivocally alludes, Gray's "On the Pleasure Arising from Vicissitude," is less central to it than other odes that it does not clearly echo. Gray's lines come near the end of his unfinished poem:

The meanest floweret of the vale,
The simplest note that swells the gale,
The common sun, the air, the skies,
To him are opening Paradise.
(Anderson 10:195)

As de Sélincourt notes, the allusion is clear in Wordsworth's final lines: "To me the meanest flower that blows can give / Thoughts that do often lie too deep for tears" (*Poetical Works* 4:467). But for Gray's "wretch, that long has tossed / On the thorny bed of pain," paradise derives from an impersonal contrast between "rosy pleasure" and "a kindred grief," between "comfort" and "misery," which leads to the sort of aesthetic distancing that is present, we shall see, at the end of the Eton College Ode, an aesthetic for which "The hues of bliss more brightly glow, / Chastis'd by sabler tints of woe. . . ." Wordsworth, in contrast, cannot see pleasure and pain in such distanced, purely aesthetic terms, and he is too acutely conscious of such a paradise as prehistorical to equate it with "The common sun, the air, the skies." This "common" world for Wordsworth cannot alone lead to "Paradise"—a deluded, pastoral claim. We recall that in *The Recluse* Prospectus manuscript, perhaps virtually contemporaneous with the ode (see Reed, *Wordsworth* 37, 663–65), "Paradise" is "the growth of common day" *only* when "this outward frame of things" is "wedded" to "minds."[30] Similarly, in the Intimations Ode the common world leads to "Thoughts," which, however—in being "too deep for tears"—remain ambiguous, perhaps "affirming a new philosophic certainty beyond grief," perhaps "admitting his overwhelming sense of loss."[31]

Recent critical emphasis on the conventionality of genre, on a "generic contract" between author and audience in which the terms are more or less clear to both parties, does not help us here, where I claim indebtedness without allusion.[32] Wordsworth may not perceive a contract specific to the ode at all, since the many uses to which the ode had been put in the eighteenth century might have inextricably snarled, or invalidated, the definition. Perhaps more important is Wordsworth's ambivalence about genre. We might remember his explicit consideration of genre in the 1798 Advertisement to *Lyrical Ballads:* "that most dreadful enemy to our pleasures, our own pre-established codes of decision." "[R]eaders, for their own sakes, should not suffer the solitary word Poetry, a word of very disputed meaning, to stand in the way of their gratification. . . ." Yet he continues, "An accurate taste in poetry . . . is an acquired talent, which can only be produced by severe thought, and a long continued intercourse with the best models of composition." Now Wordsworth did not seek only those readers who had the opportunity and means to be well acquainted with the literary tradition, as he shows by his quick qualification in the very next sentence:

"This is mentioned not with so ridiculous a purpose as to prevent the most experienced reader from judging for himself; but merely to temper the rashness of decision . . ." (*Prose* 1:116–17). This comment suggests that for Wordsworth the "severe thought" and "long continued intercourse with the best models" are the poet's—not, or at least not necessarily, the reader's.

Any reconstruction of a solitary encounter between the poet and a generic tradition must be hypothetical. Despite this reservation, I want to consider the encounter. I believe that the three most important odic "models" in Wordsworth's "long continued intercourse" are Milton's ode "On the Morning of Christ's Nativity," which we have already noted; Dryden's "Alexander's Feast"; and Gray's "Ode on a Distant Prospect of Eton College." These three are by major poets with whose works Wordsworth habitually compared his own, and their central motifs—divine birth, musical sounds, and playing children, respectively—are present in the Intimations Ode, albeit subsumed. Similar motifs occur in many odes before Wordsworth's: speculations about or praise for divinity or immortality (for example, the odes by Pomfret and Watts), praise for music (the specific tradition of the Saint Cecilia's Day odes on music), and the relating of a dramatized poetic self to a fantasied happier or more powerful self (the mideighteenth-century subjective odes).

Milton's ode is, like the child's intimations of preexistence, only a shadowy recollection hovering about the edges of Wordsworth's poem. It thereby casts into relief two important larger contexts implied throughout the Intimations Ode. First, Wordsworth's poem connects the child and his birth with the Incarnation itself—connects, not equates. "[W]e come," in words not to be glossed over as Christian anomalies in a dialectic of self and nature, "From *God*, who is our home: / *Heaven* lies about us in our infancy!" (st. 5; emphasis added). If "The Child is Father of the Man," then the poet's wish that such a connection be maintained by "natural piety" becomes not only a familial and natural devotion but specifically a religious one. That is, the poet does not worship blindly and egotistically his earlier or preexistent self; instead, he piously values his own nativity as a sign, however enigmatic, that there is something more than nature and self.

Milton's poem concerns the morning of Christ's birth and thus, broadly, nature and divinity. Necessarily the poet has some relation to this subject, Milton's being one of confidence as an observer in complete poetic control of his material. This confident control—like the virtually omnipotent control that Dryden's Timotheus has over his material, both musical (lyre) and human (Alexander)—is abandoned by Wordsworth; or, rather, it is unattainable from the start, in a poem explicitly about loss and uncertainty and implicitly about the complex and confusing internalization of Incarnation. Serene poetic control here would surely suggest the egocentric self-deception and self-worship of the omnipotent poet.

Perhaps Milton avoids such charges by restricting his overt subject to the morning (nature) rather than the Nativity (divinity); in any case, he does not seem to find the issue of poetic control a problem in this poem, as it later becomes in *Paradise Lost*. Wordsworth does, and indeed must, find it so—since, having internalized Incarnation, he cannot be restrictive—and this issue of poetic power, the second context that Milton's poem provides for the Intimations Ode, is potentially central to the genre.

Paul Fry's definition of the ode centers on this one issue and the ode's attitude toward it: "in the considerable odes of every era, a burden of doubt subverts the assertion of knowledge" (8)—a remark to which my discussion of Wordsworth's ode is seriously indebted. But this doubt is debatable in Milton and absent in Dryden. It overwhelms the mideighteenth-century odes; only Wordsworth's poem seems able intentionally to tolerate both assertion and doubt. I am not claiming that Wordsworth's is therefore more essentially an ode—only that it is different.[33] Dryden's ode, like Milton's, is primarily epideictic. Its secondary issue of poetic power takes the metaphorical form of music, which has the power—unproblematic, except perhaps in moral terms—to incite listeners to immediate passion and equally immediate action. This assertion is probably not true, but at least it makes for some action, which gives "Alexander's Feast" a plot, whatever its static (because epideictic) rhetoric. In Wordsworth's ode the relation between music and human feeling is deepened. Unlike Alexander, Wordsworth's speaker is not moved by the music in stanzas 3 and 4, although he wants to be. But he is not one of the unself-conscious "blessed Creatures," a lamb or even a shepherd, and in his self-consciousness he is cut off from their spontaneous participation in pastoral joy. Nor is he a cultural primitive like Alexander, as portrayed by Dryden. (We can see this primitivism clearly if we imagine how absurd Alexander's behavior would seem if Dryden had attributed it to William III.)

Although Gray's "Ode on a Distant Prospect of Eton College" is not quite so solipsistically subjective as the mideighteenth-century odes that invoke or elegize various personifications, it remains without a plot and offers instead only a static contrast, however learned and ironic, between happy, ignorant youth and the unhappy, wise speaker. The contrast is between youth and age, between the "little victims," who, "regardless of their doom," participate in their schoolboy pastoral of "chas[ing] the rolling circle's speed, / Or urg[ing] the flying ball," and the speaker, who knows their doom—"all are men, / Condemn'd alike to groan," for whom "Thought would destroy their paradise." To Gray's speaker this gap is unbridgeable except by wishful self-deception:

Ah, happy hills, ah, pleasing shade,
Ah, fields belov'd in vain,

Where once my careless childhood stray'd,
A stranger yet to pain?
I feel the gales, that from ye blow,
A momentary bliss bestow,
As waving fresh their gladsome wing,
My weary soul they seem to sooth,
And, redolent of joy and youth,
To breathe a second spring.

His momentary bliss and nostalgic look at the Eton schoolboys collapse in the face of adult reality, leaving him able merely to mourn the gap, his only consolation being the aesthetic irony of the final lines, "where ignorance is bliss, / 'Tis folly to be wise" (Anderson 10:216–17). The "happy hills," "fields," and "gales" blowing on the speaker find their counterparts in the Intimations Ode's "mountains," "fields of sleep," and "Winds"; however, as we have already seen, Wordsworth's speaker, instead of accepting a complete split between child and adult, sees the child as "Father of the Man" and seeks to understand the relation.[34]

Wordsworth explores the relations central to Dryden and Gray—between music and human feeling, between youth and age—as a gap between past and present, between musically inspired, unself-conscious emotional participation in action, and self-conscious inaction. In a three-part structure appropriate to its genre, the Intimations Ode pictures and elegizes the gap in stanzas 1–4, anatomizes its origin in stanzas 5–8, and finds value in that consciousness in stanzas 9–11, because that consciousness enables the poet-speaker

in thought [to] join your throng,
Ye that pipe and ye that play,
Ye that through your hearts to day
Feel the gladness of the May!

Such consciousness when—or if—matured into "the philosophic mind" becomes the catalyst for what Chayes calls a dramatic plot within a lyric frame. The progressing poem, the "lyric frame," becomes the action—the "dramatic Plot"—by which the poet discovers that growing old can also mean growing up.[35]

What must be added here to Chayes's formulation is just this maturation through time, which the poem mirrors from infancy to maturity and which gives the Intimations Ode a plot that is not only dramatic but narrative. Jeffrey Robinson denies this maturation in the poem, finding instead "a regression to an identification with the childlike" (162); by doing so, he and his students in effect read the Ode as confirming their versions of Stanley Fish's professionalism and Norman Holland's "identity theme," but with a critical edge: "New Critical study of images, patterns, rhetoric, in general the search for the poem's 'meaning' in its own terms . . . is essentially a version of the classificatory activity of Enlightenment thinking: control the object by casting light on all its dark, secret corners; remove the otherness from the poem. It is only a step from such a taming of the object to investing it with the power one wishes: that it rescue one from one's own inner turbulence" (169). They learn, necessarily and only from placing the Ode in its historical contexts, especially that of its revisions, that this rescue fantasy derives not only from their New Critical conditioning but from "Wordsworth's rhetoric of transcendence and consolation" (21). It is telling that at the book's beginning Robinson describes this thinking— "controlling (or having the fantasy of controlling) all of the work's mystery, its otherness or subjecthood"—as "what the Frankfurt critics Horkheimer and Adorno would consider *a degraded form* of Enlightenment thinking" (10; emphasis added), suggesting that formalist interpretation of the poem does not lead inevitably to "investing it with the power [that] one wishes" but that, presumably, is not really there.

The poem's true and untranscended dialectic lies in the coexistence of the value the poet discovers in growing up and the intermittent but powerful elegiac tone of the poem. This unresolved tension enables the poem to bear up under the narrative-autobiographical weight placed on it by its position at the end of Wordsworth's collected poems. A poem simple in style, lyric in substance, and resolved in argument could not bear this weight. Such a poem, placed in this summary position, would imply some corresponding simplification, and therefore falsification, of the poet's sense of his own life in relation to poetry. Here, growing up does not imply the poet's self-deceptive reduction of his complex self to doctrinal statements, idiosyncratic or orthodox. It includes instead a recognition of uncertainties and limits to human understanding: "questionings," "Fallings," "vanishings," "misgivings," "shadowy recollections, / Which, *be they what they may, / . . . /* Uphold us" are for this poet the "truths" for which he "raise[s] / The song of thanks and praise" (st. 9; emphasis added). His song, then, is not a pastoral one in praise of unambiguous feelings of pleasure and leisure, "the simple creed / Of Childhood," or a didactic one explaining immortality,[36] or an epideictic one in single-minded praise of an achieved maturity.

Perhaps because he distrusted the pastoral or the sublime lyric moment as an oversimplification, Wordsworth, who at *The Prelude*'s end sought to "teach" and "Instruct" (13.445, 446), could not present in this ode—any more than in *The Prelude* or at the ends of groups of poems in the collected poetry—a lyric summation of his, or human, existence. Perhaps because he believed that the poet is "a man speaking to men," he teaches us not about preexistence and immortality but instead about complex human responses to life, responses that involve the poet's attempted comprehension of his self. We might remember here what Wordsworth went on to say clearly in the 1802 Preface. The poet "has a greater knowledge of human nature, and a more comprehensive soul, than are supposed to be common among mankind." His poetry, whose "object is truth," "is the image of man and nature," "man and the objects that surround him . . . acting and re-acting upon each other, so as to produce an infinite complexity of pain and pleasure" (*Prose* 1:137–40). Such complexity is, I think, closely akin to the unresolved tension between loss and gain, pain and pleasure, in the Intimations Ode. If so, then for Wordsworth the poem is didactic, its truth being an irreducibly complex image of man and nature conveyed partly through the comprehensiveness of the genre. (This observation suggests in turn that the often-asserted Romantic "shift from a hierarchy adapted to didactic forms to one adjusted to lyric forms" [Cohen 62] might better be regarded, here at least, as a combining of didactic and lyric.) Central to this truth is that the self is not and cannot be a god, a perfect "favoured being" (*Prelude* [1850] 14.133), or even a master teacher. Wordsworth has not mastered his own lecture on immortality, the poem; he has not achieved the Olympian detachment that would make his ode a perfectly well wrought urn.

Wordsworth intentionally rejects such a self-image and such a poem. As poet he cannot be godlike; as auditor he can neither identify with music unselfconsciously nor, like a god, be its source; as adult he cannot cut himself off from childhood; as poet, again, he cannot achieve full identification with the power beyond his comprehension. What are these but themes transformed from the odes we have discussed—the Nativity Ode, Alexander's Feast, the Eton College Ode, and the odes addressed to personified powers? What Milton's ode avoids, that the poet cannot control Incarnation; what Dryden's ignores, that a human being is not a hypothetical primitive governed by music; what the eighteenth-century odes implicitly (though sometimes unintentionally) admit, that one cannot lose oneself in a power beyond human understanding—all these versions of inescapable self-consciousness Wordsworth's ode confronts and explores, not transcending these conditions but granting them. The elegiac tone of the poem is not unwitting evidence of the delusions that what has been lost was ever possessed and that the loss is replaced by something comfortingly called "the philosophic mind," a refuge from anxiety. Instead, the Intimations Ode's greatest strength is exactly the uneasy but essentially human coexistence of statement and uncertainty, its belief that, "be they what they may," there are "truths that [have been] wake[ned], / To perish never," along with the elegiac tone of regret for something lost. It is this awareness of coexistence, not the recognition of one and the rejection of the other, that "bring[s] the philosophic mind."

In the Intimations Ode, then, Wordsworth subsumes the typical failure of the eighteenth-century ode to achieve unself-consciousness—whether through sublime identification with power or through nostalgic participation in pastoral. His poem admits the impossibility of ever achieving that state and then seeks to understand that impossibility without transcending it. In this respect Wordsworth's ode generically overlaps pastoral elegy, presenting loss in relation to gain.[37] The speaker elegizes (a perceptual power of) his former self and then comes to terms with what has been lost, but without claiming to have achieved self-mastery by transcending the loss. This coming-to-terms recovers from nostalgia and fantasy such modes as pastoral, lyric, and elegiac. The eighteenth-century odes tend instead to reject one generic mode for another: Congreve "scorns . . . oaten reeds" in favor of "sing[ing] heroic deeds"; Young's "useful cares / Transcend diversion light"; Gray's "fields [are] belov'd in vain," providing only "momentary bliss." Wordsworth seems closer to the Nativity Ode, where Milton places pastoral, lyric, and elegy directly or indirectly at the service of religious praise. But for Wordsworth these modes are not wholly subsumed by a transcendent legitimizing purpose; his poem stops short of complete and perfect generic assimilation.

In this way of talking about the Intimations Ode, and especially about its ending, as deliberately imperfect, "imperfection" does not mean what it does in negative criticism of the poem. With a few exceptions, imperfection is generally located in the final part, stanzas 9–11. These exceptions are tonal irregularity—"a somewhat frenetically whipped-up enthusiasm" in stanza 4 and an "amused patronage" in stanza 7 (Brooks, *Well Wrought Urn* 140)—and intellectual incoherence in stanza 8—how can the child be "blindly with [its] blessedness at strife" and yet an "Eye among the blind"? While the first exceptions admittedly are tonal changes, we have seen that the genre partly justifies them. An ode is not obliged to maintain a consistently elevated tone; emotional excess in stanza 4 dramatically matches the speaker's feelings; satire in stanza 7 is appropriate not only to the speaker's need to guard against nostalgia but to the ode's generic comprehensiveness of viewpoint. The second exception, first raised by Coleridge (*Biographia* 2:138–41), has been explained subtly by Johnston: "even in childhood the recollection of immortality 'was' experienced as something 'fugitive'—fast fleeing—and made the more so by our blind childish instinct to grow up as quickly as possible. That is to say, Wordsworth joys to remember not the-thing-in-itself but its mode of being, the way in which it was apprehended and experienced" ("Recollecting Forgetting" 63).

Exceptions aside, then, we come to the most widely agreed-on imperfection, the poem's conclusion. The disappointed comments with which I began this chapter have in common their expectation of mastery, of a congruent intellectual and emotional closure. This expectation is heightened both by the poem's position in the collected poetry, at a place of closure, and by its genre, which signals confident poetic inspiration and, by including other generic modes, implies synthetic power. But I have suggested that Wordsworth sees in the odic form the possibility for an important kind of incoherence, a deliberate lack of closure. Consequently his ode both attempts and rejects complete mastery. First, it claims no transcendent sanction for the synthesis it attempts ("natural piety"); its conclusion is not otherworldly (unless we regard phrases like "Blank misgivings" as Wordsworth's unintentional flounderings for better words). Second, while the form may imply bardic confidence, the major eighteenth-century odes, as we have seen, exhibit the failure of that confidence. The poet can no longer hope or pretend that his muse or some other transcendent power, not he alone, is responsible for his poem, for both its inspired form and its possible inclusion of other genres. The modernity of Wordsworth's ode is signaled by the combination of opening self-consciousness and intellectual analysis. No muses or powers are wishfully invoked. An attempted synthesis that is not wholly resolved on the same intellectual and emotional levels, then, is not necessarily an aesthetic flaw — unless we require an inhumanly perfect poetic form and a mastery of the human in a genre that, by Wordsworth's time, hints in its form at essential imperfection.

Only a few years after the 1849–50 publication of Wordsworth's final lifetime collected poems — all forming, in his own metaphor, an incomplete "gothic church" (*Prose* 3:5–6) — Ruskin coincidentally argued that the "imperfection" of Gothic architecture is *"essential"* because "no architecture can be truly noble which is *not* imperfect." He went even farther, arguing that "the demand for perfection is always a sign of a misunderstanding of the ends of art," for two reasons: first, "no great man ever stops working till he has reached his point of failure"; second, "imperfection is in some sort essential to all that we know of life. . . . Nothing that lives is, or can be, rigidly perfect."[38] I have in effect applied Ruskin's arguments to the Intimations Ode. They necessarily apply also to the collected poetry, given the positioning of the ode at the end and the circularity of its epigraph. For Wordsworth never did regard his work as a perfectly finished artifact but saw it instead as an always imperfect form of life. So he revised until he died. But he also recognized the truth of Ruskin's justification of imperfection. Of *The Prelude* he wrote: "If when the work shall be finished it appears to the judicious to have redundancies they shall be lopped off, if possible. But this is very difficult to do when a man has written with thought, and this defect, whenever I have suspected it or found it to exist in any writings of mine, I have always found incurable. The fault lies too deep, and is in the first conception" (*WL* 1:587). Wordsworth chose both genre and place for his ode partly to highlight his sense of the imperfection intrinsic to human life. He reflects this imperfection both in his arrangement of the poems, with the Intimations Ode last, and in his two metaphors for the collection—an incomplete Gothic church and a human life.

5 *Lamia*

Attitude Is Every Thing

Keats's *Lamia* encourages its readers to take sides but makes it uncertain with whom and with what actions we are to side, morally and emotionally. Earlier readers aware of this uncertainty generally regarded it as a flaw in the poem caused by Keats's confusion or lack of narrative ability.[1] Some readers more recently have come to see it as functional;[2] we have not yet, however, investigated how much the problem is specifically a narrative one.[3] This lack of critical attention to the poem's narrator may be due largely to Bernice Slote's influential study of *Lamia*, which argues that the poem is not personal but dramatic in conception and nature. This argument solves the poem's narrative problem by mastering the narrator's comments generically as "choric comment," a distant dramatic analogue, which "summarizes and affirms the mood and accomplishment of the action itself."[4]

I shall argue instead that this uncertainty indirectly reflects Keats's narrative strategy, a strategy that denies—to his reader, to his narrator, and perhaps, paradoxically, to Keats himself—mastery of that narrative. The narrator appears to be omniscient, fully in control of his story; Keats counts on the reader's customary identification with such a narrator. Nonetheless, Keats eventually prevents such a comfortable relationship, by complicating the narrator's attitudes to the point that the reader, in order to identify again with him, must accept limits to his own desire for mastery over the story and its characters. This argument attributes an ultimately moral dimension to the "sensation" that is usually said to be the intended effect of *Lamia*.

In *The Nature of Narrative*, Robert Scholes and Robert Kellogg observe that "a narrator who is not in some way suspect, who is not in some way subject to ironic scrutiny is what the modern temper finds least bearable."[5] But whatever the modern temper may prefer, Keats's narrator seems to claim omniscience, albeit secular rather than the prophetic omniscience of Blake's Bard of Experience. He begins his story confidently, "Upon a time"—the phrase signaling a familiar genre, the fairy tale, in which, while events may be problematic, we do not expect their narrator to be so.[6] He moves untroubled into the minds of his characters ("So Hermes thought"), backs off to elaborate external description ("She was a gordian shape of dazzling hue") and dramatic presentation ("'Fair Hermes . . . / I had a splendid dream of thee last night'"), again enters into the characters' minds ("the charmed god began / An oath, and through the serpent's ears it ran / Warm, tremulous, devout, psalterian"), shifts to interpretive commentary ("It was no dream; or say a dream it was, / Real are the dreams of Gods")—all without hesitation.[7] Such narrative dexterity is coupled with what Bate has shown to be an intentional "rapidity of flow" of the Drydenesque couplets unique in Keats's later poetry (*Stylistic Development* 171, 166). The two together encourage us to accept the narrator's extranarrative commentaries in the confident, straightforward spirit in which they are given.

At first we should have no trouble agreeing with his assertions: that the dreams of gods are real (1.126–28) and that gods and their love do not grow pale (1.145); that mortal lovers do grow pale (1.145), even though we, as mortals, would naturally wish it otherwise (1.394–97); that, as every realist knows, love on this earth inevitably causes pain (2.1–6), although there is nothing like a real woman for, presumably, a real man (1.328–33). None of this is problematic so long as we take the narrator to be a real man, an uncomplicated man of the world, telling a fairy tale in a brisk, no-nonsense way. But even this conjunction should give us pause: common sense in such an overt and aggressive form is anomalous in a fairy tale. Also, while the narrator appears to assume his omniscience and the worth of his own worldliness, if he were no more than this man of confident common sense we would be faced with a difficult problem, which perhaps explains why even the best readers of the poem generally avoid its narrator. The problem can be stated simply: if the narrator is as straightforward and uncomplicated as he seems to be, to whom do we attribute the poem's astonishing subtlety and complication, which exist on all other levels of the poem—character, action, language? Evidence for its complexity of character and action needs no repetition here; criticism of the poem has gone beyond attempting to prove that, for example, Lamia is really a serpent disguised as a woman or really a woman temporarily transformed into a serpent, or that Apollonius's victory is one of truth over illusion. The poem's subtlety of language is perhaps less familiar; it should become clearer in the course of my argument.

We might hypothesize as the deus ex machina for our problem a second figure, an "implied author" standing behind the narrator like the poet behind the limited narrators of Wordsworth's experimental narratives such as *The Thorn*.[8] But those narrators are consistently present. In *Lamia* Keats does not seem concerned to maintain the consistently limited point of view that this strategy requires; such a narrator's limitations often are completely absent from a story that is still being told, presumably by the implied author. Moreover, even some of the least complicated of the passages clearly attributable to the narrator turn out to be far deeper than this limited narrator could ever be. Let us take the apparently straightforward beginning: "Upon a time, before the faery broods / Drove Nymph and Satyr from the prosperous woods" (1.1–2). "[Once] Upon a time, before [a time]" is a doubling of the fairy tale opening; it presents two mythological worlds in sequence. While neither world alone is historical, the replacement of one by the other implies that in *Lamia*, as Donald Reiman argues convincingly, "all man's gods and ideals are subject to flux and change because they are products of the human mind."[9] But our narrator seems not to understand this close relationship between the human and mythological worlds. Instead, he asserts that the Hermes-nymph episode at the poem's beginning is only an ironic contrast to mortal love: "Real are the dreams of Gods, and smoothly pass / Their pleasures in a long immortal dream" (1.127–28). Following the narrator's suggestion, readers long have seen the two loves as, in Earl Wasserman's words, "a contrast between union with essence under the conditions of the ideal world and union with essence in the world of mutability."[10]

Careful study of the two loves, however, produces a view that does not accord with the narrator's apparent understanding of their relationship: it sees instead change, and awareness of change, permeating virtually every phrase of the poem. One example, which I choose because it is clearly the narrator's comment, will suffice: "For all this came a ruin" (2.16). In his detailed study of this permeation, Garrett Stewart comments that the preposition "for" also means "in spite of" or "because of"; "the inextricable paradox of escapist fantasy" is thus "locked into the very diction." In consequence, "Metamorphosis becomes not just a theme but an epistemological mode, for the changes that Keats's rhetoric manages to ring in the progress of his narrative are dynamic, wrung from the flux of language as the reader grapples with it from moment to revisionary moment" (22, 40).

If change and ambiguity are presented so consistently and thoroughly in the poem, such presentation is almost necessarily intentional. But to whom do we attribute this intention? It is certainly not that of a narrator who implies mastery over his characters' identities by the unequivocal categories he uses for them—gods and men, Lamia a "snake" (1.88), a "serpent" (1.113) and Lamia a "lady" (1.171), a "maid" (1.185). In his use of these labels the narrator seems confidently oblivious to the possibility of paradox or inclusive alternatives: a "serpent! certes, she / Was none" (2.80–81).

The overtly contradictory nature of these characterizations should arrest us here, force us to begin to see the narrator as less than candid in his common sense, as hardly simple in his understanding, as one who has designs upon his readers, however subtle those designs. I am aware that Keats wrote, "We hate poetry that has a palpable design upon us. . . . Poetry should be great & unobtrusive, a thing which enters into one's soul, and does not startle it or amaze it with itself but with its subject."[11] But *Lamia* simply is not "unobtrusive," and it does not seem intended as such by Keats. I suggest therefore, following Hazlitt, that by "design" here he means primarily autobiographical self-expression (an argument implied by Bate, *John Keats* 259–60, 295–96, and see *KL* 1:223, n. 6). Perhaps, in addition, Keats is objecting primarily to the palpability of design, its lack of subtlety, rather than design itself—for his frequent emphasis in the letters on his poetry "doing some good for the world" implies that Keats too "has a . . . design upon us," if perhaps not a palpable one (*KL* 1:271; and see 2:139, 146).

In any case, the design is subtle. If there are no absolutes in the story for the narrator, if he is aware that the gods themselves are not metaphors for an unchanging realm of essence but reflections of human desire that alone is constant, there can be no transcendental truth that the narrator believes and is trying to reveal in his story. Indeed, "desire" is the key word here: the desire for the absolute is no less constitutive of what "human" means in this poem, and no more rational, than sexual passion itself—which is one reason why Apollonius and the philosophy he represents (and has taught to Lycius) are imaged in the same terms as Lamia and her passion.[12] Apollonius, according to Lycius, possesses the "lashless eyelids" (2.288) of a serpent, and like his pupil is "robed in philosophic gown" (1.365); his pupil's "mind [is] wrapp'd like his mantle" (1.242), "His phantasy . . . lost, where reason fades, / In the calm'd twilight of Platonic shades" (1.235–36).[13]

This curious phrase "Platonic shades" provides another example of what I am arguing is the narrator's subtlety. The phrase is paradoxical, since the basic Platonic distinction is between mutable appearance, "shades," and unchanging "Platonic" reality. The paradox can be resolved here, in the context of Lycius's behavior, only if we conclude that *Lamia* mocks such a distinction, by suggesting that such a realm of permanence is a product of human "phantasy" or desire. (The word "Platonic" is rare in Keats's poetry: the word and its variants occur only twice elsewhere, never in a significant context. On the other hand, "shades," or "shade," occurs frequently, six times in *Lamia* alone; it is used in four of those six instances with reference to a change in state of being, mental [1.236; 2.104] or physical [1.270; 2.238].[14] In no other poem is it used in this way.)

Such descriptions in the poem, which set up mutually exclusive opposites—like "Platonic" and "shades"—only to imply their hidden identity, are frequent in *Lamia*, though not always condensed into a single phrase. The emphasis elsewhere in the early descriptions of Lycius is on what sets him apart—"he made retire / From his companions . . . / Perhaps grown weary of their Corinth talk" (1.230–32). His solitude is mental as well as physical—"he pass'd, shut up in mysteries, / His mind wrapp'd like his mantle" (1.241–42)—suggesting that his thoughts are deeper than the superficial conversation of other Corinthians. But this opposition is undercut when we find that his "reason fades"; when we find that the "mysteries" in his mind amount to no more than "shades," themselves insubstantial like the "shadows" thrown by the festival lights which characterize the superficial world of Corinth (1.357–59); and when we recall that "their Corinth talk," initially in opposition to his dreaming, is itself like a dream: "As men talk in a dream, so Corinth all, / . . . Mutter'd" (1.350–53).[15]

Elsewhere Corinth seems real, reality being now that which is obtrusive, undeniable, and cannot be transcended, "the noisy world almost forsworn" (2.33), the world of "the hoarse alarm of Corinth's voice" (2.61). Corinth's reality is contrasted to the insubstantiality of Lamia's "secret bowers" (2.149), which "might fade," "A haunting music [being] sole perhaps and lone / Supportress of the faery-roof" (2.122–24). Her abode is untraceable to the inhabitants of the city: "none knew where / They could inhabit; the most curious / Were foil'd, who watch'd to trace them to their house" (1.391–93). Corinth, on the other hand, is part of plain, substantial reality, validated by intersubjective perception and memory: "they knew the street, / Remember'd it from childhood all complete / Without a gap" (2.152–54).

Amid all this confusion (or deliberate mingling) of what is dream and what is reality, most readers agree that "Only Apollonius remains surely fixed in human realities."[16] Yet his guiding principle is fundamentally unrealistic—to "preserv[e]" Lycius "from every ill / Of life" (2.296–97)—and his answer to the problem of what is real is unsatisfactory. Aside from its obviously destructive results on his pupil, his labeling fails to match reality: his eye only seems to see what really is, for instead of turning into a serpent—his answer for her identity—Lamia disappears, leaving us (as well as the friends of Lycius) with an enigma, a reality that cannot be mastered by a univocal label. The adequacy of such answers is questioned not only by the plot—Lamia's final metamorphosis—but by the poem's second possible Platonic allusion: Apollonius is called a "sophist" by the narrator three times (2.172, 291, 299). Lycius too refers to his "sophistries" (2.185). This characterization cannot, however, be explained away as a product of Lycius's delusion, since it is the narrator who insists on it. Charles Patterson is the only reader to admit the problem in point of view here, but he explains it away by concluding that "the purpose of the word 'sophist' here may well be that of echoing the earlier 'sophistries' (1.285), partly in order to sustain a one-ness of texture and tone in the poem and partly to show that the narrator is taking account of the mind of Lycius while not necessarily agreeing with his views."[17] The narrator has many and conflicting sympathies in *Lamia*, but he is not deliberately merging his point of view with that of Lycius anywhere in the poem. If we believe texture and tone to be meaningful, we must consider the possibility that the narrator means what he says. If he does, he is suggesting that Apollonius's pretension to complete knowledge is no more than a pretense.

On the other hand, as implied by the absence of further commentary on it by the poem's interpreters, the word "sophist" might be intended only as a substitution for "Greek philosopher." We should suspect such a reading, how-ever, because the problem of such substitutions is central to *Lamia*, and similar substitutions are chosen by Keats with great care in order to raise this issue: is Lamia, for example, a "snake" (1.45), a "woman" (1.117), or a "gordian shape" (1.47)? To conclude that Keats used "sophist" because he needed a two-syllable synonym for "Greek philosopher" is no different from concluding that he used "gordian shape" because he needed a three-syllable synonym for "snake"—which is a manifestly obtuse reading. (Stewart argues convincingly for the subtlety of such substitutions, esp. 10–20, 30.)

As a way of investigating how close Keats is in his intentions to his narrator, let us now seek external corroboration that Keats knew what "sophist" meant and therefore used it carefully and substantively, and that he used "Platonic shades" in full awareness of its paradoxical appearance. This investigation also will serve as an example of the kind of older historicist interpretation that recent Romantic readers reject on the grounds that its attention to authorial intention inevitably supposes, or helps create, the mystified humanist fantasy of a unified Romantic subject. I shall argue that such interpretation, like formalism that is criticized on the same grounds, does not inevitably presuppose or reify such a subject but instead can show us how the subject's intentions may indicate its consciousness of the extent to which it is—and also is not—caught up in that very fantasy of its own unity.

To begin our investigation, we might invoke what James Notopoulos has called "indirect Platonism, or the adventure of Plato's thought as a tradition in the mind and history of Europe."[18] This strategy should not be scorned, but before invoking Western literature from Plato to Keats, we should look for more direct avenues from the one to the other. There are two main avenues possible: Keats's own reading of Plato, and his conversations with Benjamin Bailey. The two are related, because the only Plato Keats is known to have had the opportunity to read before writing *Lamia* was in books belonging to Bailey, books that they probably discussed while Keats visited him at Oxford in September 1817. Prior to this time we have no evidence that Keats had read Plato, and any such reading would have been unlikely, given Keats's interests and formal education.[19]

Bailey wrote to John Taylor only a few months after Keats's visit, asking him for "translations of some of Plato's works. I have but a patchwork collection of his works—Greek & English. I have Taylor's Translation of 4 dialogues—and 2 little volumes *from the French London 1749.* of a few dialogues" (*KC* 1:10).[20] In the dialogues translated from the French, Plato explicitly distinguishes between Socrates and the Sophists, and the editor Dacier underlines the distinction in notes. All three—Socrates, Plato, and Dacier—are consistently critical of the Sophists' pretension to certain knowledge where certainty is not possible. Socrates, for example, comments: "the Sophist is but a Wholesale Merchant, and a Retailer of those Things wherewith the Soul is nourished. . . . [W]e must be very careful that the Sophist, by boasting too much of his Merchandize, do not deceive us, as those People do, who sell all that is necessary for the Nourishment of the Body: for the latter, without knowing whether the Provisions which they sell be good or bad, commend them excessively, that they may sell them the better; and those who buy them know them no better then they."[21] Therefore, if Keats read Dacier, for him to call Apollonius a Sophist implies what I have suggested about the poem itself: that Apollonius's claim to absolute knowledge is being undercut. As the Sophists mistakenly believe they understand the mystery of the poets (Dacier 2:288), so Apollonius mistakenly believes he has solved the mystery of Lamia (2.159–62). The analogy here is not far-fetched: many readers have remarked upon Lamia's kinship to Keats's conception of the poetic imagination (see for example Mellor 95). Further, if Keats was aware of this most important difference between Socrates and the Sophists, then he certainly would have seen Socrates to be a more genuine philosopher than Apollonius and the Sophists. Such a "human friend Philosopher" (*KL* 2:139) of course attends Keats's mature thinking about philosophy throughout his letters and poems. Why then Keats appears to characterize all philosophy in *Lamia* as "cold philosophy" which can "clip an Angel's wings" (2.230, 234), when clearly he has quite a different conception of philosophy, is part of a larger, complex narrative strategy. But at least we can see here that Keats, if he has read Dacier's Plato, calls Apollonius a Sophist deliberately, to undermine Apollonius's claim to know what is real and what is illusory.

Dacier's Plato does not, however—either in the dialogues included or in Dacier's introduction—present in any detail the Platonic conception of the real as opposed to the apparent, making Keats's possible reading here not a promising context for the "Platonic shades" passage. The most we find in Dacier's introductory essays is an imagistic opposition between shadows and light as a way of characterizing the relationship between heathen and Christian beliefs— Dacier is primarily interested in arguing "that Plato was an inspired witness to Christian theology" (Evans 104), which would not have interested Keats. We find also a parallel opposition between the body and soul, to the advantage of the soul. The goal of the true philosopher is, says Plato according to Dacier, "to weaken, as much as may be, the Bands that fasten the Soul to the Body; to hate and contemn this Body, which is always opposing Wisdom; to renounce all our Desires" (Dacier 1:2). "Sensual Delights," says Dacier elsewhere, to Plato "are the Consequence of human Weakness and Infirmity," and such delight "has no Essence of it self, but only springs from our Miseries and Necessities" (Dacier 1:90). Keats would hardly have been sympathetic. Instead, if we can locate his sympathies with respect to Dacier's volumes, they would have been with Socrates as he appears in the dialogues, in all his healthy skepticism of the Sophists, and with Plato insofar as he shares, in Dacier's presentation, such skepticism. Dacier comments that "*Plato* affirms that which is certain, refutes that which is false, examines that which is doubtful, and does not pronounce any Thing on that which is uncertain," and thus "he entirely followed *Socrates*'s Manner of disputing, and all along avoided the decisive Air of the Sophists and Dogmatists" (Dacier 1:71).

"Platonic shades" thus cannot be explicated from Dacier's Plato; indeed *Endymion*, the first two books of which Keats had finished before visiting Bailey, is more concerned with ontology than this Plato to which Keats may have been exposed at Oxford. Ontology is a principal interest, however, of the second book belonging to Bailey: Thomas Taylor's introductions to and translation of four dialogues.[22] The *Timaeus* especially, and Taylor's long introduction to it, make clear the primary distinction that interests us here. In words that perhaps echo ironically in *Lamia*, Taylor hopes his work to be "the means of awakening some few at least from the sleep of oblivion, of recalling their attention from fluctuating and delusive objects to permanent and real being; and thus may at length lead them back to their paternal port, as the only retreat which can confer perfect security and rest" (Taylor 435). Elsewhere in his introduction Taylor elaborates on such sleepers by quoting, as he does frequently, Plotinus: "Those who only place *being* in the genus of body, in consequence of . . . the phantasms perceived through the senses, which persuade them that sense is alone the standard of truth, are affected like those in a dream, who imagine that the perceptions of sleep are true. For sense is alone the employment of the dormant soul; since as much of the soul as is merged in body, so much of it sleeps. But true elevation and true vigilance are a resurrection from, and not with, the dull mass of body. For indeed a resurrection with body is only a transmigration from sleep to sleep, and from dream to dream" (Taylor 431–32).

If Keats read Taylor's introduction, it looks very much as if he envisioned Lycius as one of Taylor's sleepers, mistakenly believing his dream to be true, mistakenly attempting "true elevation" through "resurrection with body," which results only in a movement "from dream to dream." Lamia, in this Platonic scenario, exemplifies "matter," which, says Plotinus, "is true non-entity; the mere shadow and imagination of bulk . . . of itself invisible, and avoiding the desire of him who is anxious to perceive its nature. . . . So that it is a phantom . . . constituted in the defect and shade as it were of all real being" (Taylor 430–31). Like "matter" or "the body," Lamia deludes man into believing that she alone is real and that "sense is alone the standard of truth." Apollonius, like Taylor, seeks to awaken the sleeper from his dream.

There are only two problems with this scenario. The first is that, as I have already pointed out, while Lycius's later swoonings (1.289, 296–97; 2.22–25, 104–5) are attributed at least in part to Lamia, his first sleep is presented as a direct result of his philosophical study. The "calm'd twilight" in which Lycius is so susceptible to Lamia's charms is not presented as Lycius's rejection of his philosophical thinking—although Lycius himself and later (by implication) Apollonius see it in that light—but as a consequence of it.[23] This single, striking alteration has the effect of denying Plotinus's "resurrection from . . . body": in *Lamia*'s world, transcendence of human desire is impossible, since even the conception of such transcendence is shaped by that desire. To lose one's fantasy in Platonic shades is not to protect oneself against desire but only to become more susceptible to it. This alteration does not invalidate the scenario, however; it only changes radically its import.

A second difficulty may be more troublesome: the circumstances of Keats's stay with Bailey make it unlikely, in my opinion, that Keats read Taylor's volume. Taylor's introductions and translations both demand much of his reader: in Taylor's own words, "a legitimate student of the Platonic philosophy," to whom Taylor addresses his work, among other daunting qualifications must have "diligently studied the whole or at least the greater part of Aristotle's works, as a preparative for the more profound speculations of Plato," and must have "for many years with unabated ardour strenuously laboured through the works of Plato and his disciples" (Taylor viii). Bailey, as his scholarly and tenacious mind evidences, was quite willing to devote the time and energy necessary for such study. Keats, whether willing or not, was otherwise occupied: he writes to his sister that "we lead very industrious lives he in general Studies and I in proceeding at a pretty good rate with a Poem" (*KL* 1:154); Bailey corroborates this description, writing later of Keats's visit that "He wrote, & I read . . . from breakfast to . . . generally two or three o'clock." Whatever the "regularity" and "ease" with which he seemed to compose, Keats's primary energies and interests each day obviously were devoted to such composition.[24] "When he had finished his writing for the day, he usually read it over to me; & he read or wrote letters until we went out for a walk. This was our habit day by day" (*KC* 2:270). This description implies that Keats only browsed among Bailey's books. Neither Bailey nor Keats, then or later, even suggests that Keats studied with the time and intensity Taylor's volume requires. This does not rule out Keats's reading of Taylor, but it does make it unlikely. Dacier is another matter, because it is a different sort of book: less difficult philosophically and therefore more suitable for a browser. In addition, in the terrible last weeks of his life Keats asked Joseph Severn to locate and read Dacier to him, suggesting his earlier familiarity with it (*KC* 1:181).

In any case, Bailey was studying his own books thoroughly, and his enthusiasm for Platonic ontology makes Taylor's book a likely topic of conversation between Bailey and Keats, since their "conversation" according to Bailey "rarely or never flagged, during our walks, or boatings, or in the Evening" (*KC* 2:274). Such conversations are the second most likely means of Keats's access to Platonic ideas, then, and probably bear indirectly on the problem of "Platonic shades."

Bailey's remarks on Plato in his letters about this time show that if Keats did not read Taylor, he was exposed in Bailey at least, if not in Dacier, to an enthusiastic advocacy of the reality of Plato's world of ideas as opposed to this world of mutable appearances. Bailey's ontological certainty is reflected in his confident evaluation of Plato and Aristotle, in a passage relevant to our investigation:

I have been reading Plato whom I can sufficiently follow to fill my mind with his fine abstractions without deluding me with his errors. . . . Aristotle was doubtless a wonderful man, and perhaps a more *generally* useful one than Plato; but it seems to me that he looked very *im*perfectly *beyond* this world, but *very* perfectly *in* it. . . . Plato had "the vision and the faculty divine." He looked into . . . the inmost recesses of Truth; and wanted but the eye of Revelation to see *clearly* into the mysteries of Christianity, which he saw shadowed in the twilight. In the *greatest* Truths, in a word, Plato saw correctly—and Aristotle *in*correctly. . . . [I]t was for Plato to see the non-eternity of matter, which the other could not comprehend, but held the eternity of what is but a feeble echo or prototype of the Divine Intelligence.[25] (*KC* 1:9–10)

Bailey reconciles Platonism and Christianity by regarding the first as a shadow of the second, a metaphor we have already seen in Dacier's reading of Plato, and which Bailey may have picked up there. More important for us is the quality of Bailey's Christianized belief in Plato's world of the spirit, "the eternal mind—of which every thing that exists, it seems to my apprehension, is but the image of the Decree—the word, the Logos. Now all this," Bailey goes on to say, "*to me is clear as noonday*. But, I dare say, I have not made my notions more clear to you [John Taylor] than at best a sort of dusky twilight. Well—and so it is, I find, with every one" (*KC* 1:8). With no difficulty, we can imagine "every one" here to have included Keats, given Keats's own skepticism about "fine abstractions" in combination with Bailey's own rhapsodic and murky attempts to explain them. Keats's own such "favorite Speculation" of that time, "that we shall enjoy ourselves here after by having what we called happiness on Earth repeated in a finer tone" (*KL* 1:185), might appear similar to Bailey's "fine abstractions," but it differs fundamentally. Unlike Bailey, who makes only what Wasserman calls "easy analogical interchanges of the material and the spiritual," Keats insists upon an essential continuity between this world and a possible other world rather than a disjunction between the two: the repetition "in a finer tone," we notice, is possible only to "those who delight in sensation rather than hunger as you [Bailey] do after Truth."[26] This continuity characterizes *Lamia* as well. What Wasserman called "the conditions of the ideal world" are shaped by human desire—an answer implied by Boulger's apt question: "Is this relationship between Hermes and the Nymph intended primarily as an example of ideal love? If so, why Hermes, the rake of the gods, and a mere nymph?" ("Keats' Symbolism" 250; see Reiman, "Keats" 659–69). Lamia herself is for once unequivocal, about the sensuous nature of "the ideal world":

What taste of purer air hast thou to soothe
My essence? What serener palaces,
Where I may *all my many senses please,*
And by mysterious sleights *a hundred thirsts appease?*
(1.282–85; emphasis added)

We must suspect that Keats was not impressed with Bailey's fervent other-worldliness when it took the form, as did Dacier's version of Platonism, of an equally fervent antiworldliness. Bailey's comment to Taylor in the fall of 1818 that *Endymion* is indefensible in "the *moral* part of it," especially in "The approaching inclination it has to that abominable principle of *Shelley's*—that *Sensual Love* is the principle of *things*" (*KC* 1:34–35), reflects this antiworldliness. Consequently we may well question how much Keats and Bailey were the kindred spirits they supposed themselves to be in that idyllic month when Keats was writing Book 3 of *Endymion*. Keats had mixed feelings about the poem even during its composition (see Bate, *John Keats* 168–92). If Bailey praised it to Keats then as he did to Taylor the next spring because he found it "so etherial," because Bailey's "spirits" are "no longer mantle[d] . . . when I am in his fairy world" (*KC* 1:19), Keats could hardly have been overjoyed. It is not the sort of appreciation Keats would have sought from someone who, by the example of his scholarly devotion to Dante, Milton, and Wordsworth, was encouraging Keats to go beyond his merely sensuous appreciation of "particular passages" in Wordsworth, and his being "enamoured of the beauties of Spenser" (Bailey's descriptions of Keats [*KC* 2:274, 283]), to "the awakening of the thinking principle" (Keats's own phrase several months later [*KL* 1:281], cited also in this context by Bate, *John Keats* 215).

In short, it seems likely that during his stay with Bailey, Keats would have come into conversational—if not direct—contact with Plato's fundamental distinction between the two worlds, to the detriment of this one. But friendship does not necessitate intellectual agreement, and it seems equally likely that Keats would not have been swayed by Bailey's advocacy of Plato's distinction, since Bailey evidences not simply the high-mindedness that so impressed Keats in contrast to the pettiness of the "literary Men" of his acquaintance (*KL* 1:169) but also a fuzzy-mindedness—and a confidence (see *KC* 1:211, 232)—about the nature of things, which Keats could never bring himself to adopt or to respect without some irreverence. His reverence, if we are to trust Benjamin Haydon's account of the previous year, he reserved for the skeptic Voltaire: "Getting suddenly up, & approaching [Haydon's painting] he placed his hand on his heart, & bowing his head, 'there is the being I will bow to,' said he—he stood before Voltaire!"[27] Toward the true believer Jeremy Taylor he was less than reverent: Bailey's picture of Taylor, Keats wrote during his visit, "always looks as if he were going to hit me a rap with a Book he hold in a very threatning position" (*KL* 1:156–57).

Keats's subsequent break with Bailey, of course, cannot be used anachronistically to justify what I have been arguing as a fundamental difference between the two men. Still, a brief examination of its circumstances converges, with our earlier look at Dacier's Plato and Bailey's advocacy of a Platonic dualism, surprisingly on the "Platonic shades" of Lycius. It was Bailey's high-mindedness, we remember, that most impressed Keats—his freedom, apparently, from petty human desires. But Bailey soon enough turned out to be made of the same stuff as other men. He too not only loved women but, apparently, loved them inconstantly, switching his attentions like "a Ploughmans who wants a wife," commented Keats sardonically a few months before beginning *Lamia* (*KL* 2:67). Such a disillusionment, while hardly a cataclysmic one for Keats, nevertheless probably served to remind him as he was working on *Lamia* that Bailey's ardent love of another world was after all only love, in another of its many forms: "The man who redicules romance is the most romantic of Men" (*KL* 2:67). Bailey in Keats's life, like Lycius in his poetry, evidences the protean shape of human desire. Bailey, like Lycius, "from one trance was waken[ed] / Into another" (1.296–97).

In such an underlying unity to the different forms of desire we might find an additional, powerful, and aesthetically plausible reason for the intermittent bitterness in *Lamia*'s tone, which readers have most often attributed solely to Keats's unwilling acceptance of "the inevitable evanescence of love and beauty and illusion" when faced with real life.[28] In addition, the poem suggests that desire is not always allied, benignly or otherwise, with love and beauty. Lamia may have "tangled [Lycius] in her mesh" (1.195), but Lycius and Apollonius, at least as destructive in their passion as Lamia, each strike at another: toward Lamia, "Fine was [Lycius's] mitigated fury, like / Apollo's presence when in act to strike / The serpent" (2.78–80) and Apollonius's "eye, / Like a sharp spear, went through her utterly" (2.299–300); Lycius is "heart-struck" by Apollonius (2.293), and he wishes that Apollonius's "eyes" may be "pierce[d]" (2.277, 281). That Keats reluctantly admitted an underlying identity between two so apparently different desires—for sexual bliss and for a world divorced from such passion—is borne out by his marginal remarks to his plot source for *Lamia*, Burton's *Anatomy of Melancholy*. Sometime in 1819, in the section entitled "Loves Beginning, Object, Definition, Division," he wrote: "Nothing disgraces me in my own eyes as much as being one of a race of eyes nose and mouth beings . . . who all from Plato to Wesley have always mingled goatish winnyish lustful love with the abstract adoration of the deity. I don't understand Greek—is the love of God and the Love of Women express'd by the same word in Greek? I hope my little mind is wrong—if not I could—has Plato separated these loves?" On the next page of Burton his hope weakens: "Ha! I see how they endeavor to divide—but there appears to be a horrid relationship."[29]

Exploring the question of Platonic influence on *Lamia* has illuminated answers to two important problems that bear directly upon our understanding of *Lamia:* the meaning of "Platonic shades," and the significance of Apollonius being called a "sophist." If Keats read Dacier's Plato with any care or discussed it with Bailey, he could not fail to have understood Plato's antipathy to the Sophists. For him therefore to attribute Platonic teaching to Apollonius (Lycius is his pupil, so the "Platonic shades" would seem equally attributable to the teacher as their source) and at the same time label him a Sophist seems a paradox—resolvable only by concluding that Keats is making a rather subtle point about Platonic reality, namely that absolute belief in its ontological primacy is sophistic in claiming knowledge about that which is not certain.

There is, then, sufficient indirect evidence for us to guess that Keats meant by "Platonic shades" exactly the paradox it seems: that in this poem the ideal world of Platonic forms is as shadowy and as much a product of human desire as the world of Lamia, herself "melt[ed] into a shade" (2.238). *Lamia* makes a mockery of all attempts to divide the real and the apparent into two distinct ontological categories: *all* possible candidates for the ontologically real are imaged as dreamlike, shadowy, or enigmatic. Lamia's true nature is only the most obvious of them. The real world surrounding her unreal palace is also dreamlike, and since Apollonius's philosophy becomes "Platonic shades," it follows that Lycius does not move from illusion to reality, or vice versa, in his change of allegiance from Apollonius to Lamia, but only "from one trance . . . / Into another" (1.296–97). Replacing Apollonius's desire for intellectual fixity with Lamia's desire for perpetual sexual bliss, Lycius only changes clothing, exchanging his philosophic mantle for a "marriage robe" (2.311). In this poem there is no absolutely real world to be distinguished from the world of appearances; the two are inseparable. What most readers have seen as the poem's theme, "the clash between the logical, quantitative world of Apollonius and the symbolic mode of man's myth-making power" (Boulger, "Keats' Symbolism" 248), is thus subsumed by the poem's greater awareness that both are symbolic modes, much as a similar phrase is used by Ernst Cassirer, the best-known modern proponent of symbolic form: "The special symbolic forms are not imitations, but *organs* of reality. . . . Once language, myth, art and science are recognized as such ideational forms, the basic philosophical question is no longer that of their relation to an absolute reality. . . . [T]he central problem now is that of their mutual limitation and supplementation."[30] In *Lamia* the problem, and the main source of the poem's irony, is their "mutual limitation." Our awareness of such limitation is instigated, in part at least, by the two Platonic allusions we have traced.

I have attributed this same awareness not only to Keats but also to his narrator, making him (like his creator) an extraordinarily shifting, subtle figure rather than a fixed, two-dimensional one. This complicates "the narrator" to the point that we might be tempted simply to remove him altogether, as a redundant critical fiction, and replace him with the author, "Keats." But doing so raises another problem, which can be illustrated if we look at how "philosophy" is characterized throughout the poem. It is consistently opposed not only to "mysteries" and "charms" but to "every ill / Of life." "Philosophy will . . . / Conquer all mysteries by rule and line" (2.234–35); "Do not all charms fly / At the mere touch of cold philosophy?" (2.229–30)[31] Apollonius, who seems to represent philosophy in the poem—its apostrophe to "Philosophy" being contained within its apostrophe to Apollonius ("What [wreath] for the sage, old Apollonius?" [2.222])—states unequivocally his motive as philosopher to Lycius: "'from every ill / Of life have I preserv'd thee to this day'" (2.296–97). Virtually everything Keats says about philosophy in his letters contradicts this characterization. Nowhere does Keats regard philosophy as escapist but as a "human friend" (*KL* 2:139), in that it helps man to cope with the ills of life. This is a position Keats held to consistently, and well before writing *Lamia:* "What a happy thing it would be if we could settle our thoughts, make our minds up on any matter in five Minutes and remain content—that is to build a sort of mental Cottage of feelings quiet and pleasant—to have a sort of Philosophical Back Garden, and cheerful holiday-keeping front one—but Alas! this can never be" (*KL* 1:254, March 1818).

Such a philosophical garden is exactly what Apollonius wishes for Lycius. It is suggestive that Keats envisions this realm of permanence as a garden, the choice of image implying that the desire for such comfortable stasis is objectified not only in classical myth, as Reiman has shown of *Lamia,* but in the Christian myth of the first garden. But the serpent in Apollonius's garden imagistically transcends a single character. Lamia as serpent is a "beauteous wreath" (1.84), which image later characterizes all three major characters (2.221–29); as we have already seen, Apollonius too is serpentlike.[32] This complication implies that the serpent is not an intruder in Apollonius's garden but an inevitable inhabitant: all gardens come with snakes, and all humanly constructed worlds of permanence come with the serpent of human desire itself. The desire for such a world signals its impossibility.

Both Keats and the narrator see that such a desire, however attractive, can be destructive. Only the narrator seems to hold philosophy responsible for that destruction. But I have been arguing for a narrator who understands the nature of human desire and who should therefore understand that philosophy is not responsible for its destructiveness. Why does he then seem deliberately to mis-understand his own story, to oversimplify that which he knows to be complex? The "philosophy" passages do not constitute an isolated instance of such be-havior. If we look, for example, at his early descriptions of Lamia, we see the same pattern of mutually contradictory explanations—some of which are truer than others. As we have noticed, he frequently calls Lamia a snake, unequivo-cally (1.45, 88, 113, 132, 146), and just as unequivocally after her transformation he calls her a woman (1.171, 185, 189, 290)—both oversimplifications. Yet she is also "a gordian shape" (1.47), in a passage whose attempts at inclusiveness imply strongly the narrator's understanding that simple definitions are inadequate: "She seem'd, at once, some penanced lady elf, / Some demon's mistress, or the demon's self" (1.55–56): "Her head was serpent, but . . . / She had a woman's mouth" (1.59–60); "Her throat was serpent, but the words she spake . . ." (1.64). The narrator's hostility toward Apollonius—"Let spear-grass and the spiteful thistle wage / War on his temples" (2.228–29)—is belied by his espousal of Apollonius's reductive philosophy, as when he dismisses what "the mad poets" say about goddesses in favor of "a real woman" (1.328–33), or when he seems able to see Lamia only as a woman or only as a serpent. Yet his own desire for intellectual fixity is in turn belied by his subtle awareness of its limitation. He envies Lycius—"Ah, happy Lycius!" (1.185)—but shortly thereafter makes fun of his enchantment:

> pointing to Corinth, [he] ask'd her sweet,
> If 'twas too far that night for her soft feet.
> The way was short, for Lamia's eagerness
> Made, by a spell, the triple league decrease
> To a few paces; not at all surmised
> By blinded Lycius, so in her comprized.
> (1.342–47)

After implying that Lycius gets what he deserves—"O senseless Lycius! Mad-man!" (1.147)—he sympathizes, "let us strip for him / The thyrsus, that his watch-ing eyes may swim / Into forgetfulness" (2.225–27)—only to withdraw into impartiality, concluding with what Stewart rightly calls "this cool, measured epitaph" (35): "And Lycius' arms were empty of delight, / As were his limbs of life, from that same night" (2.307–8). Equally cool and measured is the narra-tor's "moral" from "faery land," that "Love in a palace is perhaps at last / More grievous torment than a hermit's fast" (2.8, 5, 3–4), implying his understanding that desire cannot be satisfied even in a palace because it is, finally, by nature insatiable.

But such ironic detachment is only one of the shifting attitudes of the narrator, who elsewhere — in his seemingly wholehearted, if short-lived, sympathies — appears to enact the very single-mindedness of human desire that he ironically undercuts in his characters. The overt nature of his interpretive shifts suggests that the narrator is intentionally ironic in his oversimplifications, that he puts on the mask of common sense to lure the reader into interpretations and sympathies he himself frustrates by his own contradictory responses.

To understand why Keats has created such a complex narrator, we must first take into account his readers, both as they were and as he wanted them to be. For Keats there was an important difference: "I admire Human Nature but I do not like *Men*—I should like to compose things honourable to Man—but not fingerable over by *Men*" (*KL* 1:415, December 1818).[33] Shortly after completing *Lamia*, Keats criticizes his earlier narrative poems, "intend[ing] to use more finesse with the Public" (*KL* 2:174), which suggests that he has written *Lamia* not solely for the ideal reader, "Man," but also for actual readers, "*Men*," "the Public."

Keats's equating of "Human" with "Man" is one I shall follow here in my discussion of reader response, because it seems appropriate both for the poet's increasing preference for a male audience, and for a poem that represents and critiques especially male desire. As Terence Hoagwood comments, "Lycius's fantasy has entailed from the outset the damaging impulse to imprison ('trammel up and snare') the female object of his desire, and scarcely latent violence ('Let my foes choke')."[34] But we should notice that while *Lamia* critiques this desire, it also represents Keats's own partial and sporadic identification with that desire—as suggested, for example, by the unironized nonchalance or even voyeurism with which the narrator describes the ravishment of the nymph by Hermes—and thus suggests that Keats himself is not coterminous with his imagined ideal reader. When Richard Woodhouse objected strongly to Keats's changes in *The Eve of St. Agnes* making it implicitly clear that, in Woodhouse's circumlocution, Porphyro "acts all the acts of a bona fide husband"—"tho' profanely speaking, the Interest on the reader's imagination is greatly heightened, yet I do apprehend it will render the poem unfit for ladies"—Keats, according to Woodhouse, replied that "he does not want ladies to read his poetry: that he writes for men—& that if in the former poem there was an opening for doubt what took place, it was his fault for not writing clearly & comprehensibly—that he shd despise a man who would be such an eunuch in sentiment as to leave a maid, with that Character about her, in such a situation: & shod despise himself to write about it" (*KL* 2:163).[35]

These readers were absent from Keats's mind in the writing of *Endymion* and *Isabella* but had begun to be important to him in the writing of *The Eve of St. Agnes* (see *KL* 2:174). His response to Woodhouse's objections to the revisions of this last poem suggests that he regarded Woodhouse as a kind of test case for the revised poem—as is clear from Keats's retort to Woodhouse that the "Change of Sentiment" at the poem's end "was what he aimed at, & was glad to find from my objections to it that he had succeeded" (*KL* 2:163).[36] That Woodhouse reacted as Keats apparently had expected does not, however, compliment Woodhouse or Keats's envisioned readers, since Woodhouse still cannot see *why* Keats purposed such "play[ing] with his reader" and obviously preferred *Isabella* to *The Eve of St. Agnes*, which Keats did not, the former poem now seeming "mawkish" (*KL* 2:162).

If Woodhouse's reactions represent for Keats the sort of response he counted on to his revisions of *The Eve of St. Agnes*, then it is reasonable to suppose that Woodhouse's reactions to *Lamia* also represent those expected by Keats from the readers to whom he directed the poem. Even if we bear in mind Woodhouse's self-deprecating characterization of himself in this respect—"you know how slow I am in Catching, even the sense of poetry read by the best reader for the Ist time"—and his general comprehension that "his [Keats's] poetry really must be studied to be properly appretiated" (*KL* 2:164), his description of *Lamia* in this same letter is oddly one-sided. It is almost solely of "The Story," as Woodhouse himself says, and it is a very detailed description, considering that Woodhouse apparently based it upon one reading of the poem by Keats and a brief discussion of it afterward. In addition, Woodhouse recalls being struck "every now & then" by "some beautiful poetry," for which "all these Events have given K. scope" (*KL* 2:165). In short, we have a description of the poem in terms of "Story" and "beautiful poetry." There is nothing in it of the ambivalence of response elicited by the poem from later critics, or indeed of that same response elicited—if to a lesser degree—from Woodhouse, to his dismay, by *The Eve of St. Agnes*.

Making allowances for Woodhouse's having heard the poem only once, we must still say that his response to it is devoid of any awareness that poetry for Keats is now in any serious way allied to philosophy or truth. In this sense, Woodhouse can serve as the reader to whom Keats sees he is writing: one who, whatever his good will and intelligence, comes to a narrative poem concerned with character, action, and "beautiful poetry"—and with truth, if at all, only in the shape of moral maxims. (It is this limitation of response that Woodhouse and John Taylor shared, however differing in degree—a limitation reflected in their preference for *Isabella* among Keats's narratives [see *KL* 2:162, 183]). Keats designs *Lamia* for this reader, providing him a narrator who at first seems equally interested in character, action, poetry, and truth that are unambiguous— a narrator with whom this reader would readily identify, and whose deviations from such interests this reader would find troubling. That he consciously uses Woodhouse to test such a design in *The Eve of St. Agnes* shows a rhetorical sense markedly grown from that in *Endymion* and *Isabella,* a rapidity of growth commensurate with that of his stylistic and philosophic growth. While this rhetoric also reflects his impatience with the public, significantly it reflects his increased understanding of that public.

Keats intended success with "the Public" in *Lamia:* "I am certain there is that sort of fire in it which must take hold of people in some way—give them either pleasant or unpleasant sensation. What they want is a sensation of some sort" (*KL* 2: 189). But this last verb and its object are ambiguous.[37] The public desires ("want[s]") sensational reading in the modern sense, whether of the kind Woodhouse and Taylor prudishly, if prudently, objected to in *The Eve of St. Agnes,* or of a less specifically sexual sort. In this sense sensation is wholly distinct from thought, a distinction in accord with Keats's early ideas on the subject in the letters ("O for a Life of Sensations rather than of Thoughts!" [*KL* 1:185, November 1817]). The public also lacks ("want[s]") sensation, in a deeper sense, a sense more closely tied to thought ("axioms in philosophy are not axioms until they are proved upon our pulses" [*KL* 1:279, May 1818]), a link Keats had begun to see at least a year before *Lamia,* in his well-known comparison of life to a "Mansion of Many Apartments." In the first chamber, "we remain as long as we do not think." In the second, "we become intoxicated with the light and the atmosphere . . . and think of delaying there for ever in delight." All this sounds very much like Woodhouse's stage, as a reader, of satisfaction with story, sensation of any sort, and beautiful poetry. But as is equally well known, Keats goes on: "However among the effects this breathing is father of is that tremendous one of sharpening one's vision into the heart and nature of Man—of convincing ones nerves that the World is full of Misery and Heartbreak, Pain, Sickness and oppression" (*KL* 1:280–81). The conclusions Keats thus reaches about life need no comment here, important as they are; in the context of the sensation-thought relationship, we should note that Keats consistently envisions arriving at such conclusions in terms of organic bodily processes: "breathing" an "atmosphere" sharpens one's "vision" and convinces one's "nerves." This intimate relationship between sensation and thought characterizes Keats's mature thinking about the issue. We find it elsewhere, for example in the "garden" letter quoted earlier: "if we could settle our *thoughts* . . . that is to build a sort of mental Cottage of *feelings* quiet and pleasant" (emphasis added).

The public thus gets more than it bargained for in Keats's "sensation" and the narrator who stimulates it. Wayne Booth remarks that in fiction "The author creates . . . an image of himself and another image of his reader; he makes his reader, as he makes his second self, and the most successful reading is one in which the created selves, author and reader, can find complete agreement" (*Rhetoric* 138).[38] This observation provides us a way to understand the narrator's apparent vicissitudes in *Lamia*. They may derive partly from Keats's divided mind about his poem, conflicting impulses to "'load every rift' . . . with ore" and "wipe . . . the Cits" (*KL* 2:323, 164) or to sympathize with Lamia and admit the truth of Apollonius. A divided mind is not necessarily a confused mind, however, and this chapter has shown that the vicissitudes at least partly reflect Keats's intention to construct a complex "second self," the subtle narrator, the understanding of whom makes over Keats's envisioned actual reader, like Woodhouse, into his imagined ideal reader—one who can become, as the narrator is from the beginning, aware of the world's "Misery and Heartbreak" and of their sources in human nature.

But to become aware of misery and heartbreak and their sources is not to escape them or to master them. The difference between awareness and mastery does not correspond to that between real and ideal here but instead, perhaps unexpectedly, to that between ideal and real. It is the *ideal* reader who understands and is able to accept (however unhappily) the difference between awareness and mastery. The *real* reader falls short of that ideal, to the extent that he, like Apollonius, believes he understands desire and thereby has mastered it; or to the extent that he, like Lycius, thinks he possesses desire and thereby can control it; or to the extent that he, like each wedding guest "silk-pillow'd at his ease" (2.220), only luxuriates in "beautiful poetry."

I am not arguing for a *transcendentally* ideal reader, already immune to or inoculated by the poem against desire. John Bayley asks, regarding *The Eve of St. Agnes,* "How—after we have been Madeline and Porphyro looking at Madeline—can we ration our mixture of sensations when we turn round, as we cannot help doing, and watch Keats devouring them with the eyes of his language?" We might ask a similar question of *Lamia*'s beginning: how—after we have been Hermes looking at the nymph—can we watch Keats devouring them (or her?) with the eyes of his language? The question in effect suggests the extent to which "we" are like Keats and his contemporary readers: what is "socially new" in Keats's poetry "is the way it comprehends and explores . . . the sexual fantasies and feelings of . . . the people beginning to enliven the expansion of urban middle-class culture and manners with a corresponding inner world of desire and inhibition, fantasy and wish fulfilment."[39]

Just as we are concerned here with the relation of real to ideal readers, we must concern ourselves again with the relation of poet to narrator, the relation of Keats to his constructed, complex, second self. Most modern readers have taken Keats's self-characterization in terms of "negative capability," as theoretical sanction for a formalist separation between the two (however erratically applied, and less carefully to *Lamia* than to Keats's other major poems).[40] Keats's own more direct emotional links to the poem were asserted by earlier readers who, ignoring negative capability, identified Keats with Lycius, a passive psychic battleground of eros and reality, Lamia and Apollonius (see, for example, Finney 2:698). But it is truer to a more complex conception of subjectivity to see "Keats" as the psychic site of not only the antagonists but also the mixed and uncertain attitudes toward them—attitudes that include a sometimes fitful identification with one or the other, along with the distanced, ironic recognition that both are manifestations of human desire, *and also* the recognition that such irony is neither escape from nor mastery of that desire. Such a complex conception of subjectivity comes closer to what Keats meant by negative capability than the Eliotic, aesthetic escape from personality that the phrase is often taken to warrant (see Wolfson's discussion of this point, *Questioning Presence* 31–41). Keats himself anticipates the importance of his own complex subjectivity to the poem in writing of his own "gordian complication of feelings" (*KL* 1:342) and his "own being which . . . becomes of more consequence to [him] than the crowds of shadows in the Shape of Man and women that inhabit a kingdom" (*KL* 2:246)—passages that echo his representation of Lamia and Corinth alike.[41]

It is in this sense, only, that we might identify the narrator with "Keats"—a Keats constructed primarily out of our mostly formalist reading of the poem, together with that reading's apparent impasse (in other words, the limits of our own attempted formalist mastery), a Keats compatible also with the results of our literary-historical investigations into his understanding of Plato.

Such a Keats is compatible as well not only with the heroically imaginative Keats of, for example, Bate, but with Marjorie Levinson's Keats, "a man whose almost complete lack of control over the social code kept him from living his life. He could not write his poetry in the manner he required, marry the woman he loved, claim his inheritance, hold his family together, or assist his friends" (*Keats's Life* 8). I take Levinson's central theoretical argument to be that we must understand such a Keats in his historical and social specificity in order to free ourselves from the dominant analytic method—formalist or humanist—that allegorizes his poetry "as a sweet solution to a bitter life[,] a resolution of [its] actual contradictions . . . , a transformation of experience by knowledge and by the aesthetic practice which that knowledge promotes" (2). In the case of *Lamia*, she argues, "we produce by our analytic method readings that interpret everything while explaining nothing," especially failing to explain "the poem's enigmas," such as "Lycius's sadism, Corinth's murkiness" (270), or "the strangely extended introductory narrative." But, to take only the beginning of the last of these, Levinson's own reading—that "lines 1–6 . . . are, if anything, a *problematizing*

of the once-upon-a-time motif, and, thus, a suspiciously distracting way to get going" (262)—seems little different from Reiman's reading or mine, readings produced by the very method she rejects (see p. 112 above). On one theoretical level, then, this chapter argues against this privileging of historicist investigation as the only critical way to recognize *Lamia*'s, and thus Keats's, unmasterable complexity.

Indeed, recent historicist readers of Keats seem as prone to simplifying the poem and the poet as less historically conscious, formalist readers. McGann's reception-history study of the *Lamia* volume, even while broadening our sense of other factors involved in the poem's original social context, is a case in point. "The key fact in the prepublication history of the 1820 poems," he argues persuasively of the *Lamia* volume, "is the insistence by Keats's publishers that the book not contain anything that would provoke the reviewers to attack (they were especially concerned about charges of indecency and political radicalism). Keats struggled with them over these issues, but he was eventually persuaded to follow their line." But Keats's struggle here and what I am arguing to be his complex attitude toward his audience are ironed out in what follows: "Many of the new poems were deliberately written with an eye to attracting the favourable attention of the public (this is especially apparent in the case of the three narrative poems in the book)." Finally,

> Keats's mythologically oriented works in his new book presented their early readers with ideas about art, myth, and imagination which did not open an explicit ideological attack upon the book's audience. The *Lamia* volume represented Keats's efforts to show his readers how they might, by entering his poetic space, step aside from the conflicts and tensions which were so marked an aspect of the period. The whole point of Keats's great and (politically) reactionary book was not to enlist poetry in the service of social and political causes—which is what Byron and Shelley were doing—but to dissolve social and political conflicts in the mediations of art and beauty.[42]

As I have been arguing, however, the nature of Keats's interest in the public's attention is mixed, and the poem's ideas about myth and imagination do not provide a "poetic space" that constitutes nothing more than an aesthetic escape from all "conflicts and tensions."

Conversely, it is hard to see how that poetic space constitutes a fully or even partly conscious representation of *historical* conflict and tension, as claimed by Levinson, Hoagwood, and Watkins, who ascribe *Lamia*'s theme of metamorphosis to Keats's own historical consciousness, or at least sensibility. In Watkins's words, such "change involves the dis[s]olution of a precommercial society and the emergence of a new commercial society in which wealth, private desire, and self-gratification become culturally dominant."[43] The poem's emphasis on change, however, argues not for the historical specificity of wealth, private desire, and self-gratification but for their omnipresence and insatiability. This counter-argument applies as well to Hoagwood's claim that the narrator's "doubtful tale" at the beginning of Part 2 distinguishes between "palace" and "hut" as a "classifying scheme of rich and poor" by which Keats, implicitly equating "non-elect" with "the dispossessed classes," "has imposed a class framework on the tale" and thereby "insists on the priority of material conditions of life" (691). But the distinction between "palace" and "hut" becomes a distinction with little difference: that "Love in a palace is perhaps at last / More grievous torment than a hermit's fast" (2.3–4; emphasis added) suggests instead the insatiability of desire, in that it remains ultimately impervious to wealth, and its omnipresence, in that this "moral" is a "tale from faery land."

As Watkins's own reading shows, the commercial society present in Corinth is present also in Crete, in "the opening scene of self-interest, possession, wealth, desire, and envy" (144), and of course in early-nineteenth-century England. *Lamia* thus suggests that a precommercial society, like a society free of desire, has not even a mythical existence. On the question of Keats's consciousness of change, Watkins concludes that "Keats could not speak concretely of the driving force behind the world as he was coming to know it. But he seemed to sense—or at least he was haunted by—the tremendous controlling power of history and its many contradictions and accomplishments" (155). This chapter argues that Keats did understand something about the world's driving force and his relation to it—but that he identified that force with human desire, not history. This becomes a misidentification for us only if we no longer live in a world characterized by such desire.

Lamia's poetic space then, like its author's consciousness, is mixed: it neither masters desire nor escapes from it but represents it. Although that representation is not explicitly historical, not "an explicit ideological attack" on its audience, other historicist critics than McGann have argued that the absence of such explicitness in this case does not evade or "dissolve social and political conflicts." The "narcissistic obsessions" that, I have argued, characterize Lycius and Apollonius, for Hoagwood have a "specifically political character" for Keats and are "aligned with socially injurious attitudes and acts, even with violence and war" (687). For Levinson, the poem's saturation with desire derives from Keats's position as marginally middle class, a class that "had to expose the historicity of value, clearing the ground as it were for its own violation of inherited and naturalized values. At the same time, and so as to sanction this originality and safeguard its middling position, threatened on the lower front by imitation, and the upper by assimilation, the class in the middle had to represent its own, invented values as either ahistorical or as history's telos" (*Keats's Life* 23–24). But since, at this level of generalization, these same values could be and have been located in, for example, *The Knight's Tale, King Lear,* and *The Rape of the Lock,* it seems to me what we learn is that we are still within a long-lived paradigm of the sort described by J. G. A. Pocock: in this case, a destructive desire for mastery that, as well as being political, is in this poem primarily rationalist, sexual, and social.[44]

Levinson's particular and difficult addition to this constellation is economic, based on her reading of Georg Lukacs and Georg Simmel: "If we desire to arrange human destiny according to the scheme of relationship between the wish and its object, then we must concede that, in terms of the final point in the sequence of purpose, money is the most inadequate but also the most adequate object of our endeavours."[45] Levinson explores persuasively, and in greater detail than any other reader, how Lamia is differently commodified in the poem by Hermes, Lycius, and Apollonius, respectively, but it is hard to see—except for her argument's need, and Lukacs's, to link commodification with nineteenth-century class dynamics—why Lamia should be not only a commodity, an object of desire, but ultimately an allegorical sign of money itself. According to Levinson, "Apollonius's eye ('keen, cruel, perceant, stinging') converts her from the commodity to the money form, her final incarnation. . . . No wonder he alone can penetrate her mystery" (278). But neither we nor Apollonius know a final incarnation, only an absence.

In any case, Levinson and Hoagwood alike argue that it is only "conventional criticism" and not Keats who "perform[s] that evasion," which McGann ascribes to both (Hoagwood 677). My argument is directed not so much against these historicist readings of the poem as it is against the theoretical argument, shared by Hoagwood and Levinson as well as McGann, that such a nonevasive reading is possible *only* through "a historical method [that] takes account of a poem's reception history as well as its production history," that without such a historical method we have only a formalist or a naively intentionalist criticism capable of no more than oversimplifying the poem (Hoagwood 676).

I am arguing that an intentionalist, formalist, and deconstructive reading of *Lamia* does not inevitably oversimplify the poem or Keats's intentions, which are mixed and complex. In addition they are partly moral, in the largest sense of the word. This should not surprise us, if we consider how much of his later thinking about his own narrative poetry is in terms of the good of its readers. In April 1818 he writes: "I find there is no worthy pursuit but the idea of doing

some good for the world—some do it with their society—some with their wit—
some with their benevolence. . . . [T]here is but one way for me—the road lies
th[r]ough application study and thought" (*KL* 1:271). Less than a year later, in
February 1819, he links "doing some good" explicitly with writing poetry: "I have
come to the resolution never to write for the sake of writing, or making a poem,
but from running over with any little knowlege and experience which many
years of reflection may perhaps give me—otherwise I will be dumb" (*KL* 2:43).
It is untrue to everything else Keats says about the worth of poetry to see this
affective emphasis in his narrative aesthetics as no more than a cynical and self-
protective reaction to critical and popular reception of his published poetry
(see, for example, Finney 2:686–87). In its effects poetry is instead akin to philosophy and action ("knowledge and experience"), in that it embodies comprehensive human truths read in the *"horn Book"* of the *"human heart"* (*KL* 2:102). The
act of reading is here generalized by Keats into the fundamental activity by which
man learns about his world: the heart is a book, the world a teacher. "Do you
not see how necessary a World of Pains and troubles is to school an Intelligence
and make it a soul?" (*KL* 2:102).

"Reading"—whether life or literature—is therefore not passive but active,
and the essence of such activity is the reader's imagination.[46] It may be elicited
sporadically by life ("Though a quarrel in the streets is a thing to be hated, the
energies displayed in it are fine" [*KL* 2:80]), but imaginative creations can be
designed to elicit it. (Keats found certain engravings of Italian frescoes "even finer
to me than more accomplish'd works—as there was left so much room for Imagination" [*KL* 2:19].) In narrative literature the reader's "greeting of the Spirit" (*KL*
1:243) is with the author's "second self," in *Lamia* the complex narrator.

His desire for such a narrative persona Keats presents strikingly in a self-
description shortly after finishing *Lamia*.

Writing has this disadvan[ta]ge of speaking. one cannot write a wink, or a
nod, or a grin, or a purse of the Lips, or a *smile—O law!* One can-[not] put
ones finger to one's nose, or yerk ye in the ribs, or lay hold of your button in
writing—but in all the most lively and titterly parts of my Letter you must
not fail to imagine me as the epic poets say—now here, now there, now with
one foot pointed at the ceiling, now with another—now with my pen on my
ear, now with my elbow in my mouth—O my friends you loose the action—
and attitude is every thing. . . . (*KL* 2:205, September 1819)

We should notice that here Keats does not really see this characteristic of writing, as opposed to speaking, to be a frustrating disadvantage. He is not striving

painfully for sincerity but enjoying the necessary and inevitable "disadvantage," playfully creating a persona in the very process of describing why it is so difficult.[47] While such enjoyment of indirection in a letter to "my friends" may not carry over into a poem to "the Public," that enjoyment at least suggests that "sincerity" is not an unmediated issue in *Lamia;* instead, Keats is adept, as he is in the letter just quoted, at creating the "attitude" that "is every thing," at guiding his readers to see the story and its teller in the way he wants: first as sensation in the simpler sense of the word, but eventually as a complex interplay of sensation and thought.

Such guidance is a primary purpose of the narrator's shifting stances. Wolfgang Iser explains that "modern literary works are so full of [such] apparent inconsistencies—not because they are badly constructed, but because such breaks act as hindrances to comprehension, and so force us to reject our habitual orientations as inadequate."[48] Our "habitual orientations" in the world of *Lamia* are embodied for us in the narrator's masquerade of bonhomie and common sense, in his apparent convictions that things can be understood and that we need no more than common sense to understand them. That we reject these orientations is exactly what Keats intends by his narrator's "apparent inconsistencies." It is significant that Iser finds this strategy characteristic of the novel, for Keats read widely in the eighteenth-century novel,[49] and we can sense echoes of Fielding and Sterne in his self-portrait quoted earlier. In this light, Keats's question to the George Keatses, "With what sensation do you read Fielding?" (*KL* 2:18), appreciates in meaning, suggesting perhaps both Keats's awareness of this narrative strategy in another writer and an influence on his use of the same strategy in *Lamia.* Critics often have noticed the influence of Dryden in the poem's ironic, distanced tone, as well as in its versification; this tone, however, is not consistent, and its inconsistency we might attribute partly to a second neoclassical influence, Keats's reading in the novel.

Iser's comment refocuses critical attention from the exclusively mimetic or expressive explanation of such inconsistency—that it reflects the chaos of the modern world, or the artist's psychological fragmentation—to its affective significance. The final break, at the end of the poem, is also aimed at the reader. Its abruptness comes as a surprise to us if we have not questioned the narrator's earlier confidence in his complete understanding ("the flitter-winged verse must tell, / For truth's sake, what woe afterwards befel" [1.394–95]), for the ending is without confident commentary. It is sensational enough—with Lamia's disappearance and Lycius's death—but more important is its lack of commentary, which throws us back to the actions of the poem stripped of interpretation. We might attribute its abruptness to a limited narrator's final inability to interpret his own story, but this chapter has argued its attribution to a complex narrator's refusal to oversimplify (in Wordsworth's phrase that struck Keats so forcefully) "the Burden of the Mystery" (*KL* 1:277, 281). It is a sign both of the poem's narrative complexity and of Keats's delight and involvement in such complexity that we are brought up short by such an ending, in being given both sensation and thought. We are brought up short too in realizing that no critical thought—not Apollonius's, the narrator's, Keats's, or ours—can master that Mystery.

Conclusion

This book began with a question about the usefulness of any distinction between poet and speaker (or narrator) for interpretation that no longer depends, as formalism so often has done, on a unified subject, whether poet or narrator, which thereby guaranteed the integrity of (aesthetic) intentions. Manning has asserted the necessity of the distinction, in his careful argument about Wordsworth's "Poor Susan" that "the historical situation of the text can only be reached along the treacherous, badly signposted byways of representation, and taking the circuitous route such recognition implies." Taking this route, Manning demonstrates, requires that we locate not only historical signposts but the theoretical one that distinguishes between poet and narrator; when historicist interpretation bypasses that signpost, its tendency is to restrict "the meanings of the poetic text to the generalized ideological matrix to which it is declared to belong."[1] By developing Manning's travel metaphor in this manner, I do not mean to ignore historical signposts. Following only the one, theoretical signpost would lead to a timeless world of representation, where all texts would exist in the same place—much like Eliot's "simultaneous" and "ideal order"[2]—and in which the "narrator" is always the same. At least, in that world how we characterize such a narrator in 1950, say, and how we do in 2000 reflect no more than the individual differences among "us" *in* 2000, or whenever.

But we cannot *assume* there will always be a gap between past and present that must and can be articulated only by historicist criticism. Pocock provides a brief but clear example in his discussion of the nature of historical meaning: "an utterance may, at any moment in its career, have more than one meaning and participate in more than one history. . . . Machiavelli, we say, did operate at such a level of meaning in 1513; he was interpreted at such a level of meaning in 1613; if he was interpreted in 1613 as meaning something he had or could have meant in 1513, this is to say that *the paradigm-structure had remained sufficiently stable over the intervening centuries for this to be possible*" (29–30).[3] It follows for Pocock that "paradigm-structures are historical realities, whose presence and character can be detected by the methods that historians use." But it seems also to follow that other methods, including those used here, may be at least as appropriate *within* a relatively stable paradigm. The readings offered here suggest that the past two hundred years have not altered our understanding of human subjectivity so radically that we are unable to find in these poets a similar understanding.

There may well be historically specific discursive forms that such understanding takes, still within a relatively stable paradigm of subjectivity. Here we might think, for example, of Peter de Bolla's detailed argument that "the autonomous subject" was conceptualized in and by "a set of discourses present to the period 1756–63, . . . the discourse on debt and the discourse on the sublime, . . . the combination of [which] leads to a conceptualization of the subject as . . . the remainder, that which cannot be appropriated or included within the present discursive network of control."[4] This book has made a different if complementary argument, that no *modern* discourse, or theory, is able fully to appropriate or master the subject. I do not mean thereby to imply that the problem of such appropriation is a new one. As Lee Patterson reminds us, neither subjectivity nor our interest in understanding it is new: "Insofar as we find it difficult to conceptualize the self, to that extent we think of it as unknown to earlier, simpler times. That this is not in fact the case is self-evident, but so is our need to think so." Indeed, even the need is not new: "Since at least the time of Petrarch in the mid-fourteenth century the Middle Ages has functioned as an all-purpose alternative to whatever quality the present has wished to ascribe to itself. The claim that selfhood becomes problematic only in the Renaissance"—or the eighteenth century, or the Romantic age, or the modern age—"is a prime instance of this impulse."[5]

This oversimplification of past subjectivity extends to its texts as well. It has become commonplace to distinguish between, in Belsey's version, "the interrogative text[, which] refuses a single point of view, however complex and comprehensive, but brings points of view into unresolved collision or contradiction," and "classic realism"—a product of "bourgeois ideology [that] emphasizes the fixed identity of the individual"—which "assum[es] that character, unified and coherent, is the source of action. Subjectivity is a major—perhaps the major—theme of classic realism" *and* of Romantic poetry, which, by implication also a product of bourgeois ideology, "is also based on a belief in the autonomy of the subject." "Unable to theorize the inadequacy of its concept of subjectivity, [Romantic] poetry can ultimately only present the subject as trapped between intolerable alternatives, the mortality of the material world and what Yeats calls the 'cold snows of a dream'"[6]—that is, between what Liu calls the material and the transcendental, discussed in my introduction.

The problem may be as much in the intrinsic complexity of subjectivity as in its historicity. Some readers of Romantic poetry have oversimplified this complexity; others, like Belsey, have identified the oversimplification with what the poets themselves were capable of; they have concluded from that identification the absolute need for, in McGann's words, "the hegemony of historical method to literary studies in general" (*Beauty of Inflections* 63). But oversimplification, premature and illusory mastery, exists in readers on both sides of this question of the relation between poet and "history": is the poet a subject *only* in Foucault's sense of being subjected to the (historical) forces that can be read in the poems, or is history itself subjected to (because it is present in) the poet's texts? By and large, critics until recently preferred the latter formulation; one effect of virtually every sort of critical reading since formalism has been to show how reductive is that preference. Newer historicists generally prefer the former, seeking to establish McGann's hegemonic historical method. But the very paragraph in which his argument for hegemony is most explicit reveals its own premature mastery of the human subject: "the governing context of all literary investigations must ultimately be an historical one. Literature is a human product, a humane art. It cannot be carried on (created), understood (studied), or appreciated (experienced) outside of its definitive human context. The general science governing that human context is socio-historical." Why is "human context" by definition (exclusively) "socio-historical"? Where is the "general science," socio-historical or otherwise, that *governs* (masters) that context?

Both formulations are reductive but partly true, however uncomfortably they may coexist. If, in Eagleton's words (though reversing his emphasis), the Romantic emphasis on imagination "offer[ed] the writer a comfortingly absolute alternative to history itself[,] . . . [and a]rt was becoming a commodity like anything else, and the Romantic artist little more than a minor commodity producer," it was also true that " 'Imaginative creation' [could be] an image of non-alienated labour" and "one of the few enclaves in which the creative values expunged from the face of English society by industrial capitalism [could] be celebrated and affirmed" (17–18).[7] We can see in Eagleton's formulation another version of Liu's alternatives discussed in my introduction: the poet as "a minor commodity producer" is situated firmly in the material; the poet as "imaginative creat[or]" remains, however precariously, in the transcendental. For both at the same time to be true, neither can be the whole truth.

Indeed, Eagleton's emphasis on a social and class context for the existence of these alternatives is extended by Lukacs into a context for their misunderstanding. To take either as the whole truth, argues Lukacs, is a misunderstanding itself determined by class: "As a result of its incapacity to understand history, the contemplative attitude of the bourgeoisie became polarised into two extremes: on the one hand, there were the 'great individuals' viewed as the autocratic makers of history[;] on the other hand, there were the 'natural laws' of the historical environment" (158). What Lukacs terms "natural laws" and "great individuals" have become for Liu the material and the transcendental. Whatever its origins, this polarization oversimplifies the relations between the subject and history into, at each pole, the one mastering the other.

To continue trying to map the subject's place, let us consider the following remarks by Wimsatt, Jacques Derrida, and McGann, respectively, names normally taken to stand for three modes of reading that, if sometimes mixed in critical practice, are most often represented theoretically as independent, if not incommensurate:

> We are now seeking a maximum or crucial instance where a poet's private or personal and habitual meaning . . . clearly clashed with what he managed to realize in the public materials (linguistic and cultural) of his poem. Such instances are no doubt difficult to find, because poets by and large do manage to say what they mean.[8]

> The writer writes *in* a language and *in* a logic whose proper system, laws, and life his discourse by definition cannot dominate absolutely. He uses them only by letting himself, after a fashion and up to a point, be governed by the system.[9]

Meaning, in a literary event, is a function not of "the poem itself" but of the poem's historical relations with its readers and interpreters. . . . [These] social and historical contexts, includ[e] the originary context of the author and his world. (*Beauty of Inflections* 137–38, 3)

It is worth remarking on the similarities of formalist, deconstructive, and historicist coordinates here. What Wimsatt calls "the public materials (linguistic and cultural) of [the] poem," Derrida calls "a language and . . . a logic" or "the system," and McGann calls "the poem's historical relations." For Wimsatt, "poets by and large do manage to say what they mean"; for Derrida, "the writer . . . let[s] himself, after a fashion and up to a point, be governed by the system"; and for McGann, "the originary context of the author and his world" is part of its "social and historical contexts." For all three, then, a poem exists in relation to two basic coordinates, the subject and culture. The similarity of their coordinates may seem sufficiently obvious for my point to be trivial, and I do not mean by noting it to minimize differences among formalist, deconstructive, and historicist practice. But whatever their practice, and whatever their theoretical understandings of words like "subject," "history," and "culture," all three theorists nevertheless situate that subject and the poem in relation to culture similarly: *neither* the subject *nor* culture subsumes or masters the other, but instead both coexist, with the subject as writer both using and being used by language and history.

This tension too often seems minimized or erased by adherents of any one of the three modes of reading. For example, formalist readers of Romantic poems usually have paid little attention to what Wimsatt's last sentence implies about relations between authors and narrators or speakers, except insofar as to attribute a kind of aesthetic divinity to the poets' ability "to say what they mean." Whenever such readers encounter a speaker clearly falling short of that divinity, they customarily argue, as ingeniously as is necessary to keep that divinity in place, that the speaker is being ironized by the poet. But even in the essay that provided a central theoretical rationale for the formalist split between author and speaker, and the name for its supposed violation, Wimsatt also hinted at the convergence he claims above: "The meaning of words is the history of words, and the biography of an author, his use of a word, and the associations which the word had for *him*, are part of the word's history and meaning" ("Intentional Fallacy" 10). Nevertheless, formalist and deconstructive readers, respectively, habitually have simplified Wimsatt's and Derrida's complex formulations of the relations of poet, poem, and history, enabling historicists like McGann to charge that "The famous exegetical tactic of the New Criticism and its structural and post-structural aftermath—the concentration upon a 'close reading' of 'the text'—is precisely designed to generate meaning which will establish no self-conscious or systematic relations with any of these [social and historical] contexts" (*Beauty of Inflections* 3).

Ironically, McGann's own complex thesis—that "meaning, in a literary event, is a function not of 'the poem itself' but of the poem's historical relations with its readers," while at the same time "the preparation of a finished close reading [is] not incompatible with an historical procedure" (5)—has been simplified by some Romantic historicists into the claims that there are only two alternatives, formalist or deconstructive close reading and historicist study, and that they are mutually exclusive. This is a simplification that results in attacks on such reading for inevitably violating or at least obscuring the poetry's historicity. This book has tried to show instead, in particular instances if not systematically, the extent to which the alternatives are compatible, theoretically and practically. (Here I would cite Rajan, *Supplement of Reading*, and Wolfson, *Formal Charges*, as exemplary in being at the same time formalist, deconstructive, and historicist.) It also has shown that a careful analysis of the poem's historical relations with its readers, as manifest in readings from the past several decades, reveals a spectrum of readings whose adequacy is affected positively as much by the abilities and insights of particular readers, and negatively by their relation to a desire for interpretive mastery, as by their specific theoretical allegiances.

To locate this desire and its consequences ought to encourage a rethinking of several increasingly influential formulations of Romanticism. Another way of saying that the Romantic poets dramatized but rejected mastery is to say that they continued a preference for narrative over lyric, even *in* their lyrics—by which I mean in the first case "lyric" as a mode of understanding, and only in the second case a generic mode. This preference stands diametrically opposed to what Rajan rightly calls the "lyricization" of Romantic poetry, traceable in modern interpretation not only to New Criticism's obvious preference for the lyric genre but to a pervasive ontologizing of lyric. An example is Wasserman's claim that "in the intervals between imaginative experiences there is, for Wordsworth as for Coleridge, only the chaos of aimless and bewildering multiplicity that parades before the passive senses, and for Keats and Shelley only the unreality of flux and mutability."[10] To the contrary, she argues, as I have done here, that "romantic texts" more generally "often go beyond the inclusion of [lyric] figural moments" to narration and thus "create a relationship with speaker, audience, and situation, and ask us to consider not simply the structure of signs but also the life of signs in literary communities and in psychic life" (10, 11). This lyricization, Rajan argues elsewhere, is nearly universal in modern Wordsworth studies and, she implies, in modern Romantics studies:

"The lyricization of Wordsworth has a long tradition, beginning with the New Critics"—in their "ontogenetic valorization of lyric as the mode of an autonomous and transcendental self"—"and continuing through phenomenology and deconstruction" (in its "hollow[ing] out the lyrical moment, making its paradoxes into aporias") "to New Historicism," which "simply accepts the image of Wordsworth it inherits, situating lyric as a socially symbolic act of avoidance" ("Erasure of Narrative" 366).

Such recent historicist lyricization characterizes, for example, the "lyric turn" that Clifford Siskin locates in Romantic poetry and its recent criticism, "that feature by which creative and critical narratives, from the past and from the present, veer from the generic and historical to the natural and transcendent, metamorphosing all analysis into claims for Imaginative vision."[11] In effect I have agreed only, and partly, with the second half of Siskin's argument: such a "lyric turn," implying as it does a self-deceived belief in achieved transcendence and mastery, characterizes less the poets and poems studied here than some of their readers and interpretations.

Siskin's "lyric turn" is essentially the same as McGann's influential claim that "Today the scholarship and interpretation of Romantic works is dominated by an uncritical absorption in Romanticism's own self-representations" (*Romantic Ideology* 137). Likewise, I have agreed with only half of this claim. It would be truer to say that interpretation is dominated by an uncritical absorption in what the major Romantic writers critique repeatedly (though not always and everywhere): any absorption in one's own self-representation. Why this misreading has been so pervasive and dominant is a question that may need to be studied in specific historical and cultural terms, as Mitchell has predicted from a viewpoint similar to McGann's:

> Keats's "speculations," Wordsworth's "philosophic mind," Blake's "system," Shelley's "intellectual philosophy" seem to me wonderful sites for the study of literary theorizing as an activity scarred by history. None of these Romantic theories can be taken at face value; none of their self-representations of mastery, comprehension, utopian perfection, or imaginative freedom can be accepted as reliable guides to the understanding of their work, or to our own hopes for theoretical mastery.[12]

But at least a partial answer this book has offered to the question is that our desire for mastery may be permanent and transhistorical, though not transcendent, as the poets themselves knew at least as well as their modern theorists.

Mitchell's phrasing—"*their* self-representations of mastery," "*our* own hopes for theoretical mastery"—parallels poet and reader, as subjects whose understandings of their places remain uncertainly, and permanently, short of mastery. Any such self-representation of mastery is one effect of what Richardson calls the subject's "fascination with his own imaginary ego," which returns us to the question Richardson asks, "how the subject can say 'I' independently of [this] fascination" (58). It also returns us to Lacan's comment that "there is only one method of learning that one is there, namely, to map the network. And how is a network mapped? One goes back and forth over one's ground, one crosses one's path" (*Four Concepts* 45). Not only the poet but "the critic too," remarks Jean-Pierre Mileur, "must operate in language, in a text, and, like an individual in a landscape, his (in)sight is limited to the perspective his position imposes. Error resides as a permanent possibility in the difference between a particular prospect and the actual lay of the land. But to know that our perception of the landscape is limited is not the same as to think ourselves lost. We know that a landscape is not just the possibility of error but a structure of errancy as well, that there is an account of possible perspectival errors, of versions of blindness that adds up to a 'truth'—in short, a map."[13]

Mileur's map coordinates—"critic," "language," "text"—here echo those of Wimsatt, Derrida, and McGann, and his metaphor of landscape echoes both Lacan's and Manning's travel metaphors. But I do not intend this cluster of metaphors to serve as the basis of a new model by which to explain the subject's relation to text and culture. I emphasize it instead because it is so obviously metaphoric, so obviously only a *partial* representation of relations among subject, text, and culture. In particular, it represents metaphorically the sense of the subject—poet and critic alike—of being not at home and being at home, of not knowing where one is and knowing, and especially of what it is like to be moving between those two poles, never at either one. But it is also what Booth calls one of a number of relatively "mechanized pictures of texts / webs / prison houses / mazes [perhaps closest of all in this list to "map" and "landscape"] / codes / rule systems / speech acts / semantic structures" that obscure and even prevent "a kind of critical conversation . . . , once almost universal, about the types of friendship or companionship a book provides *as* it is read" (*Company We Keep* 170). Like most of Booth's other pictures or models, it leaves out other subjects, both in its representation of the subject's acts of interpretation as solitary and in its *mis*representation of home and belonging as always equally solitary.

Booth goes on to observe that among the Romantics, "Often the language of friendship was not enough; only words of love spoke strongly enough for what books inspire" (171). This suggests strongly that his own model (or figure) of reader and book as two interacting subjects is, if only another paradigm of a particular time and culture, nevertheless a long-lived one, since it characterizes not only the Romantics but his own late-twentieth-century reading of mass-audience best-sellers, as well as of canonical works written centuries earlier.

Jon Klancher finds this paradigm no longer operative, arguing that Wordsworth and Coleridge, among others, "struggled to forge readerships in what now appears to have been a transitory, personal world of reading and writing far removed from the mass audiences and institutionalized discourses of the modern 'consciousness industry' and its ideologies."[14] Belief in such a world Klancher seems to regard as already an anachronistic faith at the time: "That the abyss between social classes and their cultures could be bridged in a heroic, high humanist act of writing, and that socially divided readers might transcend their differences in a morally renewing, redemptive act of reading—this belief failed [Wordsworth]. Yet it survives in his works, and in the faiths of many who still read him" (150). Further, Klancher suggests that this world now is, and perhaps even then was, a fantasy, arguing that belief in it has contributed to McGann's Romantic ideology by "displac[ing] the real cultural and historical conflicts of the early nineteenth century with an essentialized 'Romanticism'" (150) and an "hypostatized 'reader.'" This reader "surely," Klancher recommends, should be "abandon[ed]" by modern critics who "take their 'critical' function seriously enough to engage those discourses beyond the university that exert fantastic power upon the moral, social, and political tenor of everyday life" (177). Yet it is not at all clear that such engagement requires abandoning such belief. Booth's own project, for example, seems characterized by both, much like Wordsworth's "attempts to transform commodified textual relations into an older relation of symbolic exchange, opposing to popular German verse tragedies and the sentimental trash of the magazines new poems that call for an active, engaged response from the same readers" (143). I am suggesting that what Klancher describes as the "small, deliberative strategic world of early-nineteenth-century reading and writing[, which] still allowed for Wordsworth to imagine the reading of a poem as a personal exchange of 'power' between writer and reader" (14), remains a world that critics like Booth are attempting to (re)create; I am also suggesting that to imagine reading as such a personal exchange is neither anachronistic nor necessarily an ideologically deluded act. (By considering in detail "the particular subtlety . . . of the printed voice in poetry" [74], Griffiths argues for complex relations among writing, speech, and intention, and thus for the reading

of poetry in particular as a complex personal exchange—see esp. 13–96.) Wordsworth ends *The Prelude* with such intimacy as the necessary beginning of community, and it is not far from that to Raymond Williams's idea of "community"
that is "knowable" in, and composed by, the "creative acts" of "major individual talents."[15]

It is true that Booth's figure of book and reader as two interacting subjects is
friendlier not only than "mechanized pictures" of book and reader but than
other, equally humanized but more agonistic figures—as Klancher's "exchange
of 'power'" above might suggest. My readings have been assuming, implicitly,
one version of these figures, by using "mastery" to characterize certain imbal-
ances between authorial subject and history, subject and language, reader
and text. I have used the word deliberately, though its Hegelian undertones of
Master-Slave may seem distracting. I have preferred to let the word accumulate
its significance inductively, in relation to the readings offered here of particular
poems, but these undertones are intended to the extent they suggest that "mastery" of text or world implies a personification of what is to be mastered, however unsuccessful the mastery, and however complex the act of personification.[16]

Such personification seems in keeping with de Man's concept of the "autobiographical moment . . . as an alignment between the two subjects involved in
the process of reading" ("Autobiography" 70). But I have not been assuming
with de Man that every subject—poet, narrator, and reader alike—*must* be understood primarily as a "linguistic structure" and only secondarily on the "level
of the referent." David Hoy argues, following Hans-Georg Gadamer, that proper
"hermeneutical understanding" of the past and its texts "can best be understood by analogy with the corresponding form of the I-Thou relationship [that]
neither treats the other person as an object or a means nor tries to master the
Other by suspending his right to meaningful statement." Instead, by analogy,
"to interpret these texts is to come into dialog with them."[17] De Man in effect
makes a similar point, that the presence of meaningful language implies to us as
readers a speaking subject; his emphasis is on the extent to which that subject is
decentered and figuratively constructed. It follows that deconstruction does not
eradicate that subject: it only complicates it radically. Such complication, not
eradication, is equally the point of Derrida's remark that although deconstruction "tries to pass beyond man and humanism, the name man being the name
of that being who, throughout the history of metaphysics or of ontology—in
other words, through the history of all of his history—has dreamed of full presence, the reassuring foundation," nevertheless "The subject is absolutely indispensable. I don't destroy the subject; I situate it. That is to say, I believe that at
a certain level both of experience and of philosophical and scientific discourse
one cannot get along without the notion of subject. It is a question of knowing

where it comes from and how it functions. Therefore I keep the concept of center, which I explained was indispensable, as well as that of subject."[18]

Center and subject, I am now arguing, are indispensable to adequate conceptions not only of poet and of narrator but of the relations between readers and texts. In both contexts, decentering and centering, deconstructing and constructing, remain in tension with one another. To insist not only on the primacy of one but on the consequent marginality of the other is in effect to seek to master the subject by oversimplifying it and its relation to both activities. Versions of this form of intepretive mastery consistently have been attributed to the Romantics, as evidence of either their self-deception ("Romantic ideology") or their prophetic power ("Imagination").

In this particular context of reader and text, such insistence oversimplifies interpretation, either by evading this tension or by fantasizing its resolution. The evasion can be found throughout modern literary theory. On one side, reader-response criticism often, as exemplified by Norman Holland, simply ignores it by ignoring the cultural constraints operating on any single interpreter.[19] On the same side, Fish transfers interpretive authority from the individual to his or her "interpretive community" and thereby frees individuals of both their individual authority and any possible resulting tension with their community. For both Holland and Fish, the reader, whether purely individual (for Holland) or professionally determined (for Fish), dominates and eventually replaces with his or her own the text's cultural context (to the extent that context has not become somehow "part of" the reader or the reader's interpretive community). On the other side, for Eliot the text's cultural context (including all of its history as part of "the" collection of great works of art) dominates, even subsumes, the individual subject into its "tradition," to the point of what Eliot calls "a continual self-sacrifice, a continual extinction of personality," "depersonalization" (7).[20]

Bloom leaves in place these two opposites and even appears to fantasize the resolution of this interpretive tension, in his assertion that "No critic . . . can evade a Nietzschean will to power over a text, because interpretation is at last nothing else."[21] Though his wish is clear, at least Bloom writes about both possibilities: that the reader either replaces the text's cultural context with his or her own or is subsumed into the text's cultural context. But the two seem finally for Bloom the only—and mutually antithetical—alternatives, and they return us to my starting point in this book, Baldick's critique of Bloom's model as a "mythology of single (and mortal) combat [that] radically oversimplifies the true multiplicity and complexity of debate in the critical arena" (8).

I suggest that these theories of textual meaning, authority, and power— Bloom's in particular—fundamentally mislocate that meaning, because they suppose it to be a positivist entity, locatable "in" the reader or "in" the text; as

Hoy puts it, "the text . . . posited as an object existing at a distance from a subjective consciousness that must reach out to it . . . does not concur phenomenologically with the process of actually reading a literary work" (46–47). Bloom's own model is Oedipal: there can be only two ultimate centers or locations of meaning, authority, and power—father (text) and son (reader), and these two inevitably contest for mastery. For all Bloom's emphasis on reading as an agonistic process,[22] it always comes to an end, in that only one of the two can survive—father (Bloom's "strong precursor" writer, who subsumes the weak interpreter son) or son (Bloom's "strong misreader," who replaces, in his own mind, anyway, the father-text with his own reading or version of it). But these alternatives, father or son, winning or losing, are based on a misunderstanding of the Oedipus complex. Bloom writes: "The poetic ego is a kind of paranoid construct founded upon the ambivalency of opposition [complete independence] and identity [complete dependence] between the ephebe [later poet or reader] and the precursor."[23] His misunderstanding supposes that one subject's identity either is achieved through complete independence from its "father" or cultural context or is lost through complete dependence on that context.

These are indeed the two extremes of Oedipal "resolution." But why should we suppose that the complex is "resolved" in some final sense in every case, or even in most? Children, poets, and readers do not usually achieve some final resolution of their tension-filled relations with their parents, cultures, and poems, and those who believe that they do so may believe it out of their own desire for mastery, not because it is true. Even if we suppose such resolution, it is not necessarily the winner-take-all ending that Bloom envisions. Ricoeur hypothesizes "fatherhood as a process rather than a structure," enabling us to see how arrested is Bloom's Oedipal version of interpretation, frozen in an "infantile omnipotence" from which "proceeds the phantasm of a father who would retain the privileges which the son must seize if he is to be himself." The alternative, Ricoeur suggests, is "the degree [to which] our desire, by renouncing omnipotence, assents to the representation of a mortal father whom it is no longer necessary to kill but who can be recognized."[24] I would add here only that such recognition is itself not always free from tension.

Ricoeur's argument can be taken as an even more precise critique of Bloom's representation of Romantic poetry itself as well as how it is read. Bloom's dominant figure, among many, for poetic influence is "apophrades," the return of the dead: "A poet [is] a man rebelling against being spoken to by a dead man (the precursor) outrageously more alive than himself."[25] Ricoeur writes, "on the level of phantasm, there is a death of the father, but it is a murder; this murder is the work of omnipotent desire, which dreams of itself as immortal; it gives birth, by the interiorization of the paternal image, to a complementary phantasm, that of the father immortalized beyond the murder" (491). Throughout this book I have been arguing in effect that Bloom's, and others', reading of the entire Romantic tradition fundamentally mistakes the imagination for this fantasy of omnipotent desire.

In current Romantics studies, Bloom's Oedipal, binary opposition of mastery and slavery has become fundamental even to critics of Bloom, who see his version of Romanticism as a mystifying Romantic ideology that characterizes the (male) poets as accurately as it does Bloom himself. Marlon Ross's critique of Bloom's "gendered poetics" is a case in point.[26] "From [Bloom's] perspective," he writes, "one must either influence or be influenced. Influence is based on a hierarchized dichotomy as fundamental to Western culture as good/evil, body/soul, or male/female. The ideal state is one of absolute influence, the power to sway without ever having been swayed, the final cause that has no cause outside itself—the state of God" (88). Such "influence becomes a form of masterful self-sufficiency" (91), in effect "the power to make an object (a material thing, a vehicle for exploitation) of the other supposedly without becoming oneself an object" (89). It is, then, a form of mastery. It explains not only implicitly why Bloom relies, but explicitly "why the romantics rely[,] heavily on the prophetic stance, which itself is another instance of a masculine trope of power"; "The prophet is one who is able to enforce his vision on others" (91).

This influential, prophetic, masculine poetic subject independent of culture and history may be, according to Ross, for Bloom a tragically unachievable vision (89); for Ross, it is a profoundly deluded ideological fantasy. For Bloom and Ross alike, it characterizes canonical Romantic poetry's representation of the masterful poet; neither considers the extent to which that poetry dramatizes but also rejects such mastery, because neither considers seriously enough the complexity of narrator as well as poet. This book has sought to represent these complexities and thereby to demonstrate the continued usefulness of attempting to distinguish between poet and narrator: first, by showing that narrators *are* complex and that their complexity is made up significantly of their certainty and their uncertainty, their coherence and their incoherence, and the resulting intrasubjective tensions reflected in their narratives; second, by bringing narrator and author closer together conceptually, recognizing authors to be complex, without a unitary, pure, uncomplicated purpose; and last, by helping to show the extent to which Blake, Coleridge, Wordsworth, and Keats, in the poems studied here at least, are significantly aware of the complex relations between understanding and mastery that seem to some readers to postdate them.

I have not been arguing that Bloom's Oedipal model is irrelevant or false, *as a model:* it highlights what is agonistic in both literary influence and in interpretation, though it marginalizes what is not. Also, I am not arguing against the use of models. As Max Black puts it, "models are sometimes not epiphenomena of research," and such models are of the sort of metaphorical thought that can be "a distinctive mode of achieving insight, not to be construed as an ornamental substitute for plain thought." But models, *to be models,* should be "relatively unproblematic, more familiar, or better-organized" than their subject[27]—and they need to be seen as models and not as a replacement for that to which they refer.

Bloom's model, and the models Booth calls "pictures," have been pressed beyond their limits. It may be understandable that the more complex a model appears or becomes, the more its status as a model tends to disappear, and the more it is taken for the complex reality it models; still, such a misunderstanding is compounded by granting it mastery over its object.[28] The very point at which this mastery is assumed is most problematic, even *within the model itself* as a discipline-specific theory. I have argued this last point in chapters 2 and 3, with respect to psychoanalytic theory's intermittent assumption that it has privileged access to the origin of metaphor and metaphoric meaning. I have also argued this point throughout: with respect to formalist theory's assumption that the autonomy of the literary work results in a clear split between author and narrator, which in turn provides a comprehensive framework for understanding literary meaning through narrative point of view; and with respect to deconstructive and historicist theory's marginalizing of this split, and of narrative point of view, on the respective assumptions that textual voice is, like the subject, no more than a linguistic or an historical effect (thereby converting culture into "language" or "history").

These assumptions are at the hearts of their interpretive models. Perhaps most theoreticians would not commit themselves to the replacement of psychological, textual, and cultural reality by these models in their simplest forms but would acknowledge limits to those models. On an explicitly theoretical level, then, we find such qualifications as McGann's—"the preparation of a finished close reading [is] not incompatible with an historical procedure"; or Derrida's—"at a certain level both of experience and of philosophical and scientific discourse one cannot get along without the notion of subject," who as author "let[s] himself, after a fashion and up to a point, be governed by the system"; or Wimsatt's—although a poem "is hypostatized as an object, and metaphorically as a spatial object[,] . . . we ought not to talk as if the poem had to meet some kind of impossible angelic or metaphysical standard of absolute entity."[29]

It may be worth adding that such a metaphysical standard is itself by no means clear; the interpretive use of "object" as metaphor or model for poem or text has virtually ignored the complexity of that concept in modern philosophy of science.[30] The point is worth adding, for two reasons. First, it suggests that the positivist notion of meaning "in" the text *or* "in" the reader presupposed by theories of textual meaning, authority, and power discussed above is modeled on a concept of autonomous entities that even in its scientific origins is already, if not untenable, at least seriously oversimplified. Second, it reminds us of the need to understand as fully as possible what we take for our models, even if by doing so we diminish their apparent explanatory power—or, for that matter, their useful status as straw terms.

Learning the limits of the model of the well-wrought urn or verbal icon is akin to experiencing on a theoretical level what de Man called, in the critical interpretation of particular literary texts, formalism's metamorphosis into "a criticism of ambiguity, an ironic reflection on the absence of the unity it had postulated." My argument would qualify de Man here: the metamorphosis, or impasse for a "pure" formalism, arises from formalism's discovery that such texts are, finally, always *imperfectly* unified—not the same thing as an "*absence* of the unity it had postulated" (emphasis added) unless that unity is, in Wimsatt's words, an "impossible . . . metaphysical standard of absolute entity."

In this book we have come across other such impasses in theory, less frequently emphasized than the formalist impasse, including, for example, psychoanalytic theory's failure to account for the metaphoric power demonstrably present in *The Prelude*'s protagonist, and more generally poststructuralism's failure—on the part of deconstruction and historicism alike—to account for demonstrably complex relations between poet and narrator. Such impasses may be at times not very noticeable in interpretive practice, where we often find either a mixture or a shifting of models, or a stopping short of the impasse, however detailed in application the model might be. But perhaps it is time to acknowledge these multiple impasses and to confront the difficult problems of what happens at the intersections of formalism, deconstruction, and historicism.

I have not been comfortably balanced in my consideration of such intersections. Nor have I arrived at a theoretical position from which to determine reliably the presence or absence of irony or to predict the distance between poet and narrator. To some extent, I believe, these confessions happily enact my argument against mastery, evidenced also in the sometimes chameleon-like style of my own critical commentary, whose voice is as likely to be found in the way others' voices are brought together as in an otherwise seemingly unmediated critical voice of my own. But I am uncomfortably aware that these confessions are at least also an admission of limits to my own current understanding. (As one example, I am especially uncertain about my response to Liu's assertions about the representation of history in *The Prelude*, and I cannot yet say why.) It may be that for all of us as interpreters, no matter how profound our understanding, "World and book," as Kermode remarks, "are hopelessly plural, endlessly disappointing; we stand alone before them,"[31] as we might before culture itself or before its other personifications, as father, for example, in Ricoeur's formulation, or even as friend, in Booth's. If so, we all are enacting part of the argument made here about the Romantic poets, that we all stand in such an uncertain and uneasy place. One comfort is that we can become part of Kenneth Burke's "discussion" about world and book. That discussion might be more interesting, if more difficult, were we to acknowledge and explore the consequences of where we stand.

Notes

Introduction

1. Jerome J. McGann, *The Beauty of Inflections: Literary Investigations in Historical Method and Theory* (Oxford: Clarendon P, 1988), 137–38.

2. Chris Baldick, *Criticism and Literary Theory, 1890 to the Present* (New York: Longman, 1996), 7–8.

3. Kenneth Burke, *The Philosophy of Literary Form: Studies in Symbolic Action* (N.p.: Louisiana State UP, 1941), 110.

4. The most influential defense of intention remains that by E. D. Hirsch, Jr., *Validity in Interpretation* (New Haven, CT: Yale UP, 1967). His argument depends on his fundamental assumption that meaning requires not only a stable but a mastering subject. That assumption is reflected in his rhetoric throughout: "when critics deliberately *banished* the original author, they themselves *usurped* his place" (5; emphasis added).

5. See David Simpson, *Irony and Authority in Romantic Poetry* (Totowa, NJ: Rowman and Littlefield, 1979); Susan J. Wolfson, *The Questioning Presence: Wordsworth, Keats, and the Interrogative Mode in Romantic Poetry* (Ithaca, NY: Cornell UP, 1986), and *Formal Charges: The Shaping of Poetry in British Romanticism* (Stanford, CA: Stanford UP, 1997). Wolfson's more recent book also seeks to counter deconstructive and new historicist readers' pervasive "equation of poetic form with harmony, symmetry, and unity, and so a categorical insulation from the conflicts discovered and contemplated by" such readers, who also—mistakenly, she rightly argues— "tend to limit accounts of poetic form to the organic, the unified, the achieved, the

stable. Whatever is factitious, contradictory, and unstable is credited to the world 'outside' the poem, or is readable in its form only as the rupture of organicist desire" (13–14). My argument focuses more on relations of poet and poem to speaker than on their relations to poetic form. The two are inevitably related, though, and my readings of different poetic texts than Wolfson's should be taken as corroborating her general argument.

6. For influential examples of the former and the latter see, respectively, M. H. Abrams, *Doing Things with Texts: Essays in Criticism and Critical Theory* (New York: Norton, 1989), and Stanley Fish, *Is There a Text in This Class? The Authority of Interpretive Communities* (Cambridge, MA: Harvard UP, 1980).

7. Alan Liu, "The Power of Formalism: The New Historicism," *ELH* 56 (1989): 765.

8. Paul de Man, "Autobiography as De-Facement" (1979), *The Rhetoric of Romanticism* (New York: Columbia UP, 1984), 70–71, 76.

9. Paul Smith, *Discerning the Subject* (Minneapolis: U of Minnesota P, 1988), xxxv.

10. Paul Ricoeur, *Oneself as Another* (1990), trans. Kathleen Blamey (Chicago and London: U of Chicago P, 1992), 128.

11. Geoffrey H. Hartman, "Beyond Formalism" (1966), *Beyond Formalism* (New Haven, CT, and London: Yale UP, 1970), 42, 56.

12. "Form and Intent in the American New Criticism" (1971), *Blindness and Insight: Essays in the Rhetoric of Contemporary Criticism*, 2d rev. ed. (1971; Minneapolis: U of Minnesota P, 1983), 32, 28, 32. De Man claims that any such "totalizing principle" forms the "blindness" that enables critical "insight"—see especially "The Rhetoric of Blindness: Jacques Derrida's Reading of Rousseau" (1971), *Blindness and Insight*, 104–5, 109–10, 139; nowhere, however, does he actually make the case that New Criticism's theoretical weakness, especially its "hypostasis, which changes the literary act into a literary object by the suppression of its intentional character" (25), is *necessary* to its "practical results" (28). For a more sustained critique of de Man's claim, see Frank Lentricchia, *After the New Criticism* (Chicago: U of Chicago P, 1980), 283–84, 298–307.

13. Robert C. Elliott, *The Literary Persona* (Chicago: U of Chicago P, 1982), 18.

14. Cleanth Brooks, "Marvell's 'Horatian Ode,'" (1947), rpt. William R. Keast, ed., *Seventeenth-Century English Poetry: Modern Essays in Criticism* (New York: Oxford UP, 1962), 336–39, *The Well Wrought Urn: Studies in the Structure of Poetry* (New York: Harcourt, 1947).

15. J. Hillis Miller, *The Linguistic Moment: From Wordsworth to Stevens* (Princeton, NJ: Princeton UP, 1985), 278–79, 288–89. A similar moment occurs in Miller's reading of Yeats's poetry. To argue *against* the use of "Passages from Yeats's prose . . . to support the claim that Yeats's poems should be thought of as the intense speech of Yeats himself," Miller cites a passage from Yeats's prose—"Talk to me of originality and I will turn on you with rage. I am a crowd, I am a lonely man, I am nothing"—to argue that "The speaker of 'Nineteen Hundred and Nineteen' is not the private person William Yeats, but Yeats as a part of that *we* who is a crowd, a lonely man, nothing" (324–25). Again, this makes more sense as an argument against an oversimplified belief in a privatized biographical unity, and in favor of a complex relation of speaker to poet, than it does as an argument against all forms of biography.

1. "Introduction" to the *Songs of Experience*: The Infection of Time

1. Mary Lynn Johnson, in *The English Romantic Poets: A Review of Research and Criticism*, 4th ed., ed. Frank Jordan (New York: Modern Language Association of America, 1985), 213–14. Two notable exceptions to this generalization are Zachary Leader, *Reading Blake's "Songs"* (Boston: Routledge and Kegan Paul, 1981), and Edward Larrissy, *William Blake* (Oxford: Basil Blackwell, 1985).

2. *The Complete Poetry and Prose of William Blake*, rev. ed., ed. David V. Erdman (New York: Doubleday Anchor, 1988), 576. Subsequent references to Blake's prose are cited as, for example, *E* 576. I am not making the naively empiricist claim that we can read the *Songs* context free, only that if we become more aware of how we can read them, we can read them better. Assertions that how we read does *no more than* reflect our sociocultural or psychological context are not convincing. Fish's argument that interpretation is entirely conventional too often rests on hypothetical counterexamples that are at least whimsical: that Blake's "The Tyger" could be interpreted as an allegory of the digestive processes, for example (348–49). Norman N. Holland's argument, in "Literary Interpretation and Three Phases of Psychoanalysis," *Critical Inquiry* 2 (1976), that interpretation essentially mirrors our individual "identity theme" becomes universally but trivially true when that theme amounts to this sort of generalization: "For me, the need to see and understand is very strong" (232)—a criticism made also by Cary Nelson, "The Psychology of Criticism, Or What Can Be Said," *Psychoanalysis and the Question of the Text*, ed. Geoffrey H. Hartman (Baltimore: Johns Hopkins UP, 1978), 52–53.

3. Northrop Frye, "Blake's Introduction to Experience" (1957), rpt. *Blake: A Collection of Critical Essays*, ed. Frye (Englewood Cliffs, NJ: Prentice-Hall, 1966), 23–31. Hazard Adams, *William Blake: A Reading of the Shorter Poems* (Seattle: U of Washington P, 1963), 21–27, and D. G. Gillham, *William Blake* (Cambridge: Cambridge UP, 1973), 46–54, are representative examples of Frye's influence here.

4. *The Complete Poetry and Prose of William Blake*, ed. Erdman, 251. *Jerusalem*, plate 91, lines 20–21. Subsequent references to Blake's poetry are cited with plate and line reference when necessary—as, for example, *J* 91.20–21; *E* 251.

5. Not all readers who view the Bard as a thoroughly reliable prophet speaking for Blake ignore such details; instead, like Frye if less ingeniously, they explain them (away). Robert Gleckner for example, in *The Piper and the Bard: A Study of William Blake* (Detroit: Wayne State UP, 1959), recognizes these difficulties, but because of his thesis that the *Songs* together show the Piper "matured into the prophetic Bard or poetic character or genius" who is "the mature Blake," he creates "two voices in the poem, that of the Bard and that of the Holy Word," the second of which is "devastatingly ironic" (231–32). He thereby tries to free the Bard from any responsibility for the Genesis allusion and its father-priest-king implications. As Larrissy remarks, this creation "fails to explain how it is that the Bard should be reporting, however indirectly, sentiments which can be attributed to a tyrannical deity" (68).

6. The case for the Bard as a deluded prophet, his vision limited by Experience and subject to Blake's irony, usually has been made by citing this syntactic confusion in

conjunction with likening the Bard to other speakers in Experience whose vision seems limited. So, for example, "The Tyger" is seen as intellectual satire, because no obvious New Testament allusion provides the kind of typological recasting of the poem's Old Testament allusions that we have seen in the "Introduction," and because the speaker's questions without answers are rhetorically opposite to the Bard's confident assertions. But here too we can find the same problem: the speaker, after all, asks important questions, even if how he asks them drastically limits his possible answers. Why therefore cannot "The Tyger"'s speaker be seen as both limited and as visionary, as aspiring to vision?—a point made by John E. Grant, "The Art and Argument of 'The Tyger,'" (1960), rev. rpt. *Discussions of William Blake*, ed. Grant (Boston: D. C. Heath, 1961), 69.

7. Harold Bloom, *Blake's Apocalypse: A Study in Poetic Argument* (Ithaca, NY: Cornell UP, 1963), 130, 132.

8. This process of recognition is akin to the primary function of what Wolfgang Iser calls "negations," in *The Act of Reading: A Theory of Aesthetic Response* (1976; Baltimore: Johns Hopkins UP, 1978): "Classical and psychological aesthetics have always been at one over the postulate that the final resolution of initial tension in the work of art is coincidental with the emergence of meaning. [But] meaning as a relief from tension embodies an expectation of art which is historical in nature and consequently loses its claim to be normative. The density of negations [in modern literature] not only lays bare the historicity of our concept of meaning but also reveals the defensive nature of such a traditional expectation—we obviously anticipate a meaning that will remove the illogicalities, conflicts, and, indeed, the whole contingency of the world in the literary work. To experience meaning as a defence, or as having a defensive structure, is, of course, also a meaning, which, however, the reader can only become conscious of when the traditional concept of meaning is invoked as a background, in order for it to be discredited" (223). I would add only that the concept of meaning as defence against "the whole contingency of the world" has always been with us, deriving from our permanent desire for a simpler world, and that textual negations, often lurking in the most classical of texts, always have been able to frustrate this desire more or less.

9. Heather Glen, *Vision and Disenchantment: Blake's "Songs" and Wordsworth's "Lyrical Ballads"* (Cambridge: Cambridge UP, 1983), esp. 1–33, 57–223. Glen builds on the work of Vivian de Sola Pinto, "William Blake, Isaac Watts, and Mrs. Barbauld" (1944), rev. rpt. *The Divine Vision: Studies in the Poetry and Art of William Blake*, ed. de Sola Pinto (London: Victor Gollancz, 1957), 65–87; John Holloway, *Blake: The Lyric Poetry* (London: Edward Arnold, 1968); Nick Shrimpton, "Hell's Hymnbook: Blake's *Songs of Innocence and of Experience* and Their Models," *Literature of the Romantic Period, 1750–1850*, ed. R. T. Davies and B. G. Beatty (New York: Barnes and Noble, 1976), 19–35; and Leader, *Reading Blake's "Songs."*

10. Tilottama Rajan, *The Supplement of Reading: Figures of Understanding in Romantic Theory and Practice* (Ithaca, NY: Cornell UP, 1990), 200. Rajan argues in detail that while the *Songs* are "Individually simple, they become ambiguous at the point where we try to connect them so as to make them yield a narrative or an argument. Instead of being an expression of the system, their very form as a collection that can be put together from more than one perspective raises the problem of system: of how parts are organized into wholes and of

how evidence is generalized into explanatory structures" (222). My only qualification is that at least some of the *Songs*, including especially the "Introduction" to *Experience*, are *not* "individually simple"; the problem Rajan convincingly points out is itself replicated within individual poems.

11. Nelson Hilton, *Literal Imagination: Blake's Vision of Words* (Berkeley: U of California P, 1983), 3, 8.

12. Compare Miller's remark about Wordsworth's poems: "Each new poem turns out, when it is scrutinized, to be another expression of the same alternations between one meaning and another that it may have been called upon to control in the first poem examined" (*Linguistic Moment* 75, n. 20).

13. Michel Foucault, "What Is an Author?" *Textual Strategies: Perspectives in Post-Structuralist Criticism*, ed. Josue V. Harari (Ithaca, NY: Cornell UP, 1979), 160. Equally misleading is his methodological conclusion in favor of "depriving the subject (or its substitute) of its role as originator, and [instead] of analyzing the subject as a variable and complex function of discourse" (158); I do not understand why the second necessarily precludes the first—that is, why "the subject as . . . function of discourse" precludes "the subject . . . as originator." In this book I am attempting to explore relations between the two. Foucault hints at such relations when, envisioning discourse about which we no longer ask questions like "Who really spoke?", he imagines not only questions like "What are the modes of existence of this discourse?" but also *these* questions: "What are the places in it where there is room for possible subjects? Who can assume these various subject-functions?" (160).

14. Robert N. Essick, *William Blake and the Language of Adam* (Oxford: Clarendon P, 1989), 191, 26. I am extending a part of Essick's argument about Blake's kerygmatic language to *Songs of Experience*. Essick's own argument is more complicated; see note 17, below.

15. Joseph Viscomi, *Blake and the Idea of the Book* (Princeton, NJ: Princeton UP, 1993), 162, 155, 157, 175.

16. W. J. T. Mitchell, *Blake's Composite Art: A Study of the Illuminated Poetry* (Princeton, NJ: Princeton UP, 1978), 4, 6–8. Such ambiguity is compounded by different versions of the frontispiece, two of which I discuss briefly on p. 24.

17. Other readers have noticed the same ambiguities; see, for example, Larrissy 26–28. Essick is the most recent of readers who excise such ambiguities from the poem and from other poems in *Songs of Innocence*: "Writing has not replaced voice but has, *in this innocent context*, continued and preserved it for recreation by the audience" (183; emphasis added). Essick is also the most theoretically sophisticated of these readers, not simply assuming this context to be innocent on the basis of the collection's title but arguing for it on the basis that Blake is deliberately recreating a language appropriate to such a context: "The differences between the linguistic landscape of innocence and of experience derive in large measure from the structural and functional distinction between two states of semiotic consciousness, one that unself-consciously perceives (and hence creates) incarnational signs as the embodiment and expression of the spirit immanent within the material, and another that is self-consciously aware of the differential nature of language" (128). Essick shows that these two "states of semiotic consciousness" derive from

linguistic concepts of Blake's time, and he argues persuasively that Blake critiques both concepts; still, his own argument suggests more that linguistic "innocence" is *represented* in the *Songs of Innocence* than that it provides the definitive interpretive context of, and thereby conjoins writing and voice in, the poems.

18. Glen is unusually sensitive to this paradox in "The Chimney Sweeper," for example (95–102), and to other forms this paradox takes, such as between the written word as potentially both redemptive and hegemonic (66–73). Indeed, she eventually argues that the *Songs of Innocence* "offer a powerful affirmation of the way in which a sense of possibility beyond the status quo may be threatened by but *may also be formed and shaped within* an exploitative and alienating society" (111).

19. M. M. Bakhtin, *The Dialogic Imagination*, ed. Michael Holquist, trans. Caryl Emerson and Holquist (Austin: U of Texas P, 1981), 294. Despite his insight into "The importance of struggling with another's discourse, its influence in the history of an individual's coming to ideological consciousness" (348), Bakhtin seems to assume that literary texts reflect not the process but the end of that struggle, a consciousness already completed: the "languages of heteroglossia . . . may all be drawn in by the novelist for the orchestration of his themes and for the refracted (indirect) expression of his intentions and values" (292); "He can make use of language without wholly giving himself up to it, he may treat it as semi-alien or completely alien to himself, while compelling language ultimately to serve all his own intentions" (299). Despite his insistence that the novelist and the poet differ fundamentally in their use of heteroglossia, Bakhtin's rhetoric here — "*may* all be drawn in," "the *refracted (indirect)* expression of his intentions," "*can* make use of language," "*may* treat it" — barely disguises his presumption that they are both masters of their own texts: "The prose writer makes use of words that are already populated with the social intentions of others and compels them to serve his own new intentions, to serve a second master" (299–300). In Bakhtin's terms, I am arguing that Blake's struggle with biblical discourse is part of his coming to ideological consciousness and that Blake makes use of that language without wholly giving himself up to it. But I am arguing also that it does not ultimately serve all his own intentions — that, in other words, he is not fully the master of his allusions.

20. George Orwell, "Politics and the English Language" (1946), rpt. *In Front of Your Nose, 1945–1950, The Collected Essays, Journalism and Letters of George Orwell*, ed. Sonia Orwell and Ian Angus (New York: Harcourt, Brace and World, 1968), 4:138, 137.

21. For more detailed descriptions of the changes, see Blake, *Songs of Innocence and of Experience*, ed. Andrew Lincoln (Princeton, NJ: William Blake Trust, Princeton UP, 1991), 17–18, and Viscomi 271–75.

22. The following account of neoclassical art theory of line, and Blake's response to it, is drawn from Morris Eaves, *William Blake's Theory of Art* (Princeton, NJ: Princeton UP, 1982).

23. Glen argues throughout that this is one of the distinctions marking "the real originality" both of the *Songs* and of Wordsworth's *Lyrical Ballads* (7).

24. Lincoln 19. See Lincoln, plate 28 (Copy W, King's College) and figure 6 (Copy T, British Museum Print Room).

25. Stewart Crehan, *Blake in Context* (Dublin and Atlantic Highlands, NJ: Gill and Macmillan, Humanities P, 1984), 199–200. See especially 192–238 for a discussion of English art in a world of aristocracy, patronage, and the Academy.

26. Specifically, Milton's uncertainties in the invocations to *Paradise Lost,* especially to Books 3 and 7, and in the Old Testament's anxiety about false and true prophets. The view that Milton's anxiety here is only an inherited motif, whose seriousness is drained off by his aesthetic control of everything in the poem, including his role as prophet-narrator, makes formalist sense but not human sense. The question is not, for example, whether we would read Milton's invocation to Book 3 differently if we knew he was not going blind; it is, whether Milton would have written it differently if he were not.

27. "From this subjection," Shelley continues, "the loftiest do not escape." "Preface" to *Prometheus Unbound, Shelley's Poetry and Prose,* ed. Donald H. Reiman and Sharon B. Powers (New York: Norton, 1977), 135, and quoted by Marilyn Butler as the epigraph to her *Romantics, Rebels, and Reactionaries: English Literature and its Background, 1760–1830* (Oxford: Oxford UP, 1981).

28. Foucault, *The History of Sexuality,* Vol. 1: *An Introduction* (1976), trans. Robert Hurley (1978; New York: Random House, 1980), 85. Again, Larrissy is an exception. I am arguing throughout this book that every poet discussed here understands, if sometimes in different ways, his analogous cultural position—understands, that is, without transcending that position.

29. McGann, *Social Values and Poetic Acts: The Historical Judgment of Literary Work* (Cambridge, MA: Harvard UP, 1988), 234.

30. Blake wrote this in his mid-forties, in 1803; clearly it is not an isolated sentiment, since he reiterates it over twenty years later, in an 1826 letter: "No discipline will turn one Man into another even in the least particle. & such Discipline I call Presumption & Folly I have tried it too much not to know this" (*E* 775).

31. See *U* 10.1–13.40, *E* 74–77; *M* 3.6–29, *E* 96–97; *FZ* 55.16–23, *E* 338. Leader anticipates my argument in his point that "Prophecy leads to imposition; prophets become (or beget) priests" (*Reading Blake's "Songs"* 142); Leader cites David Bindman's interpretation—in *Blake as an Artist* (Oxford: Phaidon, 1977)—of Blake's 1805 watercolors of Moses as presenting "Moses' opposing roles of prophet and law-giver" (143). Leader and I differ in where we find Blake: for him, Blake is here (if "not always or everywhere") "in control of the conflict between poetic and prophetic impulse," "framing [this conflict] within the larger dramatic context of the Piper's growth into Bard, and the Bard's gradual realization of the dangers and deficiencies of the prophetic mode" (143).

32. Mark L. Reed, "The Speaker of *The Prelude,*" *Bicentenary Wordsworth Studies in Memory of John Alban Finch,* ed. Jonathan Wordsworth (Ithaca, NY: Cornell UP, 1970), 291.

33. Robert Scholes, *Textual Power: Literary Theory and the Teaching of English* (New Haven, CT: Yale UP, 1985), 47.

34. Here, my argument becomes part of a larger interest in specifically Romantic irony. For example, Anne K. Mellor argues in *English Romantic Irony* (Cambridge, MA: Harvard UP, 1980) that "romantic irony[,] grow[ing] out of philosophical skepticism and the social turbulence of the French Revolution and the American War of Independence[,]

posits a universe founded in chaos and incomprehensibility rather than in [the] divinely ordained teleology" of "secularized Judeo-Christian traditions," as summarized by Abrams in *Natural Supernaturalism: Tradition and Revolution in Romantic Literature* (New York: Norton, 1971). She argues further that "the romantic ironist's enthusiastic response to process and change terminates where the perception of a chaotic universe arouses either guilt or fear" (vii). Whatever its origins, irony as I have described it posits neither the chaotic nor the teleological universe in Mellor's either/or scenario but is no less fundamental to Romantic texts; further, I believe we shall see that the Romantic poets' responses to such irony are often undeterminable, and in every case more complex than either enthusiasm or guilt and fear.

35. Despite my one example, Frye, Erdman—in *Blake: Prophet against Empire*, rev. ed. (Garden City, NY: Doubleday Anchor, 1969), and Michael Ferber—in *The Social Vision of William Blake* (Princeton, NJ: Princeton UP, 1985), have shown how wide-ranging is Blake's understanding of cultural mastery, an understanding not only literary, philosophical, religious, political, and social but sexual. Perhaps in this last category is shown most clearly the coexistence of Blake's understanding and its limits; David Aers argues— in "Blake: Sex, Society and Ideology," *Romanticism and Ideology: Studies in English Writing, 1765–1830*, ed. Aers, Jonathan Cook, and David Punter (London: Routledge and Kegan Paul, 1981)—that "Blake's overall exploration of contemporary sexual being comprises an extra-ordinary intelligent and radical critique of his culture," while at the same time he "seems not to have focused on the repressive male traditions actually affirmed in his work" (36, 43).

36. Geoffrey H. Hartman, "Envoi: 'So Many Things,'" *Unnam'd Forms: Blake and Textuality*, ed. Nelson Hilton and Thomas A. Vogler (Berkeley: U of California P, 1986), 244–45.

37. *The Sense of an Ending: Studies in the Theory of Fiction* (New York: Oxford UP, 1967), 39. Kermode echoes Philip Rahv's distinction—in "The Myth and the Powerhouse" (1953), rpt. *The Myth and the Powerhouse* (New York: Farrar, Straus and Giroux, 1965)— between "the mythic imagination," which is "a believing imagination," and "the imagination of art," that "achieves independence as it gradually detaches itself from myth" (10). For Rahv, "the craze for myth is the fear of history" (13), which is "the fear of the hazards of freedom" (20), and he cites Blake in his final sentence: "Eternity is in love with the productions of time" (*E* 36).

2. *The Rime of the Ancient Mariner:* Distinguishing the Certain from the Uncertain

1. Robert Penn Warren, "A Poem of Pure Imagination: An Experiment in Reading" (1946), rev. rpt. *Selected Essays* (New York: Random House, 1958), 198–305, esp. 214.

2. Homer Obed Brown, "The Art of Theology and the Theology of Art: Robert Penn Warren's Reading of Coleridge's *The Rime of the Ancient Mariner*," *Boundary 2* 8, no. 1 (Fall 1979): 237–60; McGann, "The Ancient Mariner: the Meaning of the Meanings" (1981), rpt. *Beauty of Inflections* 135–72.

3. Walter Jackson Bate, *Coleridge* (New York: Macmillan, 1968), 56.

4. Humphrey House, *Coleridge: The Clark Lectures, 1951–52* (Philadelphia: Dufour, 1965), 89, 103.

5. This first argument complements those of Frances Ferguson, "Coleridge and the Deluded Reader: 'The Rime of the Ancient Mariner,'" *Georgia Review* 38 (1977): 617–35, and Raimonda Modiano, "Words and 'Languageless' Meanings: Limits of Expression in *The Rime of the Ancient Mariner*," *MLQ* 38 (1977): 40–61. Only our emphases differ: mine is on the Neoplatonic elements in the gloss.

6. *The Critical Review*, 2d Ser., 24 (1798): 200. As Lawrence Lipking observes, in "The Marginal Gloss," *Critical Inquiry* 3 (1977), Wordsworth echoes Southey in his note on the poem's "great defects" in the second edition of *Lyrical Ballads* (1800), among them that "the events having no necessary connection do not produce each other" (*"Lyrical Ballads" and Other Poems, 1797–1800, by William Wordsworth*, ed. James Butler and Karen Green [Ithaca, NY: Cornell UP, 1992], 791). Lipking goes on to suggest that Coleridge added the gloss "to demonstrate that [what Wordsworth saw as] the brilliant fragments of 'The Ancient Mariner' made one great whole," because Coleridge feared that Wordsworth's detailing of the poem's defects by analogy reflected on "the failure of [Coleridge's] *personality* to make a whole" (613–14; emphasis added). If Lipking's suggestion is valid, it does not cancel additional, more traditionally aesthetic motives for adding the gloss— although I shall argue that such motives do not finally reduce to Coleridge's desire to master his own text.

7. *The Letters of Charles and Mary Anne Lamb*, ed. Edwin W. Marrs, Jr. (Ithaca, NY: Cornell UP, 1975), 1:142.

8. B. R. McElderry, Jr., "Coleridge's Revision of 'The Ancient Mariner,'" *SP* 29 (1932): 68–94, esp. 70–79.

9. A few readers have regarded the machinery as neither perplexing nor flawed but as interpretable and functional. See J. B. Beer, *Coleridge the Visionary* (London: Chatto and Windus, 1959), 133–74; and James Twitchell, "The World above the Ancient Mariner," *TSLL* 17 (1975): 103–17. Beer contends that "the core of the poem [is] a body of organized symbolism" based in part on "the concept of the ideal Sun and seraphs, where pure intelligences are in communion with a Deity who is source of light and harmony" (173–74); Twitchell holds that Coleridge "adopt[ed] the Neoplatonic system," because "It provided an invisible but graduated system of life above man" enabling us, "if we can only read this super-Nature carefully enough," to "find the keys to unlock the mind" (116). I shall argue that the machinery is functional without being interpretable. My argument is indebted to Richard Haven's more general study of the poem in *Patterns of Consciousness: An Essay on Coleridge* ([Amherst]: U of Massachusetts P, 1969), 18–42.

10. *Collected Letters of Samuel Taylor Coleridge*, ed. Earl Leslie Griggs (Oxford: Clarendon P, 1956–1971), 1:260. For a clear presentation of Coleridge's early philosophical beliefs, see John H. Muirhead, *Coleridge as Philosopher* (New York: Humanities P, 1930), 35–59; for a clear presentation of the complexities involved in trying to establish influences on these beliefs, see G. N. G. Orsini, *Coleridge and German Idealism* (Carbondale: Southern Illinois UP, 1969), 3–56.

11. The centrality of affective value to Coleridge's thinking has been shown best by Gordon McKenzie, *Organic Unity in Coleridge* (Berkeley: U of California P, 1939), and Haven, *Patterns of Consciousness*.

12. *The Notebooks of Samuel Taylor Coleridge*, ed. Kathleen Coburn (New York: Bollingen Foundation, 1957–), 3:3881.

13. See Muirhead 118–36; Coleridge did not credit Neoplatonism with such understanding—see Haven, *Patterns of Consciousness* 16, 86.

14. *The Rime of the Ancyent Marinere* (1798), in Jack Stillinger, *Coleridge and Textual Instability: The Multiple Versions of the Major Poems* (New York: Oxford UP, 1994), 179. Subsequent references to *The Rime of the Ancient Mariner* (1834) are to this edition.

15. *Biographia Literaria*, ed. James Engell and W. Jackson Bate (Princeton, NJ: Princeton UP, 1983), 2:6. Here I accept Reed's argument—in "Wordsworth, Coleridge, and the 'Plan' of the *Lyrical Ballads*," *UTQ* 34 (1965): 238–53—that their subsequent remarks about the volume probably indicate more a later "attempt to adjust and clarify their own attitudes towards [*Lyrical Ballads*]" (243), than an accurate recollection of their conscious intentions at the time. Whatever their recollective accuracy Coleridge's statements in the *Biographia* about *The Ancient Mariner* clearly emphasize affective value and not systematic truth.

16. McElderry admits that "most of the gloss is artistic restatement and ornament of what is obvious in the text." His final explanation for this curious redundancy, that "Once [Coleridge] hit on the idea of writing a gloss there was a chance for him to relive the creative joy of his youth" (91), while psychologically plausible, credits Coleridge in his creation of the gloss with none of the artistic control that McElderry himself demonstrates so convincingly is Coleridge's in his other revisions of the same period. For additional evidence of the care with which he revised the poem, see Richard Payne, "'The Style and Spirit of the Elder Poets': The *Ancient Mariner* and English Literary Tradition," *MP* 75 (1978): 368–84.

17. Martin Wallen, *Coleridge's "Ancient Mariner": An Experimental Edition of Texts and Revisions, 1798–1828* (Barrytown, NY: Station Hill Literary Editions, 1993), 112.

18. See Stillinger 60–73 for description of, and commentary on, the poem's versions. Stillinger himself appears to qualify his own argument at the end: the gloss "introduce[s] themes, moral judgments, and religious ideas that are not present *(or at least not immediately obvious)* in the verse" (72; emphasis added).

19. See Huntington Brown, "The Gloss to *The Rime of the Ancient Mariner*," *MLQ* 6 (1945): 319–24.

20. Interestingly, this conclusion, inevitable I believe to any careful study of point of view in the poem, is a throwback to much early criticism of the poem. See Haven, "The Ancient Mariner in the Nineteenth Century," *SIR* 11 (1972): 360–74, esp. 372.

21. Sarah Dyck, in "Perspective in 'The Rime of the Ancient Mariner,'" *SEL* 13 (1973): 591–604, finds a "four-fold perspective" (591): the Mariner's, the Wedding-Guest's, the glossator's, and the narrator's.

22. Warren, "Preface," *Selected Essays* xi–xii. Compare H. Aram Veeser's demonstration that "crisis not consensus surrounds the New Historicist project," in his "Introduction" to *The New Historicism*, ed. Veeser (New York: Routledge, 1989), xv, and Miller's remark that "The diversity of 'deconstruction' is so great that it would be better to speak

of '*deconstructionisms* in America,'" in his *Theory Now and Then* (Durham, NC: Duke UP, 1991), ix. To see diversity among readers of one's own persuasion seems easier than to see it among others.

23. Daniel P. Watkins, "History as Demon in Coleridge's *The Rime of the Ancient Mariner*," *PLL* 24 (1988): 30–31.

24. Peter L. Berger and Thomas Luckmann, *The Social Construction of Reality: A Treatise in the Sociology of Knowledge* (1966; Garden City, NY: Doubleday Anchor, 1967), 103.

25. Patrick J. Keane, *Coleridge's Submerged Politics: "The Ancient Mariner" and "Robinson Crusoe"* (Columbia and London: U of Missouri P, 1994), 172, 202. See esp. 177–211 for a consideration of contemporary historicist study of Romanticism. Watkins's crosscurrents originated in the argument of Edward E. Bostetter, "The Nightmare World of *The Ancient Mariner*" (1962), rpt. *Coleridge: A Collection of Critical Essays*, ed. Kathleen Coburn (Englewood Cliffs, NJ: Prentice-Hall, 1967)—cited by Keane at this point in his own essay. As Keane suggests, his rhetorical question and answer amount to an historicist corroboration of Bostetter's argument, which I shall discuss later in this chapter.

26. W. K. Wimsatt, Jr.; and Monroe C. Beardsley, "The Intentional Fallacy" (1946), rev. rpt. Wimsatt, *The Verbal Icon: Studies in the Meaning of Poetry* (Lexington: UP of Kentucky, 1954), 10.

27. John Livingston Lowes, *The Road to Xanadu: A Study in the Ways of the Imagination*, rev. ed. (1930; Princeton, NJ: Princeton UP, 1986), 274–75. Lowes himself is not always aware of this freedom. He repeatedly asserts that in *The Ancient Mariner* "the associated images of memory" are "masterfully curbed" by a "conscious imaginative moulding" (366–67)—see 61, 67, 85, 105–6, 131, 149–50, 201–2, 268–69, 278–81, 311, 375–77, and 394–96. But this assertion is belied by his argument, which mostly has the opposite effect. Christopher Norris observes, in *The Deconstructive Turn: Essays in the Rhetoric of Philosophy* (New York: Methuen, 1983), that "There is a deep-rooted conflict . . . between the materialist-associative psychology which Lowes adopts for all practical purposes, and the strain of idealist philosophy which his argument can never entirely subdue"; "'Imagination' is progressively decomposed into the elements of 'fancy.' The ideology of Symbol and Metaphor—the 'unmediated vision' of Romantic asp[ir]ation—is . . . reduced to a matter of discrete and piecemeal perception" (137, 136). Similarly, Rajan argues in detail that for Coleridge, "As the guarantor of poetic identity, imagination is also the antidote for an associationism that seems the equivalent in psychology to poststructuralism in semiotics" (*Supplement of Reading* 104).

28. This assertion lives on: to Wallen in 1993, for example, "*Scholarship* has obscured the gap between the gloss and the Mariner's narration by accepting the gloss as a clarification" (138; emphasis added).

29. E. S. Shaffer, *"Kubla Khan" and "The Fall of Jerusalem": The Mythological School in Biblical Criticism and Secular Literature, 1770–1880* (Cambridge: Cambridge UP, 1975).

30. My argument should not be taken as dependent historically on McGann's, perhaps thereby indirectly validating his larger claim about the primacy of "the poem's historical relations with its readers." The original form of the first part of this chapter, a

"close reading," appeared in 1981—see "'Unmeaning Miracles' in 'The Rime of the Ancient Mariner,'" *South Atlantic Review* 46 (1981): 16–26—as did the original form of McGann's "historical procedure."

31. I omit consideration of nonpsychoanalytic critics who seek illuminating parallels between the poem and Coleridge's own scattered remarks about dreaming. See R. C. Bald, "Coleridge and *The Ancient Mariner*: Addenda to *The Road to Xanadu*," *Nineteenth-Century Studies*, ed. Herbert Davis, William C. DeVane, and R. C. Bald (Ithaca, NY: Cornell UP, 1940), 1–45; Haven, *Patterns of Consciousness* 1–42; Paul Magnuson, *Coleridge's Nightmare Poetry* (Charlottesville: UP of Virginia, 1974), 50–84; John Beer, *Coleridge's Poetic Intelligence* (London: Macmillan, 1977), 70–94, 147–84; and David S. Miall, "The Meaning of Dreams: Coleridge's Ambivalence," *SIR* 21 (1982): 57–71. Coleridge himself was not only fascinated by his own dreams, as his notebooks make obvious, but interested in the nature of dreaming, as his addition—whatever its other purposes—in 1800 to *The Ancient Mariner* of the subtitle "A Poet's Reverie" might suggest. See Bald 37–40.

32. *The Interpretation of Dreams* (1900), *The Standard Edition of the Complete Psychological Works of Sigmund Freud*, ed., trans. James Strachey (London: Hogarth Press and The Institute of Psycho-Analysis, 1953–74), 5:589, 4:277–78, 5:506, 19:128–29. Subsequently abbreviated *SE*.

33. James D. Boulger, "'The Rime of the Ancient Mariner'—Introduction," *Twentieth Century Interpretations of "The Rime of the Ancient Mariner*," ed. Boulger (Englewood Cliffs, NJ: Prentice-Hall, 1969), 7. Such major commentators include Lowes, Warren, House 84–113, and Bate 55–65. I have called Boulger's consensus a formalist one because, whatever their use of Coleridge's life or other writings, these interpretations do appeal finally to the poem. In this sense even Lowes, in his analysis of the structure of the voyage, is formalist.

34. Mary Jane Lupton, "'The Rime of the Ancient Mariner': The Agony of Thirst," *American Imago* 27 (1970): 146.

35. David Beres, "A Dream, a Vision, and a Poem: A Psychoanalytic Study of the Origins of *The Rime of the Ancient Mariner*," *International Journal of Psycho-Analysis* 32 (1951): 111. An exception to this identification of Coleridge with the Mariner is Leon Waldoff, "The Quest for Father and Identity in 'The Rime of the Ancient Mariner,'" *Psychoanalytic Review* 58 (1971): 439–53.

36. See Douglas Angus, "The Theme of Love and Guilt in Coleridge's Three Major Poems," *JEGP* 59 (1960): 655–68; Beverly Fields, *Reality's Dark Dream: Dejection in Coleridge* (Kent, OH: Kent State UP, 1967), 84–91. In any case, Wordsworth originally suggested the albatross to Coleridge for his poem—see *The Poetical Works of William Wordsworth*, rev. ed. Ernest de Sélincourt and Helen Darbishire (Oxford: Clarendon P, 1952–59) 1:361; subsequently cited as *Poetical Works*.

37. D. W. Harding, "The Theme of 'The Ancient Mariner'" (1941), rev. rpt. Coburn, ed., *Coleridge* 62, 61.

38. See also A. M. Buchan, "The Sad Wisdom of the Mariner" (1964), rpt. Boulger, ed., *Interpretations of "The Rime"* 92–110. On this point, and generally, Waldoff seems the least reductive of the psychoanalytic interpreters: "There is no reason to insist that the

albatross is a father-figure; it is sufficient that it is closely associated with the God of the Mariner's universe" ("Quest for Father" 443). But while apparently admitting in the poem adult religious experience as well as—rather than as a mere derivative of—infantile fantasy, he mingles the two indiscriminately: "The Oedipal conflict with the Father is resolved through a new attitude of prayer and submissiveness, thereby bridging an emotional and cosmic gulf" (447).

39. Overdetermination is not limited to dream interpretation and thus is not exclusively a corollary to dream condensation—see Robert Waelder, "The Principle of Multiple Function: Observations on Over-Determination," *Psychoanalytic Quarterly* 5 (1936): 45–62. Overdetermination has been discussed above in connection with the ambivalence of the albatross as a psychic symbol.

40. Pinchas Noy, "A Revision of the Psychoanalytic Theory of the Primary Process," *International Journal of Psycho-Analysis* (1969): 157.

41. An explanation of Noy's assigning self-integration to the primary process is necessary here. In *Beyond the Pleasure Principle* (1920), *SE* 18:1–64, Freud hypothesizes a "compulsion to repeat" as the motive force behind recurrent painful dreams "impossible to classify as wish-fulfilments." They are found in "traumatic neuroses" or when "the psychical traumas of childhood" are brought to memory (32), and they appear to be caused by "fright . . . the state a person gets into when he has run into danger without being prepared for it" (12). Fright, then, is the emotion attendant upon an experience, real or fantasied, that cannot immediately be assimilated because of its unforeseen, threatening nature. The repetition of such painful experience may be the result of an "instinctual" (35) "impulse to work over in the mind some overpowering experience so as to make oneself master of it" (16). Since "all instinctual impulses . . . obey the primary process" (34), the assimilation of experience into the self necessitates the work of the primary process.

42. Charles A. Owen, Jr., emphasizes that the world of the Mariner is not the world of the poem, in "Structure in *The Ancient Mariner*," *CE* 23 (1962): 261–67.

43. Magnuson's is the most detailed nonpsychoanalytic discussion of the Mariner's psychic disintegration, although—like the psychoanalytic interpretations discussed above—it slights the importance of the moral. That this disintegration is the source of the Mariner's apparent lack of personality was noticed first by Lamb; see *Letters* 1:266.

44. See, for example, Bostetter 72–73; Fields 91; Lupton 142.

45. Milton Teichman, "The Marriage Metaphor in the *Rime of the Ancient Mariner*," *Bulletin of the New York Public Library* 73 (1969): 47. Teichman here extends and distorts Warren 255–57.

46. Bostetter 70–71; Lupton 143–44; Magnuson 84.

47. "Christian Skepticism in *The Rime of the Ancient Mariner*," *From Sensibility to Romanticism*, ed. Frederick W. Hilles and Harold Bloom (New York: Oxford UP, 1965), 443.

48. Forest Pyle, *The Ideology of Imagination: Subject and Society in the Discourse of Romanticism* (Stanford, CA: Stanford UP, 1995), 57, 34–35. Pyle's word is "nation" not "society"; he argues that for Coleridge the imagination is "the foundation and model" for constructing a specifically *English* subject and society (55).

3. *The Prelude*: Still Something to Pursue

1. Melvin Rader, *Wordsworth: A Philosophical Approach* (Oxford: Clarendon P, 1967), 113; Hartman, *Wordsworth's Poetry, 1787–1814* (1964; New Haven, CT: Yale UP, 1971); Thomas P. Weiskel, *The Romantic Sublime: Studies in the Structure and Psychology of Transcendence* (Baltimore: Johns Hopkins UP, 1976), 49, 53; Charles Altieri, "Wordsworth's Wavering Balance: The Thematic Rhythm of *The Prelude*," *WC* 4 (1973): 229.

2. McGann, *The Romantic Ideology: A Critical Investigation* (Chicago: U of Chicago P, 1983), 91.

3. Catherine Belsey, "The Romantic Construction of the Unconscious," *Literature, Politics and Theory: Papers from the Essex Conference, 1976–84*, ed. Francis Barker et al. (New York: Methuen, 1986), 58.

4. Richard J. Onorato, *The Character of the Poet: Wordsworth in* The Prelude (Princeton, NJ: Princeton UP, 1971), 272, 271.

5. *The Thirteen-Book "Prelude" by William Wordsworth*, ed. Mark L. Reed (Ithaca, NY, and London: Cornell UP, 1991), Book 1, l. 373. All references to *The Prelude* are to the 1805 text unless otherwise noted.

6. David Collings, *Wordsworthian Errancies: The Poetics of Cultural Dismemberment* (Baltimore: Johns Hopkins UP, 1994), 136, 137. See also James A. W. Heffernan, "The Presence of the Absent Mother in Wordsworth's *Prelude*," *SIR* 27 (1988): 253–72, esp. 259–60.

7. Timothy Bahti, "Wordsworth's Rhetorical Theft," *Romanticism and Language*, ed. Arden Reed (Ithaca, NY: Cornell UP, 1984), esp. 110–24. Similarly, Cathy Caruth, in *Empirical Truths and Critical Fictions: Locke, Wordsworth, Freud* (Baltimore: Johns Hopkins UP, 1991), argues that the Infant Babe passage in Book 2 "locates the origins of 'our first poetic spirit' in a 'being' whose history moves from 'mute dialogues with my mother's heart' to 'conjectures' that 'trace' this progress" (45), which "suggests that the mother, while designating an empirical beginning, can also be read as the figure of an 'origin' that cannot be located temporally or spatially" (56).

8. In "The Erasure of Narrative in Post-Structuralist Representations of Wordsworth," *Romantic Revolutions: Criticism and Theory*, ed. Kenneth R. Johnston et al. (Bloomington and Indianapolis: Indiana UP, 1990), Rajan observes that "first-generation deconstruction explored the fissures in textual identity without giving up the idea of a consciousness enmeshed in its representation, [while] a second generation of deconstructive critics including . . . Bahti see constructs of *self* as figures produced by language, and thus place rhetoric in a relation of supposed undecidability but actual priority to psychology" (350–51). For other significant examples of such placing, see the complex readings of the Arab Dream episode in Book 5 by Bahti, "Figures of Interpretation, The Interpretation of Figures: A Reading of Wordsworth's 'Dream of the Arab,'" *SIR* 18 (1979): 601–27, and Andrzej Warminski, "Missed Crossing: Wordsworth's Apocalypses," *MLN* 99 (1984): 983–1006.

9. See *Ecrits: A Selection* (1966), trans. Alan Sheridan (New York: Norton, 1977), 66–67, 199, 218, 285, 310–11.

10. See Jerome C. Christensen, "The Sublime and the Romance of the Other," *Diacritics* (Summer 1978): 10–23, whose discussion of the Infant Babe passage anticipates my later conclusion about the child's metaphoric power.

11. Mary Jacobus, *Romanticism, Writing, and Sexual Difference: Essays on "The Prelude"* (Oxford: Clarendon P, 1989), 271, 273.

12. Compare Leo Bersani's remark, in *A Future for Astyanax: Character and Desire in Literature* (New York: Columbia UP, 1984), that "The game can also be looked at as evidence of the child's awareness that the world exists beyond his perception of it. The child 'knows' that the world exists, and that he is not the entire world. And this awareness is the necessary condition for imagination and desire: without a sense of realities beyond us, we would be incapable of experiencing the lack without which desire is inconceivable" (207).

13. Foucault, *Sexuality* 85. On the fort-da game, see also Lacan, *The Four Fundamental Concepts of Psycho-Analysis* (1973), trans. Alan Sheridan (New York: Norton, 1978), 61–63; John P. Muller and William J. Richardson, *Lacan and Language: A Reader's Guide to "Ecrits"* (New York: International Universities P, 1982), 9–23; Muller, "Language, Psychosis, and the Subject in Lacan" 29–31, and Richardson, "Lacan and the Subject of Psychoanalysis" 57–58, both in *Interpreting Lacan*, ed. Joseph H. Smith and William Kerrigan (New Haven, CT: Yale UP, 1982).

14. Alphonse de Waelhens, *Schizophrenia: A Philosophical Reflection on Lacan's Structuralist Interpretation* (1972), trans. W. Ver Eecke (Pittsburgh: Duquesne UP, 1978), 118.

15. Robert Young, "The Eye and Progress of His Song: A Lacanian Reading of *The Prelude*," *Oxford Literary Review* 3, no. 3 (1979): 79–80, 85, 89, 88; rev. rpt. *William Wordsworth's "The Prelude,"* ed. Harold Bloom (New York: Chelsea House, 1986).

16. I take Simpson to argue that Wordsworth suspects metaphor because "The making of metaphor serves to bind the subject into a wished-for relation to its context, in that the conjunctions which it establishes are the wished-for features of an imaginary world which the subject can then reflect back in order to constitute itself" (153). I have been arguing for *The Prelude* what Simpson claims to characterize not Wordsworth but Shelley: "a more complex use of metaphor where the illusion of the stable subject and the fixing of its environment is not encouraged" (160), or, I would say, is not assumed or achieved but is explored. The subject's "wished-for relation to its context" here seems to me to result precisely from the subject's *inability* to understand metaphor as metaphoric, not literal.

17. One way of characterizing the psychotic is that he is not a subject, being in possession of no life story—see Muller 28–30.

18. It remains a lure throughout life. For horrible confirmation of the whole body-image persisting in adult life, see the account of the execution by mutilation and dismemberment of Damiens the regicide in 1757, quoted by Foucault, *Discipline and Punish: The Birth of the Prison* (1975), trans. Alan Sheridan (1978; New York: Random House, 1979), 3–6; see also *Ecrits* 28.

19. Martin Price, "The Sublime Poem: Pictures and Powers," *Yale Review* 58 (1968): 194–213.

20. Karl R. Johnson, Jr., *The Written Spirit: Thematic and Rhetorical Structure in Wordsworth's "The Prelude"* (Salzburg: Inst. für Englische Sprache und Literatur, U Salzburg, 1978), 12.

21. *The Prose Works of William Wordsworth*, ed. W. J. B. Owen and Jane Worthington Smyser (Oxford: Clarendon P, 1974) 1:138, 142, 148; subsequently cited as *Prose*. I understand Wordsworth here to identify or ally closely metaphoric with imaginative power. My use of "imaginative," then, is Romantic and fundamentally different from Lacan's "imaginary," which he equates with "phantasies" (*Ecrits* 35).

22. James K. Chandler, *Wordsworth's Second Nature: A Study of the Poetry and Politics* (Chicago and London: U of Chicago P, 1984), 210–11.

23. *The Fourteen-Book "Prelude" by William Wordsworth*, ed. W. J. B. Owen (Ithaca, NY: Cornell UP, 1985).

24. See in particular Herbert Lindenberger, *On Wordsworth's "Prelude"* (Princeton, NJ: Princeton UP, 1963).

25. *The Letters of William and Dorothy Wordsworth*, ed. Ernest de Sélincourt, 2d ed. rev. Chester L. Shaver (Oxford: Clarendon P, 1967–93), 1:101, 154, 518; subsequently abbreviated *WL*. See Abbie Findlay Potts, *Wordsworth's "Prelude": A Study of Its Literary Form* (Ithaca, NY: Cornell UP, 1953), 63, 68–76; Everard H. King, *James Beattie's "The Minstrel" and the Origins of Romantic Autobiography* (Lewiston, NY: Edwin Mellen P, 1992), 61–111. Text of *The Minstrel* (1774) cited from King 244–75.

26. T. S. Eliot, "Hamlet and His Problems" (1919), *Selected Essays* (New York: Harcourt, Brace and World, 1950), 124–25.

27. See Kenneth R. Johnston, "Recollecting Forgetting: Forcing Paradox to the Limit in the 'Intimations Ode,'" *WC* 2 (1971): 59–64.

28. Josephine Miles, *Eras and Modes in English Poetry*, 2d ed. (Berkeley: U of California P, 1964), 56, 57.

29. See Jonathan Wordsworth, *William Wordsworth: The Borders of Vision* (Oxford: Clarendon P, 1982), 303–39, esp. 310–12.

30. James Beattie, *The Minstrel* (1774), *Poetical Works* (London: George Bell, 1894), xxi.

31. Theresa M. Kelley, *Wordsworth's Revisionary Aesthetics* (Cambridge: Cambridge UP, 1988), 91–92; emphasis added.

32. Howard Erskine-Hill, *Poetry of Opposition and Revolution: Dryden to Wordsworth* (Oxford: Clarendon P, 1996), 184, 208, 189–90. Collings too finds a fundamental continuity between the two versions but for exactly the opposite reason: the earlier version is definitive—"Wordsworth writes the self in the 1799 *Prelude* as something that takes shape not through autobiographical development but rather through deviant, anxious pleasures"—because the later versions only reinscribe that unchanged self in a history that seems unrelated or even opposed to narrative—"For [Wordsworth, in his representation of revolutionary France in the 1805 *Prelude*], lived history, like autobiography, is the pure disruption of narrative" (211).

33. "Time and History in Wordsworth" (1967), *Romanticism and Contemporary Criticism* (Baltimore: Johns Hopkins UP, 1993), 90–91, 93. In *Wordsworth: The Sense of History* (Stanford, CA: Stanford UP, 1989), Liu reads both the Simplon and Snowdon episodes

as essentially historical (esp. 21–31, 446–52), although for him "history" is, first, Napoleonic and, second, in his initial formulation "a sense, not yet formulated into idea, that the completion of the present depends perpetually upon something beyond" (5). Wordsworth is *aware* of such a "sense," but I do not yet understand how it is specifically historical in Liu's sense. His evidence for a significant, even determining Napoleonic presence — or significant "absence" — in the two episodes, despite the remarkable detail of that evidence in itself, does not yet seem to me "evidence." Liu's own method here he describes as "not so much positivistic method as a deflected or denied positivism able to discriminate absence" (24). I do not reject this method categorically — and I use a version of it in the next chapter to argue for Wordsworth's "indebtedness without influence" — but I do not find it persuasive here, perhaps because de Man's and Erskine-Hill's histories seem always presences in the poem and thus diminish the force of an hypothesized repressed absence. Pyle argues implicitly against such absence, in arguing, like Wordsworth himself, for "The role of the imagination in the intertwining of poetry and politics"; the poet's "internalization [is] something considerably more complicated, and something considerably more powerful, than a mystified withdrawal from the social and political world" (61, 62). In *The Return of the Visible in English Romanticism* (Baltimore: Johns Hopkins UP, 1993), William H. Galperin also argues against such absence, in a somewhat different way: "the experience of France at the time of the Revolution, which Wordsworth recollects in books 9 and 10 of *The Prelude,* is more accurately represented in the earlier description of London where the Poet's complicity with the Revolution . . . is less a matter of displacement or of guilt than of being caught up in a 'moving pageant' in which the word and the world, self and society, are continually indistinguishable" and which thus threatens the poet's individuality. Further, there is a "consciousness" on the poet's part of the poem's "contradictions" between his individuality and such a threat, a consciousness "that recognizes all too well the truth of being made 'subservient . . . to the great ends of liberty and power' (11.182–83)" (124, 128).

34. John Sitter, *Literary Loneliness in Mid-Eighteenth-Century England* (Ithaca, NY: Cornell UP, 1982), 214, 158.

35. Peter Brooks, *Reading for the Plot: Design and Intention in Narrative* (New York: Knopf, 1984), xii. This is also the conclusion reached about all narrative history by Louis O. Mink, "Narrative Form as a Cognitive Instrument," *The Writing of History: Literary Form and Historical Understanding,* ed. Robert H. Canary and Henry Kosicki (Madison: U of Wisconsin P, 1978), 129–49; about psychoanalytic narrative by Donald P. Spence, *Narrative Truth and Historical Truth: Meaning and Interpretation in Psychoanalysis* (New York: Norton, 1982) — see also *Ecrits* 51–55; and about philosophical discourse on subjectivity by Anthony J. Cascardi, *The Subject of Modernity* (Cambridge: Cambridge UP, 1992), esp. 57–65.

36. Terry Eagleton, *Literary Theory,* 2d ed. (Minneapolis: U of Minnesota P, 1996), 160.

37. Kermode, *The Classic: Literary Images of Permanence and Change* (Cambridge, MA: Harvard UP, 1983), 114, 113, 75. Kermode's distinction and my argument here cast doubt on de Man's claim, in *Allegories of Reading* (New Haven, CT: Yale UP, 1979), that "*all* literary language . . . is the most advanced and refined mode of deconstruction" (17;

emphasis added). I have argued, as has de Man elsewhere (see p. 85), that Wordsworth's text is not baffled or entranced by the dream of a perfectly coherent subject, or theory about that subject, and thus that it is at least as advanced as its deconstructors. Beattie's text is clearly not so advanced.

4. The Intimations Ode: An Infinite Complexity

1. Barbara Herrnstein Smith, *Poetic Closure* (Chicago: U of Chicago P, 1968), 253.

2. Brooks, *Well Wrought Urn* 148; Florence G. Marsh, "Wordsworth's *Ode:* Obstinate Questionings," *SIR* 5 (1966): 230; G. Wilson Knight, *The Starlit Dome* (1941; London: Methuen, 1959), 48; Colin Clarke, *Romantic Paradox* (New York: Barnes, 1963), 92.

3. Rosalie L. Colie, *The Resources of Kind: Genre-Theory in the Renaissance* (Berkeley: U of California P, 1973), 29.

4. *Lectures 1808–1819: On Literature,* ed. R. A. Foakes (Princeton, NJ: Princeton UP, 1987), 1:495.

5. Abrams, "Structure and Style in the Greater Romantic Lyric," *From Sensibility to Romanticism,* ed. Frederick W. Hilles and Harold Bloom (New York: Oxford UP, 1965), 528.

6. Irene M. Chayes, "Rhetoric as Drama: An Approach to the Romantic Ode," *PMLA* 79 (1964): 67. See Norman Maclean, "From Action to Image: Theories of the Lyric in the Eighteenth Century," *Critics and Criticism,* ed. R. S. Crane (Chicago: U of Chicago P, 1952), 408–60.

7. The significant exceptions to this emphasis on generic independence in Romantic poetry are Bate, *The Stylistic Development of Keats* (1945; New York: Humanities P, 1962); Stuart Curran, *Poetic Form and British Romanticism* (New York: Oxford UP, 1986); and Brennan O'Donnell, *The Passion of Meter: A Study of Wordsworth's Metrical Art* (Kent, OH: Kent State UP, 1995).

8. Robert Anderson, ed., *The Works of the British Poets,* 13 vols. (London, 1795); Eric Rothstein, *Restoration and Eighteenth-Century Poetry 1660–1780* (Boston: Routledge, 1981), 7.

9. Coleridge applies this phrase to Wordsworth's ode in the *Biographia:* "The ode was intended for such readers only as had been accustomed to watch the flux and reflux of their inmost nature" (2:147). I cite Wordsworth instead to point out the striking similarity between his explanation of the phrase and his much later discussion of the Intimations Ode. Wordsworth continues, " . . . by the great and simple affections of our nature. This object I have endeavoured in these short essays to attain by various means; [among others,] by shewing . . . the perplexity and obscurity which in childhood attend our notion of death, or rather our utter inability to admit that notion." This explanation suggests that Wordsworth, as well as Coleridge, found the "fluxes and refluxes of the mind" reflected specifically in his ode.

10. See, respectively, Marsh 219–30; Peter J. Manning, "Wordsworth's Intimations Ode and Its Epigraphs" (1983), rev. rpt. *Reading Romantics: Texts and Contexts* (New York: Oxford UP, 1990), 68–84; Paul H. Fry, *The Poet's Calling in the English Ode* (New Haven, CT: Yale UP, 1980); Paul McNally, "Milton and the Immortality Ode," *WC* 11 (1980):

28–33; and Anne Williams, "Wordsworth's *Intimations Ode:* The Fortunate Fall" (1981), rev. rpt. *Prophetic Strain: The Greater Lyric in the Eighteenth Century* (Chicago and London: U of Chicago P, 1984), 140–51. Fry is a partial exception to my final remark.

11. David Trotter, *The Poetry of Abraham Cowley* (Totowa, NJ: Rowman, 1979), 119.

12. Ralph Cohen, "On the Interrelations of Eighteenth-Century Literary Forms," *New Approaches to Eighteenth-Century Literature,* ed. Phillip Harth (New York: Columbia UP, 1974), 36, 35.

13. See Maclean 423. Since the "eighteenth-century intermixtures extended far beyond those specified in the Renaissance" (Cohen 52), it is not surprising that Cowley's pseudo-Pindaric odes were seen as a new genre less because of their subject matter than because of their frequent transitions (a notion implied by Maclean 420–21, and stated by Cohen 47). Defending the ode—Wordsworth's in particular—against the charge of incoherence elicited by such frequent transitions, modern critics tend to argue on the grounds of "dominating images, emotional relationships between subjects, and complex metrical organization" (S[tephen] F. F[ogle] and P[aul] H. F[ry], "Ode," *The New Princeton Encyclopedia of Poetry and Poetics,* ed. Alex Preminger and T. V. F. Brogan [Princeton, NJ: Princeton UP, 1993], 855). Cohen's argument suggests that generic inclusiveness ought to be an equally important ground for defense.

14. See Reed, *Wordsworth: The Chronology of the Middle Years, 1800–1815* (Cambridge, MA: Harvard UP, 1975), 11–12, 27.

15. Manning perceptively discusses this epigraph as Vergilian allusion. Quotations from the Ode are from the text in *"Poems, in Two Volumes" and Other Poems, 1800–1807 by William Wordsworth,* ed. Jared Curtis (Ithaca, NY: Cornell UP, 1983), 269–77.

16. Pastoral and elegy are almost ubiquitously mentioned in criticism of the Intimations Ode, for good reason—see p. 107. Epithalamium is suggested by the joyful union with nature from which the speaker feels excluded in stanzas 1–4—see Williams 148–49. Satire is rarely noticed—but see Helen Vendler, "Lionel Trilling and the *Immortality Ode,*" *Salmagundi* 41 (1978): 73–75. Allegorical romance is suggested by Dorothy Wordsworth's reading of Book 1 of *The Faerie Queene* to Wordsworth on 16 June 1802—see Jared Curtis, *Wordsworth's Experiments with Tradition* (Ithaca, NY: Cornell UP, 1971), 129–31, and Reed, *Wordsworth* 181.

17. In *"The Prelude:* Wordsworth's Metamorphic Epic," *Genre* 14 (1981), Stuart Peterfreund argues that stanza 7 incorporates "the Virgilian progression of genres"—pastoral, satire, epic (and drama)—to show that "the history of the individual internalizes and recapitulates larger histories, such as the history of literature, of which the progression of genres is a special case" (447–48).

18. Not all editions treat the Intimations Ode in the same way. In 1815 it appears separately in the table of contents and has a separate title page, as specified by Wordsworth—see Curtis, ed., 269, 375. In no subsequent edition is the ode clearly a separate category in the table of contents, although its title is printed in large and small capitals, the only poem of its length so treated. In 1820 it has a separate title page. In 1827 and 1832 it is numbered as the last poem in "Epitaphs and Elegiac Poems." In all subsequent editions—1837,

1845, 1849–50—it is not numbered, as are all other poems in that section—a distinction suggesting that it is again separate. Such nuances of placement characterize other poems —for example, "Peter Bell," which in 1849–50 is last in "Poems of the Imagination" in the table of contents but is not numbered with the others and is given a separate title page. In addition, the Intimations Ode is last only among the completed poems, in all the editions from 1815 on (except 1820, which does not include *The Excursion*). *The Excursion*, which follows it in a separate volume (except in the one-volume 1845 edition) and which is always described in its preface as "only a portion of a poem," undercuts our sense of closure in the Intimations Ode.

I am grateful to my colleague Paul Betz for his generosity in letting me examine his Wordsworth collection, which provides evidence for my observations on the positioning of the poems.

19. William Knight, ed., *The Poetical Works of William Wordsworth* (London: Macmillan, 1896), 8:199.

20. Wordsworth obviously arranged his poems for publication with great care (see, for example, Reed, *Wordsworth* 338–39, 488, 572, 574, 578, 687–93). In *Wordsworth: Language as Counter-Spirit* (New Haven, CT: Yale UP, 1977), Ferguson argues that "Although Wordsworth's suggestion (in a letter to Coleridge of May 1809) that the poems in the various categories would ascend in a 'gradual scale of imagination' might be taken to imply a movement from simple to complex, he seems by 1815 to have given first place in each of the facultative categories [affections, fancy, imagination, sentiment, and reflection] to poems markedly problematic" (42). My argument implicitly disagrees, since it supports Wordsworth's suggestion and claims that the final poems are generally more narrative than lyric in mode, in that Wordsworth seeks to reflect a complexity in human life for which the lyric mode is inadequate.

21. "The pattern established in book 1 of *The Prelude*, of intensely emotional concrete descriptions alternated with highly rhetorical abstract interpretations, pervades all fourteen books in some degree"—Kenneth R. Johnston, "The Idiom of Vision," *New Perspectives on Coleridge and Wordsworth*, ed. Geoffrey H. Hartman (New York: Columbia UP, 1972), 5. Analysis and narrative are often mixed in *The Prelude*, but despite some oversimplification I cite them separately here. For analysis, see 1.429, 5.140, 7.624, 8.586, 10.940, 11.385, and 13.66. For narrative, see 3.195, 4.268, 5.414, 10.38 and 657, and 12.354. Analysis and narrative imply the inclusion of lyric in larger intellectual and temporal contexts, respectively—an inclusion whose importance is argued for also by Rajan, "Erasure of Narrative."

22. See also David Ferris, "Where Three Paths Meet: History, Wordsworth, and the Simplon Pass," *SIR* 30 (1991): "Not only is [the Simplon Pass episode] evoked repeatedly in the interpretation of *The Prelude* but more significant than the fact of this repetition is the tendency to put aside the discursive position of this episode" (392, n. 2).

23. While Lindenberger rightly criticizes John Jones, in Jones's *The Egotistical Sublime: A History of Wordsworth's Imagination* (London: Chatto, 1954), 125–26, for suggesting that Wordsworth uses interpolation to keep the story going (102), he later takes much the

same position: "There is no real progression in *The Prelude*, but only restatements of the poet's efforts to transcend the confines of the temporal order" (188).

For the argument that Wordsworth is avoiding confrontation with apocalypse, see Hartman, *Wordsworth's Poetry*, whose reading of this part of Book 6 seems contradictory. He remarks that "the tempo of the whole journey . . . is often neglected for the striking events that detach themselves only partially from it" (54). Yet he apparently considers "the tempo" and "the striking events" experientially and ontologically incompatible, since on the other hand he argues that the apostrophe to Imagination halts the "song's progress . . . because the poet is led beyond nature. Unless he can respect the natural (which includes the temporal) order, his song, at least as narrative, must cease" (46). "Though his discovery [of "the independence of imagination from nature" (41)] shakes the foundation of his poem, he returns after a cloudburst of verses to the pedestrian attitude of 1790, when the external world and not imagination seemed to be his guide ('Our journey we renewed, / Led by the stream,' etc.)" (48). But the "pedestrian attitude" is demonstrably not the narrator's, literally or metaphorically.

For a detailed reading of Book 6, see the undeservedly neglected work by Karl Johnson, 22–72, 279–85.

24. Jonathan Bishop, "Wordsworth and the 'Spots of Time,'" *ELH* 26 (1959): 52.

25. Hugh Blair, *Lectures on Rhetoric and Belles Lettres* (1783), ed. Harold F. Harding (Carbondale: Southern Illinois UP, 1965), 2:322–23.

26. See Harvey D. Goldstein, "*Anglorum Pindarus:* Model and Milieu," *Comparative Literature* 17 (1965): 299–310.

27. Bate, *The Burden of the Past and the English Poet* (1970; New York: Norton, 1972), 4; Sitter 84.

28. Edmund Burke, *A Philosophical Enquiry into the Origin of Our Ideas of the Sublime and Beautiful* (1759), ed. J. T. Boulton (New York: Columbia UP, 1958), 39, 58, 57.

29. In *Wordsworth's Great Period Poems* (Cambridge and New York: Cambridge UP, 1986), Marjorie Levinson argues that the words "tree" and "field" are "draw[n] from the dictionary of eighteenth-century libertarian discourse" (90) — Tree of Liberty, Champ de Mars — there "signif[ying] an apocalyptic idea and its imminent fulfillment" (94) but here evidencing the narrator's "attempt to liberate the fond, pastoral memory from its original, political context," although he fails: "The historicity of the imagery is as a return of the repressed" (94). This argument parallels Liu's about *The Prelude* and Keane's about *The Rime of the Ancient Mariner* (though Keane's is less confident): "the literary work . . . speaks of one thing because it cannot articulate another — presenting formally a sort of allegory by absence, where the signified is indicated by an identifiably absented signifier" (9). The claim appears more axiomatic than inductive here, since Levinson does not explain why or how history becomes primary and nature secondary in this poem. She observes that "The dark ground which defines Wordsworth's poetry is, first or finally, that sense of lost things which engenders all human creation, but the form which those losses assume through the language of the poetry and of the age is deeply specific" (11–12), which ground is akin to de Man's (and other, formalist readers') articulation of "history"

in *The Prelude*. But she then gives "that sense of lost things" an unequivocally Revolutionary origin: "The poet's nostalgia, *then,* for a vivid experience of Nature, *must* be the reflex and expression of his nostalgia for the particular idea of Nature which informed the Revolution and its philosophic discourse" (85; emphasis added).

30. Text from Abrams, *Natural Supernaturalism* 473.

31. Stephen Prickett, *Coleridge and Wordsworth: The Poetry of Growth* (Cambridge: Cambridge UP, 1970), 127.

32. See, for example, Heather Dubrow, *Genre* (New York: Methuen, 1982), 31–44.

33. For arguments against teleological and normative genre definition, see Hans Robert Jauss, *Toward an Aesthetic of Reception,* trans. Timothy Bahti (Minneapolis: U of Minnesota P, 1982), 76–109, and Alastair Fowler, *Kinds of Literature* (Cambridge, MA: Harvard UP, 1982), 37–53, 235–55.

34. Jeffrey C. Robinson, in *Radical Literary Education: A Classroom Experiment with Wordsworth's "Ode"* (Madison: U of Wisconsin P, 1987), 81–91, discusses Gray's ode in terms similar to mine, but he finds a generic continuity from Gray's ode to Wordsworth's, in their "peculiar combination of life seen as a falling off from edenic happiness and the presentation of this loss denuded of historical and biographical detail" (86).

35. Here I synthesize Lionel Trilling's alternatives in "The Immortality Ode" (1942), *The Liberal Imagination* (New York: Viking, 1950), 131, as does Curtis, *Wordsworth's Experiments* 114, 138. I am indebted especially to Trilling; Curtis; Brooks, *Well Wrought Urn*; and Vendler for their readings of Wordsworth's Ode.

36. On the ambiguities of the seemingly explanatory title, see Ferguson, *Wordsworth* 100–101.

37. Here we see an interplay of genre (elegy) with genre (ode), rather than an inclusion of modes (pastoral, song, satire; narrative, lyric) within a genre (ode). This distinction between genre and mode is Fowler's: "modal terms never imply a complete external form" (107).

38. John Ruskin, *The Stones of Venice,* vol. 2 (1853), in *The Works of John Ruskin,* ed. E. T. Cook and Alexander Wedderburn (New York: Longmans, 1904), 10:202–3. In *Revision and Authority in Wordsworth: The Interpretation of a Career* (Philadelphia: U of Pennsylvania P, 1989), Galperin characterizes Wordsworth's sense of human imperfection in terms of the poet's recognition of the extent to which he is constituted by language and culture, by arguing that Wordsworth's gothic metaphor indicates "the consignment of the self to the status of ruin, replete with its confinement to a rhetoric of temporality (youth, old age, death and so on)," but also indicates "a *conscious* effort to return power—such shaping authority embodied in the gothic or sublime self—to a totality or to a textuality of which the self itself is no longer an extrapolation" (210).

5. *Lamia*: Attitude Is Every Thing

1. See, for example, Sidney Colvin, *John Keats* (London: Macmillan, 1917), 408. This attitude has not disappeared—see, for example, Miriam Allott, ed., *The Poems of John Keats* (1970; rpt. with corrections New York: Longman, 1975): "the diversity of critical opinion points to K[eats]'s uncertain intentions in the poem" (615).

2. See especially Bate, *John Keats* (1963; rpt. with corrections New York: Oxford UP, 1966), 543–61; Richard Harter Fogle, "Keats's *Lamia* as Dramatic Illusion," *Nineteenth-Century Literary Perspectives*, ed. Clyde de L. Ryals (Durham, NC: Duke UP, 1974), 65–75; and Garrett Stewart, "*Lamia* and the Language of Metamorphosis," *SIR* 15 (1976): 3–41.

3. In "The Performing Narrator in Keats's Poetry," *KSJ* 26 (1977), William C. Stephenson remarks that "The poem's main interpretative problems . . . stem directly from the *narrator's* seemingly ambiguous role in the poem" (60)—but we disagree completely about that role. The one significant exception to my generalization is Wolfson, *Questioning Presence* 333–43.

4. Bernice Slote, *Keats and the Dramatic Principle* (Lincoln: U of Nebraska P, 1958), 152; see 123–92.

5. Robert Scholes and Robert Kellogg, *The Nature of Narrative* (New York: Oxford UP, 1966), 277.

6. Our expectation does not make it so. The fairy tale narrator may be complex, a conclusion implicit throughout the study by Max Lüthi, *Once Upon a Time: On the Nature of Fairy Tales* (New York: Ungar, 1970).

7. All *Lamia* quotations are from *The Poems of John Keats*, ed. Jack Stillinger (Cambridge, MA: Harvard UP, 1978). Where useful, line numbers are cited: for example (2.123).

8. The phrase "implied author" is Wayne Booth's, in *The Rhetoric of Fiction* (Chicago: U of Chicago P, 1961), 70–71, passim.

9. Donald H. Reiman, "Keats and the Humanistic Paradox: Mythological History in *Lamia*," *SEL* 11 (1971): 659. See also Stuart M. Sperry, Jr., *Keats the Poet* (Princeton, NJ: Princeton UP, 1973), 295.

10. Earl R. Wasserman, *The Finer Tone* (Baltimore: Johns Hopkins UP, 1953), 158.

11. *The Letters of John Keats, 1814–1821*, ed. Hyder Edward Rollins (Cambridge, MA: Harvard UP, 1958), 1:224; subsequently abbreviated *KL*, with approximate dates where relevant to the argument: for example (*KL* 2:123, July 1819).

12. These similarities have, of course, been remarked upon by others, in different argumentative contexts. See for example Slote 145–47, Stewart 33, and especially Marjorie Levinson, *Keats's Life of Allegory: The Origins of a Style* (Oxford: Basil Blackwell, 1988), 270–87, esp. 282–85. I shall consider Levinson's argument later in this chapter.

13. The proof reads "platonian," which Woodhouse altered to "Platonic" (Stillinger, *Poems of Keats* 458). While William Allan Coles, in "The Proof Sheets of Keats's 'Lamia,'" *Harvard Library Bulletin* 8 (1954), suggests "the strong possibility that the alterations in Woodhouse's hand . . . are by him and not by Keats" (116), the source of the change is unimportant for my argument. First, Keats probably agreed or would have agreed with it, since, as de Sélincourt remarks in *The Poems of John Keats*, 5th ed. (London: Methuen, 1926), some of the poem's variant readings "are made in order to secure a correct quantity to a classical proper noun," and Keats probably "referred such matters" to Woodhouse: "At the beginning of the proof sheets of *Lamia*, corrected by Woodhouse, is a list of all the classical names in the poem with their quantities carefully marked" (454). Second, there is no record, in the *OED* at least, of "platonian" meaning anything but "Platonic."

14. The other two occurrences are at 1.360 and 2.212. See *A Concordance to the Poems of John Keats,* ed. Michael G. Becker, Robert J. Dilligan, Todd K. Bender (New York: Garland, 1981), 404, 460, 461.

15. Stephenson, in "The Fall from Innocence in Keats's 'Lamia,'" *PLL* 10 (1974), notes that Lycius "is closely identified, through imagery, with the society of Corinth: his 'silent sandals swept the mossy green' (l. 239), just as the men and women of Corinth 'shuffled their sandals o'er the pavement white' (l. 356)" (36).

16. David Perkins, *The Quest for Permanence* (Cambridge, MA: Harvard UP, 1959), 275. See also, for example, Waldoff, *Keats and the Silent Work of Imagination* (Urbana: U of Illinois P, 1984): although "the narrator takes a critical attitude toward him," Apollonius "represents the inescapability of reality" (175).

17. Charles I. Patterson, Jr., *The Daemonic in the Poetry of John Keats* (Urbana: U of Illinois P, 1970), 207–8.

18. James A. Notopoulos, *The Platonism of Shelley* (Durham, NC: Duke UP, 1949), 3.

19. See Charles Cowden Clarke's notes on Keats, in *The Keats Circle,* ed. Hyder Edward Rollins, 2d ed. (Cambridge, MA: Harvard UP, 1965), 2:147–50; subsequently abbreviated as *KC.* Excluding Bailey, there are other conversational contexts that might have afforded Keats some knowledge of Plato. The widest-ranging case is made by Clarence DeWitt Thorpe, in *The Mind of John Keats* (New York: Oxford UP, 1926), 148–50, who argues, in addition to Bailey's, the likely influence of Leigh Hunt and the possible influence of Cowden Clarke, Haydon, Reynolds, Severn, and Lamb — "all of whom were unquestionably familiar with the Platonic doctrines" (150). All of this may be true, but there is no written evidence to substantiate it. The most exciting possible conversational source is of course Shelley, but the written evidence is unconvincing. Keats and Shelley were together several times from December 1816 to February 1818, but the only specific record of Plato being discussed is that of a conversation between Shelley and Horace Smith, which Keats left behind — see Arthur H. Beavan, *James and Horace Smith* (London: Hurst and Blackett, 1899), 138. From a careful examination of the evidence, Donald H. Reiman, in *Shelley and His Circle, 1773–1822,* ed. Reiman (Cambridge, MA: Harvard UP, 1973), 5:399–411, concludes "that Keats did not particularly enjoy Shelley's company" (405).

20. In his note to this passage, Rollins identifies the two volumes as "a translation from Anne Lefèvre Dacier, perhaps the so-called third London edition, 1772." The French translation is actually by her husband, André Dacier — see Frank B. Evans III, "Platonic Scholarship in Eighteenth-Century England," *MP* 41 (1943): 108 — and why Rollins surmises that Bailey owned the 1772 edition is not clear, since Bailey specifies the 1749 edition. I shall therefore quote from the 1749 edition, which in any case differs from the 1772 edition only in accidentals of punctuation and capitalization. I am indebted to my colleague Leona Fisher for a bibliographic description of the 1772 edition.

21. *The Works of Plato Abridg'd,* trans. "from the French, by several Hands," 4th ed. (London, 1749), 2:246. See also 1:261, 271; 2:219.

22. *The Cratylus, Phaedo, Parmenides and Timaeus of Plato,* trans. Thomas Taylor (London, 1793). Bernard Blackstone, in *The Consecrated Urn* (London: Longmans, Green, 1959), believes that "No book exercised a profounder influence on Keats's mind,"

finding "The indirect evidence" to be "overwhelming" while admitting that "There is no direct evidence that Keats read Plato in Taylor's translation" (165). His indirect evidence consists of unconvincing verbal parallels between Keats's poetry and the dialogues, mostly the *Timaeus;* none of the passages I present here from Taylor or from *Lamia* are included in his discussion.

23. This conclusion is one that Boulger, for example, cannot believe; in "Keats' Symbolism," *ELH* 28 (1961), he assumes (with no textual support) that the "Platonic shades" passage "in other words [means that Lycius] bore some secret, perhaps unrecognized, grudge against his educational training with Apollonius" (253). Other readers consider the passage even less seriously. Patterson wonders in passing "Whether or not this seemingly trivial remark indicates Keats's considered view of Platonic thought" (199) but does not stop to answer. Allott's gloss only paraphrases it: "Lycius sets out on his walk in an unthinking mood, but as evening comes on his thoughts are lost in high Platonic speculations" (627). Other readers paraphrase "twilight of Platonic shades" quite differently, as "a state of reverie bordering on dream" (Mario L. D'Avanzo, *Keats's Metaphors for the Poetic Imagination* [Durham, NC: Duke UP, 1967], 62) or "the twilight of the dream world" (Boulger 253). The different paraphrases only help, unwittingly, to point out the problem: how can "high Platonic speculations" be at the same time a "dream world"? Yet the poem suggests that this is the case.

24. Bate comments sensibly, "That Bailey should have recalled the rate of Keats's writing so exactly after thirty-one years suggests how much of a point Keats had made of it as a goal" (*John Keats* 207). I am generally indebted to Bate's sympathetic portrayal of Bailey and Keats's relationship with him (196–218).

25. Some of Bailey's assured tone is understandable as a rhetorical reaction to the dominance of Aristotle and neglect of Plato he probably had encountered at Oxford in his previous year's study. See Charles Edward Mallet, *A History of the University of Oxford* (1927; rpt. New York: Barnes and Noble, 1968), 3:127–28; Notopoulos 31, 395–96.

26. Wasserman, "Keats and Benjamin Bailey on the Imagination," *MLN* 68 (1953): 363. "Bailey can claim only that the experiences of the imagination with the material world bear an analogy to (ultimate) truth. . . . Keats, on the other hand, is replying that our mortal and postmor[t]al existences are not merely analogous, but are causally connected" (365).

27. *The Diary of Benjamin Robert Haydon,* ed. Willard Bissell Pope (Cambridge, MA: Harvard UP, 1960) 2:317; cited by Sperry, "Keats's Skepticism and Voltaire," *KSJ* 12 (1963): 78. Bate (*John Keats* 111–12) considers Keats's behavior here a joke on Haydon, which Haydon failed to see—if so, my point about Keats's playful irreverence is strengthened.

28. Georgia S. Dunbar, "The Significance of the Humor in 'Lamia,'" *KSJ* 8 (1959): 26.

29. Quoted by Claude Lee Finney, *The Evolution of Keats's Poetry* (Cambridge, MA: Harvard UP, 1936), 1:296. I have not seen Keats's copy of the *Anatomy;* Blackstone (304–5, n. 2) describes Keats's final sentence as separated from his question and as located on the following page of Burton.

30. Ernst Cassirer, *Language and Myth,* trans. Susanne K. Langer (1946; rpt. New York: Dover, n.d.), 8–9.

31. To argue that (Keats is the narrator because) the narrator means only "*cold* philosophy" here and implicitly distinguishes it from "Philosophy" is ingenious (Slote 168–70). Clearly, however, the narrator does not distinguish between the two, since he uses them interchangeably: for him, all philosophy is "cold."

32. See Stewart 17, 29–31. Wolfson notes that "perhaps the narrator wants to show the insidious effect of the reptiles of the mind, for Lycius' final appearance, too, is eerily snaky" (*Questioning Presence* 342). Gene M. Bernstein, in "Keats' 'Lamia': The Sense of a Non-Ending," *PLL* 15 (1979), argues that Apollonius and Lamia "are in fact very similar: both are serpentine, both function as mediators, and both are either possessed by, or are themselves, the demon" (190); he concludes from such similarities only that the poem "is deliberately indeterminate and conveys the sense of a non-ending" (192).

33. The distinction is hardly original with Keats. Wordsworth, for example, makes a similar one, between "the People," to whom "his devout respect, his reverence, is due," and "the Public," to whom he "hopes that he feels as much deference as it is entitled to . . . " ("Essay, Supplementary to the Preface" [1815], in *Prose* 3:84).

34. Terence Allan Hoagwood, "Keats and Social Context: *Lamia*," *SEL* 29 (1989): 693.

35. Leader argues persuasively, in *Revision and Romantic Authorship* (Oxford: Clarendon P, 1996), 298–307, that by the time of the *Lamia* volume at least, Keats's gendering of his audience is complicated: "Some part of Keats's ambivalence towards his audience — including his reluctance to revise to meet its needs and tastes — derives from issues of gender, issues already hinted at not only in [Keats's] phrases like 'manly singleness' and 'manly vigour' but in [his] association of public favour with 'the love of a woman'" (298). See also Margaret Homans, "Keats Reading Women, Women Reading Keats," *SIR* 29 (1990): 341–70.

36. See Michael Ragussis, "Narrative Structure and the Problem of the Divided Reader in *The Eve of St. Agnes*," *ELH* 42 (1975): 378.

37. The ambiguity of "sensation" for Keats, and its importance, are discussed usefully by Sperry, *Keats* 3–29. For Sperry "the task of rendering a satisfactory account, sufficiently definite and at the same time inclusive, of sensation" was "the major problem confronting [both] English philosophy in the Enlightenment" and "poets in the main movement of English Romanticism" (28). My own brief remarks on sensation are of more limited scope. They seek only to point to the range of its uses that Sperry details in the letters — where Keats frequently emphasizes one or another aspect of sensation, "a highly complicated process, sensory, emotional, and intellectual" (8) — and then apply that range to Keats's remark about *Lamia*'s audience.

38. Booth's terms clarify my argument here, but I would stop short of agreeing with him about what constitutes "the most successful reading." First, the relations, harmonious and uneasy, between selves and second selves, and their respective disagreement, are as important as the second selves and their agreement. Second, a critical history of interpretation suggests that what constitutes a "successful" reading depends at least in part on its various contexts.

39. John Bayley, *The Uses of Division: Unity and Disharmony in Literature* (New York: Viking, 1976), 153, 146.

40. In the best recent example, Wolfson finds Keats's "interrogative poetics" to be "deliberately avoiding the idiom that animates Wordsworth's most probing inquiries: the mysteries of his own selfhood, of his life in time and history" (*Questioning Presence* 41). Nevertheless, she emphasizes as I do that both poets are centrally concerned with subjectivity, however differently mediated: "If the mysteries that absorb Wordsworth's attention are those that arise from the depths of his selfhood, those that perplex Keats involve the operation of his 'camelion' self" (37; see *KL* 1:387).

41. Leader cites the second passage as evidence for a "'late' Keats": "in the letters of 1819, as opposed to those of 1818 in which the theory of 'negative capability' is evolved, the poet is seen as both active and male" (*Revision* 308). This late Keats, he argues, evidences a "new valuing of self or personal identity" (309) congruent with the preferences of Taylor, Woodhouse, and other readers; "Once impeding political associations had been severed, or at least muted, along with a related indelicacy, the advisers focused exclusively on 'style,' which is to say, on the creation of a poetic voice that was both correct and controlled—stable, sound, single" (311). I am arguing that "negative capability" and "personal identity" are not antithetical in Keats and that *Lamia*'s poetic voice, while *stylistically* "controlled," is far from being "stable, sound, and single."

42. McGann, "Keats and the Historical Method" 52, 53. Later McGann qualifies his argument, without however discussing how the argument and its qualification might interact: "Romanticism . . . was unwilling to make contracts with the audiences available to it. Keats, who is especially typical of this Romantic line, showed how poetry could establish 'a world elsewhere.' In that alternative geography, personal and social tensions could be viewed with greater honesty and intellectual rigour" (57). This qualification is being explored in historicist detail by others; see Nicholas Roe, ed., *Keats and History* (Cambridge: Cambridge UP, 1995), esp. Roe, "Keats's Commonwealth," 194–211, and Kelley, "Keats, Ekphrasis, and History," 212–37.

43. Watkins, *Keats's Poetry and the Politics of the Imagination* (Rutherford, NJ: Fairleigh Dickinson UP, 1989), 142. See also Levinson, *Keats's Life* 255–68.

44. See J. G. A. Pocock, *Politics, Language, and Time: Essays on Political Thought and History* (New York: Atheneum, 1971), 29–30, and my concluding chapter. The presence of this complex desire in Shakespeare's play hardly needs noting; for Chaucer's poem, see Stephen Knight, *Geoffrey Chaucer* (Oxford: Basil Blackwell, 1986), 83–90; for Pope's, see C. J. Nicholson, "A World of Artefacts: *The Rape of the Lock* as Social History," *Literature and History* 5 (1979): 67–79. We might also be reminded here of Blake's cultural conflation of father-priest-king, whose existence Blake does not confine to his own time.

45. Georg Lukacs, *History and Class Consciousness: Studies in Marxist Dialectics* (1968), trans. Rodney Livingstone (Cambridge, MA: MIT P, 1971); Georg Simmel, *The Philosophy of Money*, trans. T. Bottomore and D. Frisby (London: Routledge and Kegan Paul, 1978), 161, quoted by Levinson, *Keats's Life* 255.

46. See Donald C. Goellnicht, "Keats on Reading: 'Delicious Diligent Indolence,'" *JEGP* 88 (1989): 190–210; and Andrew Bennett's discussion of "Keats and Reading: The Reader as Lover," in *Keats, Narrative and Audience: The Posthumous Life of Writing* (Cambridge: Cambridge UP, 1994), 53–58.

47. For a similar reading of Keats's self-description here, see Eric Griffiths, *The Printed Voice of Victorian Poetry* (Oxford: Clarendon P, 1989), 36–37.

48. Wolfgang Iser, *The Act of Reading: A Theory of Aesthetic Response* (1976; Baltimore: Johns Hopkins UP, 1978), 18. Although Iser has studied carefully a wide range in function of such textual inconsistencies, his theory is often virtually reduced by its critics to its admitted but more limited origin, Ingarden's "places of indeterminacy," which are to be "removed, filled in or even glossed over" in the service of aesthetic "harmony" (175). (This is no more than a reader-response version of New Critical unity—or, in the terms of my argument, simplification of what is irreducible complexity.) For example, see Jane Tompkins, "An Introduction to Reader-Response Criticism," *Reader-Response Criticism: From Formalism to Post-Structuralism*, ed. Tompkins (Baltimore: Johns Hopkins UP, 1980), xv; or Eagleton, summarizing Iser's "liberal humanism": "Textual indeterminacies just spur us on to the act of abolishing them, replacing them with a stable meaning" (71). In spite of Eagleton's claim that Iser's description of the reading process amounts to no more than reaffirming a weak "liberal humanism" (69), that process can contribute to changing our lives, although the contribution is not unidirectional; that is, what we learn in reading needs to be confirmed in other aspects of our lives, and vice versa. On this last point see Booth, *The Company We Keep: An Ethics of Fiction* (Berkeley: U of California P, 1988), esp. 264–91, 324–73.

49. See *KL*, "General Index," "novelists, K's references to," 421.

Conclusion

1. Manning, "Placing Poor Susan: Wordsworth and the New Historicism" (1986), rev. rpt. *Reading Romantics: Texts and Contexts* (New York: Oxford UP, 1990), 300. Manning also argues that "The problem of critical discourse, how we see Susan, mirrors and reduplicates the problem of how Susan sees" (304), so that "The poem attracts our common gaze and throws us back on our differences, enacting both our desire to understand the mute figures before us and its frustration" (319). I have made a similar argument about the poems read here, that the problem of narrative mastery within them reflects the problem of our interpretive mastery of them.

2. Eliot, "Tradition and the Individual Talent" (1919), rpt. *Selected Essays* (New York: Harcourt, 1950), 4–5.

3. Pocock explicitly makes use of Thomas S. Kuhn's concept of paradigm in *The Structure of Scientific Revolutions*, 2d ed. (Chicago: U of Chicago P, 1970).

4. Peter de Bolla, *The Discourse of the Sublime: Readings in History, Aesthetics and the Subject* (Oxford: Basil Blackwell, 1989), 6.

5. Lee Patterson, *Chaucer and the Subject of History* (Madison: U of Wisconsin P, 1991), 8, 12. Such oversimplification extends from "selfhood" to "society": "approaches to the problem of modernity that presuppose the unity of 'traditional' society fail to recognize the fact that concepts like 'tradition' . . . may be the inventions of a modernizing historical ideology" (Cascardi 4).

6. Belsey, *Critical Practice* (New York: Methuen, 1980), 92, 64, 73, 122, 123. Belsey repeatedly makes this distinction between the interrogative text and the classic realist

text, in spite of her qualification that "a different way of reading, a different critical approach can transfer a text from one modality to another" (92), a qualification that if taken seriously would undermine the distinction altogether. For a critique not so much of the distinction itself but of "the human mind['s tendency] to invest [such] binary oppositions with a moral evaluation," see Fredric Jameson, "The Ideology of the Text," *The Ideologies of Theory: Essays, 1971–86, Vol. 1: Situations of Theory* (Minneapolis: U of Minnesota P, 1988), esp. 54–71. Of the cognate opposition, modernism versus realism, he observes that "like so many oppositions of this kind, to the negative or straw term has been attributed everything that is error, illusion, and the like" (58).

7. A similar point is made earlier and in greater detail by Raymond Williams, in *Culture and Society, 1780–1950* (New York: Columbia UP, 1958): the Romantic "idea of art as a superior reality . . . offered an immediate basis for an important criticism of industrialism[, but also] it tended, as both the situation and the opposition hardened, to isolate art, to specialize the imaginative faculty to this one kind of activity" (43).

8. Wimsatt, "Genesis: An Argument Resumed" (1968), rpt. *Day of the Leopards: Essays in Defense of Poems* (New Haven, CT: Yale UP, 1976), 30.

9. Jacques Derrida, *Of Grammatology* (1967), trans. Gayatri Chakravorty Spivak (Baltimore: Johns Hopkins UP, 1976), 158.

10. Wasserman, *The Subtler Language: Critical Readings of Neoclassic and Romantic Poems* (Baltimore: Johns Hopkins P, 1959), 186.

11. Clifford Siskin, *The Historicity of Romantic Discourse* (New York and Oxford: Oxford UP, 1988), 12.

12. Mitchell, "Visible Language: Blake's Wond'rous Art of Writing," *Romanticism and Contemporary Criticism*, ed. Morris Eaves and Michael Fischer (Ithaca, NY: Cornell UP, 1986), 95.

13. Jean-Pierre Mileur, *The Critical Romance: The Critic as Reader, Writer, Hero* (Madison: U of Wisconsin P, 1990), 114–15.

14. Jon P. Klancher, *The Making of English Reading Audiences, 1790–1832* (Madison: U of Wisconsin P, 1987), 172.

15. Raymond Williams, *Problems in Materialism and Culture* (London: Verso, 1982), 25; commented on by George Levine, in his "Introduction: Reclaiming the Aesthetic," *Aesthetics and Ideology*, ed. Levine (New Brunswick, NJ: Rutgers UP, 1994), who describes Williams's position as "altogether another take on the Foucauldian perspective that, in effectively denying 'major individual talent,' in finding all individual acts of imagination determined by larger constricting social systems, makes community simply oppressive, and makes imagination not liberatory but delusive." He goes on to remark that Williams's "knowable community to which we aspire may be self-deluding and provincial. It's a risk worth taking" (21). Rajan argues against Klancher, specifically about the *Lyrical Ballads*, that "We cannot determine what Wordsworth's real audience was, and if we could, that would not establish what his real audience *is*. . . . Though reader-response theory is often accused of approaching the reader in an insufficiently materialist way, literalizing the notion of audience by identifying it with a specific historical group is equally essentialist" (*Supplement of Reading* 165–66).

16. Not to consider German philosophy in writing about reader-response theory may seem hopelessly naive. Rajan is correct that her "decision to focus on English romantic texts but to develop a historically grounded framework for their analysis from German theory of the period is probably no longer something that needs to be defended" (*Supplement of Reading* 4), and the framework she develops is sophisticated. But in going on to argue that such texts are "an increasingly metafictional literature that makes theory a subject of reflection within the text itself" (4), she seems to me to imply in effect that such a framework is neither necessary nor sufficient for interpretation. In any case, I am concerned with how the poets and their poems imply their readers.

17. David Couzens Hoy, *The Critical Circle: Literature, History, and Philosophical Hermeneutics* (Berkeley: U of California P, 1978), 61, 63–64.

18. "Structure, Sign, and Play in the Discourse of the Human Sciences," in *The Structuralist Controversy: The Languages of Criticism and the Sciences of Man*, ed. Richard Macksey and Eugenio Donato (1970; Baltimore: Johns Hopkins UP, 1972), 264–65, 271–72.

19. See *5 Readers Reading* (New Haven, CT: Yale UP, 1975). One of Holland's chapters *is* titled "From Subjectivity to Collectivity" (232–49). But he moves untroubled from one to the other, using the same model of an "identity theme," a particular "constancy that informs everything a human being says or does" (56) and that determines how each person interprets a text: "The individual (considered as the continuing creator of variations on an identity theme [stemming from "a pleasure principle of change"] relates to the world as he does to a poem or a story: he uses its physical reality as grist with which to re-create himself, that is, to make yet another variation in his single, enduring identity" (128–29). "One can then understand the group as a macroperson, having an identity theme. . . . In this sense, one grasps the whole style of the group outright, as one would abstract the personality of one of these five readers" (245). Tension in this model, we should notice, exists only to be overcome or avoided. Holland does not change his model substantially in *The I* (New Haven, CT: Yale UP, 1985).

20. Eliot says that the tradition, the "ideal order" of artworks, "is modified by the introduction of the new (the really new) work of art among them," and thus that "the past [is] altered by the present as much as the present is directed by the past" ("Tradition" 5). But his insistence on the artist's (and reader's) "extinction of personality" prevents any explanation of how that qualification might seriously affect that order.

21. Bloom, "From J to K, Or the Uncanniness of the Yahwist," *The Bible and the Narrative Tradition*, ed. Frank McConnell (New York: Oxford UP, 1986), 21.

22. For example, Bloom, "The Breaking of Form," *Deconstruction and Criticism* (New York: Seabury P, 1979), 5–6, and *The Breaking of the Vessels* (Chicago: U of Chicago P, 1982), 104.

23. Bloom, *Poetry and Repression: Revisionism from Blake to Stevens* (New Haven, CT: Yale UP, 1976), 145.

24. Ricoeur, "Fatherhood: From Phantasm to Symbol," *The Conflict of Interpretations*, ed. Don Ihde (Evanston, IL: Northwestern UP, 1974), 469, 470, 473.

25. Bloom, *A Map of Misreading* (New York: Oxford UP, 1974), 19.

26. Marlon B. Ross, *The Contours of Masculine Desire: Romanticism and the Rise of Women's Poetry* (New York and Oxford: Oxford UP, 1989), 6. For Ross, the exemplary case of this prophetic mastery is Wordsworth, whom Ross characterizes exclusively in the binary terms I am discussing: "For Wordsworth, the domesticated poet is only weak if he is mastered—by emotion, by chaos, by domestic trials, by political strife, by men in other vocations, by the reading public, by past poets, or by poets to come. Conversely, to the extent that he masters the domestic situation in which he finds himself, he is strong and worthy of serving as a founding patriarch of and above culture, despite any salient flaws that may mar his character as a mere man living within that culture" (21). Ross produces yet another binary opposition in his gendered alternative: "whereas the male romantic sees his problem primarily as the capacity to break continuity in order to establish the self-fathering strength of his own voice over culture, the female writer's problem is primarily one of establishing continuity in the midst of her own attempt to give birth to a new voice, the feminine poet, who wants her power to emanate not from the isolated experience of self but from the vested authority of culture as a whole" (192–93).

27. Max Black, "Models and Archetypes" (1960), rpt. *Models and Metaphors* (Ithaca, NY: Cornell UP, 1962), 236, 237, 230.

28. The complexity of Bloom's formulations of literary influence, as compared to the relative simplicity but equal explanatory power of Bate's—see especially *Burden of the Past*—may help to explain the far greater critical attention paid to, if not the greater influence of, the former.

29. Wimsatt, "Battering the Object" (1970), rpt. *Day of the Leopards*, 194–95.

30. For one example of this complexity, see Ivor Leclerc, *The Nature of Physical Existence* (New York: Humanities P, 1972), esp. 311–12, 314, 328–29.

31. Kermode, *The Genesis of Secrecy: On the Interpretation of Narrative* (Cambridge: Harvard UP, 1979), 145.

Works Cited

Abrams, M. H. *Doing Things with Texts: Essays in Criticism and Critical Theory*. New York: Norton, 1989.

———. *Natural Supernaturalism: Tradition and Revolution in Romantic Literature*. New York: Norton, 1971.

———. "Structure and Style in the Greater Romantic Lyric." *From Sensibility to Romanticism*. Ed. Frederick W. Hilles and Harold Bloom. New York: Oxford UP, 1965. 527–60.

Adams, Hazard. *William Blake: A Reading of the Shorter Poems*. Seattle: U of Washington P, 1963.

Aers, David. "Blake: Sex, Society and Ideology." *Romanticism and Ideology: Studies in English Writing, 1765–1830*. Ed. Aers, Jonathan Cook, David Punter. London: Routledge and Kegan Paul, 1981. 27–43.

Allott, Miriam, ed. *The Poems of John Keats*. 1970. Rpt. with corrections. New York: Longman, 1975.

Altieri, Charles. "Wordsworth's Wavering Balance: The Thematic Rhythm of *The Prelude*." *WC* 4 (1973): 226–40.

Anderson, Robert, ed. *The Works of the British Poets*. 13 vols. London, 1795.

Angus, Douglas. "The Theme of Love and Guilt in Coleridge's Three Major Poems." *JEGP* 59 (1960): 655–68.

Bahti, Timothy. "Figures of Interpretation, the Interpretation of Figures: A Reading of Wordsworth's 'Dream of the Arab.'" *SIR* 18 (1979): 601–27.

——. "Wordsworth's Rhetorical Theft." *Romanticism and Language*. Ed. Arden Reed. Ithaca, NY: Cornell UP, 1984. 86–124.

Bakhtin, M. M. *The Dialogic Imagination*. Ed. Michael Holquist. Trans. Caryl Emerson and Michael Holquist. Austin: U of Texas P, 1981.

Bald, R. C. "Coleridge and *The Ancient Mariner:* Addenda to *The Road to Xanadu.*" *Nineteenth-Century Studies*. Ed. Herbert Davis, William C. DeVane, and R. C. Bald. Ithaca, NY: Cornell UP, 1940. 1–45.

Baldick, Chris. *Criticism and Literary Theory, 1890 to the Present*. London: Longman, 1996.

Bate, Walter Jackson. *The Burden of the Past and the English Poet*. 1970. New York: Norton, 1972.

——. *Coleridge*. New York: Macmillan, 1968.

——. *John Keats*. 1963. Rpt. with corrections. New York: Oxford UP, 1966.

——. *The Stylistic Development of Keats*. 1945. New York: Humanities Press, 1962.

Bayley, John. *The Uses of Division: Unity and Disharmony in Literature*. New York: Viking P, 1976.

Beattie, James. *The Minstrel*. 1774. *Poetical Works*. London: George Bell, 1894.

Beavan, Arthur H. *James and Horace Smith*. London: Hurst and Blackett, 1899.

Becker, Michael G., Robert J. Dilligan, and Todd K. Bender, eds. *A Concordance to the Poems of John Keats*. New York: Garland, 1981.

Beer, J[ohn] B. *Coleridge the Visionary*. London: Chatto and Windus, 1959.

——. *Coleridge's Poetic Intelligence*. London: Macmillan, 1977.

Belsey, Catherine. *Critical Practice*. New York: Methuen, 1980.

——. "The Romantic Construction of the Unconscious." *Literature, Politics and Theory: Papers from the Essex Conference, 1976–84*. Ed. Francis Barker et al. New York: Methuen, 1986. 57–76.

Bennett, Andrew. *Keats, Narrative and Audience: The Posthumous Life of Writing*. Cambridge: Cambridge UP, 1994.

Beres, David. "A Dream, a Vision, and a Poem: A Psychoanalytic Study of the Origins of *The Rime of the Ancient Mariner*." *International Journal of Psycho-Analysis* 32 (1951): 97–116.

Berger, Peter L. and Thomas Luckmann. *The Social Construction of Reality: A Treatise in the Sociology of Knowledge*. 1966. Garden City, NY: Doubleday Anchor, 1967.

Bernstein, Gene M. "Keats' 'Lamia': The Sense of a Non-Ending." *PLL* 15 (1979): 175–92.

Bersani, Leo. *A Future for Astyanax: Character and Desire in Literature*. New York: Columbia UP, 1984.

Bindman, David. *Blake as an Artist*. Oxford: Phaidon, 1977.

Bishop, Jonathan. "Wordsworth and the 'Spots of Time.'" *ELH* 26 (1959): 45–65.

Black, Max. "Models and Archetypes." 1960. *Models and Metaphors: Studies in Language and Philosophy*. Ithaca, NY: Cornell UP, 1962. 219–43.

Blackstone, Bernard. *The Consecrated Urn*. London: Longmans, Green, 1959.

Blair, Hugh. *Lectures on Rhetoric and Belles Lettres*. 1783. Ed. Harold F. Harding. 2 vols. Carbondale: Southern Illinois UP, 1965.

Blake, William. *The Complete Poetry and Prose of William Blake*. Rev. ed. Ed. David V. Erdman. New York: Doubleday Anchor, 1988.

Bloom, Harold. *Blake's Apocalypse: A Study in Poetic Argument.* Ithaca, NY: Cornell UP, 1963.
———. "The Breaking of Form." *Deconstruction and Criticism.* New York: Seabury P, 1979. 1–37.
———. *The Breaking of the Vessels.* Chicago: U of Chicago P, 1982.
———. "From J to K, Or the Uncanniness of the Yahwist." *The Bible and the Narrative Tradition.* Ed. Frank McConnell. New York: Oxford UP, 1986. 19–35.
———. *A Map of Misreading.* New York: Oxford UP, 1974.
———. *Poetry and Repression: Revisionism from Blake to Stevens.* New Haven, CT: Yale UP, 1976.
Booth, Wayne. *The Company We Keep: An Ethics of Fiction.* Berkeley: U of California P, 1988.
———. *The Rhetoric of Fiction.* Chicago: U of Chicago P, 1961.
Bostetter, Edward E. "The Nightmare World of *The Ancient Mariner.*" 1962. Rpt. in Coburn, ed. 65–77.
Boulger, James D. "Christian Skepticism in *The Rime of the Ancient Mariner.*" *From Sensibility to Romanticism.* Ed. Frederick W. Hilles and Harold Bloom. New York: Oxford UP, 1965. 439–52.
———. "Keats' Symbolism." *ELH* 28 (1961): 244–59.
———, ed. *Twentieth Century Interpretations of "The Rime of the Ancient Mariner."* Englewood Cliffs, NJ: Prentice-Hall, 1969.
Brooks, Cleanth. "Marvell's 'Horatian Ode.'" 1947. *Seventeenth-Century English Poetry: Modern Essays in Criticism.* Ed. William R. Keast. New York: Oxford UP, 1962. 321–40.
———. *The Well Wrought Urn: Studies in the Structure of Poetry.* New York: Harcourt, 1947.
Brooks, Peter. *Reading for the Plot: Design and Intention in Narrative.* New York: Knopf, 1984.
Brown, Homer Obed. "The Art of Theology and the Theology of Art: Robert Penn Warren's Reading of Coleridge's *The Rime of the Ancient Mariner.*" *Boundary 2* 8, no. 1 (Fall 1979): 237–60.
Brown, Huntington. "The Gloss to *The Rime of the Ancient Mariner.*" *MLQ* 6 (1945): 319–24.
Buchan, A. M. "The Sad Wisdom of the Mariner" (1964). Rpt. in Boulger, ed. 92–110.
Burke, Edmund. *A Philosophical Enquiry into the Origin of Our Ideas of the Sublime and Beautiful.* 1759. Ed. J. T. Boulton. New York: Columbia UP, 1958.
Burke, Kenneth. *The Philosophy of Literary Form: Studies in Symbolic Action.* [Baton Rouge]: Louisiana State UP, 1941.
Butler, Marilyn. *Romantics, Rebels, and Reactionaries: English Literature and Its Background, 1760–1830.* Oxford: Oxford UP, 1981.
Caruth, Cathy. *Empirical Truths and Critical Fictions: Locke, Wordsworth, Kant, Freud.* Baltimore and London: Johns Hopkins UP, 1991.
Cascardi, Anthony J. *The Subject of Modernity.* Cambridge: Cambridge UP, 1992.
Cassirer, Ernst. *Language and Myth.* Trans. Susanne K. Langer. 1946. Rpt. New York: Dover, n.d.
Chandler, James K. *Wordsworth's Second Nature: A Study of the Poetry and Politics.* Chicago and London: U of Chicago P, 1984.
Chayes, Irene M. "Rhetoric as Drama: An Approach to the Romantic Ode." *PMLA* 79 (1964): 67–79.

Christensen, Jerome C. "The Sublime and the Romance of the Other." *Diacritics* (Summer 1978): 10–23.

Clarke, C. C. *Romantic Paradox.* New York: Barnes, 1963.

Coburn, Kathleen, ed. *Coleridge: A Collection of Critical Essays.* Englewood Cliffs, NJ: Prentice-Hall, 1967.

Cohen, Ralph. "On the Interrelations of Eighteenth-Century Literary Forms." *New Approaches to Eighteenth-Century Literature.* Ed. Phillip Harth. New York: Columbia UP, 1974. 33–78.

Coleridge, Samuel Taylor. *Biographia Literaria.* 1817. Ed. James Engell and W. Jackson Bate. 2 vols. Princeton, NJ: Princeton UP, 1983.

——. *Collected Letters of Samuel Taylor Coleridge.* Ed. Earl Leslie Griggs. Vol. 1. Oxford: Clarendon P, 1956–1971.

——. *Lectures 1808–1819: On Literature.* Ed. R. A. Foakes. Vol. 1. Princeton, NJ: Princeton UP, 1987.

——. *The Notebooks of Samuel Taylor Coleridge.* Ed. Kathleen Coburn. 4 vols. to date. New York: Bollingen Foundation, 1957–.

Coles, William Allan. "The Proof Sheets of Keats's 'Lamia.'" *Harvard Library Bulletin* 8 (1954): 114–19.

Colie, Rosalie L. *The Resources of Kind: Genre-Theory in the Renaissance.* Berkeley: U of California P, 1973.

Collings, David. *Wordsworthian Errancies: The Poetics of Cultural Dismemberment.* Baltimore: Johns Hopkins UP, 1994.

Colvin, Sidney. *John Keats.* London: Macmillan, 1917.

Crehan, Stewart. *Blake in Context.* Dublin and Atlantic Highlands, NJ: Gill and Macmillan, Humanities P, 1984.

Curran, Stuart. *Poetic Form and British Romanticism.* New York: Oxford UP, 1986.

Curtis, Jared. *Wordsworth's Experiments with Tradition.* Ithaca, NY: Cornell UP, 1971.

[Dacier, André, trans. and ed.] *The Works of Plato Abridg'd.* Trans. "from the French, by several Hands." 4th ed. London, 1749.

D'Avanzo, Mario L. *Keats's Metaphors for the Poetic Imagination.* Durham, NC: Duke UP, 1967.

De Bolla, Peter. *The Discourse of the Sublime: Readings in History, Aesthetics and the Subject.* Oxford: Basil Blackwell, 1989.

De Man, Paul. *Allegories of Reading.* New Haven, CT: Yale UP, 1979.

——. "Autobiography as De-Facement." 1979. *The Rhetoric of Romanticism.* New York: Columbia UP, 1984. 67–81.

——. "Criticism and Crisis." 1967. *Blindness and Insight: Essays in the Rhetoric of Contemporary Criticism.* 2d rev. ed. 1971. Minneapolis: U of Minnesota P, 1983. 3–19.

——. "Form and Intent in the American New Criticism." *Blindness and Insight.* 20–35.

——. "The Rhetoric of Blindness: Jacques Derrida's Reading of Rousseau." 1971. *Blindness and Insight.* 102–41.

——. "Time and History in Wordsworth." 1967. *Romanticism and Contemporary Criticism.* Baltimore: Johns Hopkins UP, 1993. 74–94.

Derrida, Jacques. *Of Grammatology.* 1967. Trans. Gayatri Chakravorty Spivak. Baltimore: Johns Hopkins UP, 1976.

———. "Structure, Sign, and Play in the Discourse of the Human Sciences." *The Structuralist Controversy: The Languages of Criticism and the Sciences of Man.* Ed. Richard Macksey and Eugenio Donato. 1970. Baltimore: Johns Hopkins UP, 1972. 247–72.

De Sélincourt, Ernest. *The Poems of John Keats.* 5th ed. London: Methuen, 1926.

De Sola Pinto, Vivian. "William Blake, Isaac Watts, and Mrs. Barbauld." 1944. Rev. rpt. *The Divine Vision: Studies in the Poetry and Art of William Blake.* Ed. de Sola Pinto. London: Victor Gollancz, 1957. 65–87.

De Waelhens, Alphonse. *Schizophrenia: A Philosophical Reflection on Lacan's Structuralist Interpretation.* 1972. Trans. W. Ver Eecke. Pittsburgh: Duquesne UP, 1978.

Dubrow, Heather. *Genre.* New York: Methuen, 1982.

Dunbar, Georgia S. "The Significance of the Humor in 'Lamia.'" *KSJ* 8 (1959): 17–26.

Dyck, Sarah. "Perspective in 'The Rime of the Ancient Mariner.'" *SEL* 13 (1973): 591–604.

Eagleton, Terry. *Literary Theory: An Introduction.* 2d ed. Minneapolis: U of Minnesota P, 1996.

Eaves, Morris. *William Blake's Theory of Art.* Princeton, NJ: Princeton UP, 1982.

Eliot, T. S. "Hamlet and His Problems." 1919. *Selected Essays.* New York: Harcourt, Brace and World, 1950. 121–26.

———. "Tradition and the Individual Talent." 1919. *Selected Essays.* 3–11.

Elliott, Robert C. *The Literary Persona.* Chicago: U of Chicago P, 1982.

Erdman, David V. *Blake: Prophet against Empire.* Rev. ed. Garden City, NY: Doubleday Anchor, 1969.

Erskine-Hill, Howard. *Poetry of Opposition and Revolution: Dryden to Wordsworth.* Oxford: Clarendon P, 1996.

Essick, Robert N. *William Blake and the Language of Adam.* Oxford: Clarendon P, 1989.

Evans, Frank B., III. "Platonic Scholarship in Eighteenth-Century England." *MP* 41 (1943): 103–10.

Ferber, Michael. *The Social Vision of William Blake.* Princeton, NJ: Princeton UP, 1985.

Ferguson, Frances. "Coleridge and the Deluded Reader: 'The Rime of the Ancient Mariner.'" *Georgia Review* 38 (1977): 617–35.

———. *Wordsworth: Language as Counter-Spirit.* New Haven, CT: Yale UP, 1977.

Ferris, David. "Where Three Paths Meet: History, Wordsworth, and the Simplon Pass." *SIR* 30 (1991): 391–438.

Fields, Beverly. *Reality's Dark Dream: Dejection in Coleridge.* Kent, OH: Kent State UP, 1967.

Finney, Claude Lee. *The Evolution of Keats's Poetry.* 2 vols. Cambridge, MA: Harvard UP, 1936.

Fish, Stanley. *Is There a Text in This Class? The Authority of Interpretive Communities.* Cambridge, MA: Harvard UP, 1980.

Fogle, Richard Harter. "Keats's *Lamia* as Dramatic Illusion." *Nineteenth-Century Literary Perspectives.* Ed. Clyde de L. Ryals. Durham, NC: Duke UP, 1974. 65–75.

F[ogle], S[tephen] F., and P[aul] H. F[ry]. "Ode." *The New Princeton Encyclopedia of Poetry and Poetics.* Ed. Alex Preminger and T. V. F. Brogan. Princeton, NJ: Princeton UP, 1993. 855–57.

Foucault, Michel. *Discipline and Punish: The Birth of the Prison.* 1975. Trans. Alan Sheridan. 1978. New York: Random House, 1979.

———. *The History of Sexuality, Vol. 1: An Introduction.* 1976. Trans. Robert Hurley. 1978. New York: Random House, 1980.

———. "What Is an Author?" *Textual Strategies: Perspectives in Post-Structuralist Criticism.* Ed. Josue V. Harari. Ithaca, NY: Cornell UP, 1979. 141–60.

Fowler, Alastair. *Kinds of Literature.* Cambridge, MA: Harvard UP, 1982.

Freud, Sigmund. *The Standard Edition of the Complete Psychological Works of Sigmund Freud.* Ed. and trans. James Strachey. London: Hogarth P and The Institute of Psycho-Analysis, 1953–74.

Fry, Paul H. *The Poet's Calling in the English Ode.* New Haven, CT: Yale UP, 1980.

Frye, Northrop. "Blake's Introduction to Experience." 1957. *Blake: A Collection of Critical Essays.* Ed. Frye. Englewood Cliffs, NJ: Prentice-Hall, 1966. 23–31.

Galperin, William H. *The Return of the Visible in English Romanticism.* Baltimore: Johns Hopkins UP, 1993.

———. *Revision and Authority in Wordsworth: The Interpretation of a Career.* Philadephia: U of Pennsylvania P, 1989.

Gillham, D. G. *William Blake.* Cambridge: Cambridge UP, 1973.

Gleckner, Robert. *The Piper and the Bard: A Study of William Blake.* Detroit: Wayne State UP, 1959.

Glen, Heather. *Vision and Disenchantment: Blake's "Songs" and Wordsworth's "Lyrical Ballads."* Cambridge: Cambridge UP, 1983.

Goellnicht, Donald C. "Keats on Reading: 'Delicious Diligent Indolence.'" *JEGP* 88 (1989): 190–210.

Goldstein, Harvey D. "Anglorum Pindarus: Model and Milieu." *Comparative Literature* 17 (1965): 299–310.

Grant, John E. "The Art and Argument of 'The Tyger.'" 1960. Rev. rpt. *Discussions of William Blake.* Ed. Grant. Boston: D. C. Heath, 1961. 64–82.

Griffiths, Eric. *The Printed Voice of Victorian Poetry.* Oxford: Clarendon P, 1989.

Harding, D. W. "The Theme of 'The Ancient Mariner.'" 1941. Rev. rpt. in Coburn, ed. 51–64.

Hartman, Geoffrey H. "Beyond Formalism." 1966. *Beyond Formalism: Literary Essays 1958– 1970.* New Haven, CT: Yale UP, 1970. 42–57.

———. "Envoi: 'So Many Things.'" *Unnam'd Forms: Blake and Textuality.* Ed. Nelson Hilton and Thomas A. Vogler. Berkeley: U of California P, 1986. 242–48.

———. *Wordsworth's Poetry, 1787–1814.* 1964. New Haven, CT: Yale UP, 1971.

Haven, Richard. "The Ancient Mariner in the Nineteenth Century." *SIR* 11 (1972): 360–74.

———. *Patterns of Consciousness: An Essay on Coleridge.* [Amherst]: U of Massachusetts P, 1969.

Haydon, Benjamin Robert. *The Diary of Benjamin Robert Haydon.* Ed. Willard Bissell Pope. Vol. 2. Cambridge, MA: Harvard UP, 1960.

Heffernan, James A. W. "The Presence of the Absent Mother in Wordsworth's *Prelude*." *SIR* 27 (1988): 253–72.

Hilton, Nelson. *Literal Imagination: Blake's Vision of Words*. Berkeley: U of California P, 1983.

Hirsch, E. D., Jr. *Validity in Interpretation*. New Haven, CT: Yale UP, 1967.

Hoagwood, Terence Allan. "Keats and Social Context: *Lamia*." *SEL* 29 (1989): 675–97.

Holland, Norman N. *5 Readers Reading*. New Haven, CT: Yale UP, 1975.

———. *The I*. New Haven, CT: Yale UP, 1985.

———. "Literary Interpretation and Three Phases of Psychoanalysis." *Critical Inquiry* 2 (1976): 221–33.

Holloway, John. *Blake: The Lyric Poetry*. London: Edward Arnold, 1968.

Homans, Margaret. "Keats Reading Women, Women Reading Keats." *SIR* 29 (1990): 341–70.

House, Humphrey. *Coleridge: The Clark Lectures, 1951–52*. Philadelphia: Dufour, 1965.

Hoy, David Couzens. *The Critical Circle: Literature, History, and Philosophical Hermeneutics*. Berkeley: U of California P, 1978.

Iser, Wolfgang. *The Act of Reading: A Theory of Aesthetic Response*. 1976. Baltimore: Johns Hopkins UP, 1978.

Jacobus, Mary. *Romanticism, Writing, and Sexual Difference: Essays on "The Prelude."* Oxford: Clarendon P, 1989.

Jameson, Fredric. "The Ideology of the Text." 1975–76. *The Ideologies of Theory: Essays, 1971–86, Vol. 1: Situations of Theory*. Minneapolis: U of Minnesota P, 1988. 17–71.

Jauss, Hans Robert. *Toward an Aesthetic of Reception*. Trans. Timothy Bahti. Minneapolis: U of Minnesota P, 1982.

Johnson, Karl R., Jr. *The Written Spirit: Thematic and Rhetorical Structure in Wordsworth's "The Prelude."* Salzburg: Inst. für Englische Sprache und Literatur, U Salzburg, 1978.

Johnson, Mary Lynn. "William Blake: Studies of Individual Works: *Songs of Innocence and of Experience*." *The English Romantic Poets: A Review of Research and Criticism*. 4th ed. Ed. Frank Jordan. New York: Modern Language Association of America, 1985. 202–14.

Johnston, Kenneth R. "The Idiom of Vision." *New Perspectives on Coleridge and Wordsworth*. Ed. Geoffrey H. Hartman. New York: Columbia UP, 1972. 1–39.

———. "Recollecting Forgetting: Forcing Paradox to the Limit in the 'Intimations Ode.'" *WC* 2 (1971): 59–64.

Jones, John. *The Egotistical Sublime: A History of Wordsworth's Imagination*. London: Chatto, 1954.

Keane, Patrick J. *Coleridge's Submerged Politics: "The Ancient Mariner" and "Robinson Crusoe."* Columbia: U of Missouri P, 1994.

Keats, John. *The Letters of John Keats, 1814–1821*. Ed. Hyder Edward Rollins. 2 vols. Cambridge, MA: Harvard UP, 1958.

———. *The Poems of John Keats*. Ed. Jack Stillinger. Cambridge, MA: Harvard UP, 1978.

Kelley, Theresa M. "Keats, Ekphrasis, and History." *Keats and History*. Ed. Nicholas Roe. Cambridge: Cambridge UP, 1995. 212–37.

———. *Wordsworth's Revisionary Aesthetics*. Cambridge: Cambridge UP, 1988.

Kermode, Frank. *The Classic: Literary Images of Permanence and Change.* Cambridge, MA: Harvard UP, 1983.

——. *The Genesis of Secrecy: On the Interpretation of Narrative.* Cambridge, MA: Harvard UP, 1979.

——. *The Sense of an Ending: Studies in the Theory of Fiction.* New York: Oxford UP, 1967.

King, Everard H. *James Beattie's "The Minstrel" and the Origins of Romantic Autobiography.* Lewiston, NY: Edwin Mellen P, 1992.

Klancher, Jon P. *The Making of English Reading Audiences, 1790–1832.* Madison: U of Wisconsin P, 1987.

Knight, G. Wilson. *The Starlit Dome.* 1941. London: Methuen, 1959.

Knight, Stephen. *Geoffrey Chaucer.* Oxford: Basil Blackwell, 1986. 83–90.

Knight, William, ed. *The Poetical Works of William Wordsworth.* 8 vols. London: Macmillan, 1896.

Kuhn, Thomas S. *The Structure of Scientific Revolutions.* 2d ed. Chicago: U of Chicago P, 1970.

Lacan, Jacques. *Ecrits: A Selection.* 1966. Trans. Alan Sheridan. New York: Norton, 1977.

——. *The Four Fundamental Concepts of Psycho-Analysis.* 1973. Trans. Alan Sheridan. New York: Norton, 1978.

Lamb, Charles. *The Letters of Charles and Mary Anne Lamb.* Ed. Edwin W. Marrs, Jr. Vol. 1. Ithaca, NY: Cornell UP, 1975.

Larrissy, Edward. *William Blake.* Oxford: Basil Blackwell, 1985.

Leader, Zachary. *Reading Blake's "Songs."* Boston: Routledge and Kegan Paul, 1981.

——. *Revision and Romantic Authorship.* Oxford: Clarendon P, 1996.

Leclerc, Ivor. *The Nature of Physical Existence.* New York: Humanities P, 1972.

Lentricchia, Frank. *After the New Criticism.* Chicago: U of Chicago P, 1980.

Levine, George. "Introduction: Reclaiming the Aesthetic." *Aesthetics and Ideology.* Ed. Levine. New Brunswick, NJ: Rutgers UP, 1994. 1–28.

Levinson, Marjorie. *Keats's Life of Allegory: The Origins of a Style.* Oxford: Basil Blackwell, 1988.

——. *Wordsworth's Great Period Poems.* Cambridge and New York: Cambridge UP, 1986.

Lincoln, Andrew, ed. *Songs of Innocence and of Experience.* Princeton, NJ: William Blake Trust, Princeton UP, 1991.

Lindenberger, Herbert. *On Wordsworth's "Prelude."* Princeton, NJ: Princeton UP, 1963.

Lipking, Lawrence. "The Marginal Gloss." *Critical Inquiry* 3 (1977): 609–55.

Liu, Alan. "The Power of Formalism: The New Historicism." *ELH* 56 (1989): 721–71.

——. *Wordsworth: The Sense of History.* Stanford, CA: Stanford UP, 1989.

Lowes, John Livingston. *The Road to Xanadu: A Study in the Ways of the Imagination.* Rev. ed. 1930. Princeton, NJ: Princeton UP, 1986.

Lukacs, Georg. *History and Class Consciousness: Studies in Marxist Dialectics.* 1968. Trans. Rodney Livingstone. Cambridge, MA: MIT P, 1971.

Lupton, Mary Jane. "'The Rime of the Ancient Mariner': The Agony of Thirst." *American Imago* 27 (1970): 140–59.

Lüthi, Max. *Once upon a Time: On the Nature of Fairy Tales.* New York: Ungar, 1970.

Maclean, Norman. "From Action to Image: Theories of the Lyric in the Eighteenth Century." *Critics and Criticism.* Ed. R. S. Crane. Chicago: U of Chicago P, 1952. 408–60.

Magnuson, Paul. *Coleridge's Nightmare Poetry.* Charlottesville: UP of Virginia, 1974.

Mallet, Charles Edward. *A History of the University of Oxford.* Vol. 3. 1927. New York: Barnes and Noble, 1968.

Manning, Peter J. "Placing Poor Susan: Wordsworth and the New Historicism" 1986. Rev. rpt. *Reading Romantics: Texts and Contexts.* 300–320.

———. "Wordsworth's Intimations Ode and Its Epigraphs." 1983. *Reading Romantics: Texts and Contexts.* New York and Oxford: Oxford UP, 1990. 68–84.

Marsh, Florence G. "Wordsworth's Ode: Obstinate Questionings." *SIR* 5 (1966): 219–30.

McElderry, B. R., Jr. "Coleridge's Revision of 'The Ancient Mariner.'" *SP* 29 (1932): 68–94.

McGann, Jerome J. "The Ancient Mariner: The Meaning of the Meanings." 1981. Rpt. *Beauty of Inflections.* 135–72.

———. *The Beauty of Inflections: Literary Investigations in Historical Method and Theory.* Oxford: Clarendon P, 1988.

———. "Keats and the Historical Method in Literary Scholarship." 1979. Rpt. *Beauty of Inflections.* 15–65.

———. *The Romantic Ideology: A Critical Investigation.* Chicago and London: U of Chicago P, 1983.

———. *Social Values and Poetic Acts: The Historical Judgment of Literary Work.* Cambridge, MA, and London: Harvard UP, 1988.

McKenzie, Gordon. *Organic Unity in Coleridge.* Berkeley: U of California P, 1939.

McNally, Paul. "Milton and the Immortality Ode." *WC* 11 (1980): 28–33.

Mellor, Anne K. *English Romantic Irony.* Cambridge, MA: Harvard UP, 1980.

Miall, David S. "The Meaning of Dreams: Coleridge's Ambivalence." *SIR* 21 (1982): 57–71.

Miles, Josephine. *Eras and Modes in English Poetry.* 2d ed. Berkeley: U of California P, 1964.

Mileur, Jean-Pierre. *The Critical Romance: The Critic as Reader, Writer, Hero.* Madison: U of Wisconsin P, 1990.

Miller, J. Hillis. *The Linguistic Moment: From Wordsworth to Stevens.* Princeton, NJ: Princeton UP, 1985.

———. *Theory Now and Then.* Durham, NC: Duke UP, 1991.

Mink, Louis O. "Narrative Form as a Cognitive Instrument." *The Writing of History: Literary Form and Historical Understanding.* Ed. Robert H. Canary and Henry Kosicki. Madison: U of Wisconsin P, 1978. 129–49.

Mitchell, W. J. T. *Blake's Composite Art: A Study of the Illuminated Poetry.* Princeton, NJ: Princeton UP, 1978.

———. "Visible Language: Blake's Wond'rous Art of Writing." *Romanticism and Contemporary Criticism.* Ed. Morris Eaves and Michael Fischer. Ithaca, NY: Cornell UP, 1986. 46–95.

Modiano, Raimonda. "Words and 'Languageless' Meanings: Limits of Expression in *The Rime of the Ancient Mariner.*" *MLQ* 38 (1977): 40–61.

Muirhead, John H. *Coleridge as Philosopher.* New York: Humanities P, 1930.

Muller, John P. "Language, Psychosis, and the Subject in Lacan." *Interpreting Lacan.* Ed. Joseph H. Smith and William Kerrigan. New Haven, CT: Yale UP, 1982. 21–32.

Muller, John P., and William J. Richardson. *Lacan and Language: A Reader's Guide to "Ecrits."* New York: International Universities P, 1982. 9–23.

Nelson, Cary. "The Psychology of Criticism, Or What Can Be Said." *Psychoanalysis and the Question of the Text.* Ed. Geoffrey H. Hartman. Baltimore: Johns Hopkins UP, 1978. 45–61.

Nicholson, C. J. "A World of Artefacts: *The Rape of the Lock* as Social History." *Literature and History* 5 (1979): 67–79.

Norris, Christopher. *The Deconstructive Turn: Essays in the Rhetoric of Philosophy.* New York: Methuen, 1983.

Notopoulos, James A. *The Platonism of Shelley.* Durham, NC: Duke UP, 1949.

Noy, Pinchas. "A Revision of the Psychoanalytic Theory of the Primary Process." *International Journal of Psycho-Analysis* (1969): 155–78.

O'Donnell, Brennan. *The Passion of Meter: A Study of Wordsworth's Metrical Art.* Kent, OH: Kent State UP, 1995.

Onorato, Richard J. *The Character of the Poet: Wordsworth in* The Prelude. Princeton, NJ: Princeton UP, 1971.

Orsini, G. N. G. *Coleridge and German Idealism.* Carbondale: Southern Illinois UP, 1969.

Orwell, George. "Politics and the English Language." 1946. *In Front of Your Nose, 1945–1950, The Collected Essays, Journalism and Letters of George Orwell.* Ed. Sonia Orwell and Ian Angus. Vol. 4. New York: Harcourt, Brace and World, 1968. 127–40.

Owen, Charles A., Jr. "Structure in *The Ancient Mariner.*" *CE* 23 (1962): 261–67.

Patterson, Charles I., Jr. *The Daemonic in the Poetry of John Keats.* Urbana: U of Illinois P, 1970.

Patterson, Lee. *Chaucer and the Subject of History.* Madison: U of Wisconsin P, 1991.

Payne, Richard. "'The Style and Spirit of the Elder Poets': The *Ancient Mariner* and English Literary Tradition." *MP* 75 (1978): 368–84.

Perkins, David. *The Quest for Permanence.* Cambridge, MA: Harvard UP, 1959.

Peterfreund, Stuart. "*The Prelude:* Wordsworth's Metamorphic Epic." *Genre* 14 (1981): 441–72.

Pocock, J. G. A. *Politics, Language, and Time: Essays on Political Thought and History.* New York: Atheneum, 1971.

Potts, Abbie Findlay. *Wordsworth's "Prelude": A Study of Its Literary Form.* Ithaca, NY: Cornell UP, 1953.

Price, Martin. "The Sublime Poem: Pictures and Powers." *Yale Review* 58 (1968): 194–213.

Prickett, Stephen. *Coleridge and Wordsworth: The Poetry of Growth.* Cambridge: Cambridge UP, 1970.

Pyle, Forest. *The Ideology of Imagination: Subject and Society in the Discourse of Romanticism.* Stanford, CA: Stanford UP, 1995.

Rader, Melvin. *Wordsworth: A Philosophical Approach.* Oxford: Clarendon P, 1967.

Ragussis, Michael. "Narrative Structure and the Problem of the Divided Reader in *The Eve of St. Agnes.*" *ELH* 42 (1975): 378–94.

Rahv, Philip. "The Myth and the Powerhouse." 1953. *The Myth and the Powerhouse.* New York: Farrar, Straus and Giroux, 1965. 3–21.

Rajan, Tilottama. "The Erasure of Narrative in Post-Structuralist Representations of Wordsworth." *Romantic Revolutions: Criticism and Theory.* Ed. Kenneth R. Johnston et al. Bloomington and Indianapolis: Indiana UP, 1990. 350–70.

———. *The Supplement of Reading: Figures of Understanding in Romantic Theory and Practice.* Ithaca, NY: Cornell UP, 1990.

Reed, Mark L. "The Speaker of *The Prelude.*" *Bicentenary Wordsworth Studies in Memory of John Alban Finch.* Ed. Jonathan Wordsworth. Ithaca, NY: Cornell UP, 1970. 276–93.

———. "Wordsworth, Coleridge, and the 'Plan' of the *Lyrical Ballads.*" *UTQ* 34 (1965): 238–53.

———. *Wordsworth: The Chronology of the Middle Years, 1800–1815.* Cambridge, MA: Harvard UP, 1975.

Reiman, Donald H. "Keats and the Humanistic Paradox: Mythological History in *Lamia.*" *SEL* 11 (1971): 659–69.

———, ed. *Shelley and His Circle, 1773–1822.* Vol. 5. Cambridge, MA: Harvard UP, 1973.

Richardson, William J. "Lacan and the Subject of Psychoanalysis." *Interpreting Lacan.* Ed. Joseph H. Smith and William Kerrigan. New Haven, CT: Yale UP, 1982. 51–74.

Ricoeur, Paul. "Fatherhood: From Phantasm to Symbol." *The Conflict of Interpretations.* Ed. Don Ihde. Evanston, IL: Northwestern UP, 1974. 468–97.

———. *Oneself as Another.* 1990. Trans. Kathleen Blamey. Chicago and London: U of Chicago P, 1992.

Robinson, Jeffrey C. *Radical Literary Education: A Classroom Experiment with Wordsworth's "Ode."* Madison: U of Wisconsin P, 1987.

Roe, Nicholas. "Keats's Commonwealth." *Keats and History.* Ed. Roe. Cambridge: Cambridge UP, 1995. 194–211.

Rollins, Hyder Edward, ed. *The Keats Circle.* 2d ed. 2 vols. Cambridge, MA: Harvard UP, 1965.

Ross, Marlon B. *The Contours of Masculine Desire: Romanticism and the Rise of Women's Poetry.* New York: Oxford UP, 1989.

Rothstein, Eric. *Restoration and Eighteenth-Century Poetry, 1660–1780.* Boston: Routledge, 1981.

Ruskin, John. *The Stones of Venice.* Vol. 2. 1853. Vol. 10 of *The Works of John Ruskin.* Ed. E. T. Cook and Alexander Wedderburn. New York: Longmans, 1904.

Scholes, Robert. *Textual Power: Literary Theory and the Teaching of English.* New Haven, CT: Yale UP, 1985.

Scholes, Robert, and Robert Kellogg. *The Nature of Narrative.* New York: Oxford UP, 1966.

Shaffer, E. S. *"Kubla Khan" and "The Fall of Jerusalem": The Mythological School in Biblical Criticism and Secular Literature.* Cambridge: Cambridge UP, 1975.

Shelley, Percy Bysshe. "Preface" to *Prometheus Unbound, Shelley's Poetry and Prose.* Ed. Donald H. Reiman and Sharon B. Powers. New York: Norton, 1977. 132–36.

Shrimpton, Nick. "Hell's Hymnbook: Blake's *Songs of Innocence and of Experience* and Their Models." *Literature of the Romantic Period, 1750–1850.* Ed R. T. Davies and B. G. Beatty. New York: Barnes and Noble, 1976. 19–35.

Simmel, Georg. *The Philosophy of Money.* Trans. T. Bottomore and D. Frisby. London: Routledge and Kegan Paul, 1978.

Simpson, David. *Irony and Authority in Romantic Poetry.* Totowa, NJ: Rowman and Littlefield, 1979.

Siskin, Clifford. *The Historicity of Romantic Discourse.* New York, Oxford: Oxford UP, 1988.

Sitter, John. *Literary Loneliness in Mid-Eighteenth-Century England.* Ithaca, NY: Cornell UP, 1982.

Sitterson, Joseph C., Jr. "'Unmeaning Miracles' in 'The Rime of the Ancient Mariner.'" *South Atlantic Review* 46 (1981): 16–26.

Slote, Bernice. *Keats and the Dramatic Principle.* Lincoln: U of Nebraska P, 1958.

Smith, Barbara Herrnstein. *Poetic Closure.* Chicago: U of Chicago P, 1968.

Smith, Paul. *Discerning the Subject.* Minneapolis: U of Minnesota P, 1988.

Southey, Robert. *The Critical Review.* 2d Ser. 24 (1798): 200.

Spence, Donald P. *Narrative Truth and Historical Truth: Meaning and Interpretation in Psychoanalysis.* New York: Norton, 1982.

Sperry, Stuart M., Jr. *Keats the Poet.* Princeton, NJ: Princeton UP, 1973.

———. "Keats's Skepticism and Voltaire." *KSJ* 12 (1963): 75–93.

Stephenson, William C. "The Fall from Innocence in Keats's 'Lamia.'" *PLL* 10 (1974): 35–50.

———. "The Performing Narrator in Keats's Poetry." *KSJ* 26 (1977): 51–71.

Stewart, Garrett. "*Lamia* and the Language of Metamorphosis." *SIR* 15 (1976): 3–41.

Stillinger, Jack. *Coleridge and Textual Instability: The Multiple Versions of the Major Poems.* New York: Oxford UP, 1994.

Taylor, Thomas, ed. and trans. *The Cratylus, Phaedo, Parmenides and Timaeus of Plato.* London, 1793.

Teichman, Milton. "The Marriage Metaphor in the *Rime of the Ancient Mariner*." *Bulletin of the New York Public Library* 73 (1969): 40–48.

Thorpe, Clarence DeWitt. *The Mind of John Keats.* New York: Oxford UP, 1926.

Tompkins, Jane P. "An Introduction to Reader-Response Criticism." *Reader-Response Criticism: From Formalism to Post-Structuralism.* Ed. Tompkins. Baltimore: Johns Hopkins UP, 1980. ix–xxvi.

Trilling, Lionel. "The Immortality Ode." 1942. *The Liberal Imagination.* New York: Viking, 1950. 129–59.

Trotter, David. *The Poetry of Abraham Cowley.* Totowa, NJ: Rowman, 1979.

Twitchell, James. "The World above the Ancient Mariner." *TSLL* 17 (1975): 103–17.

Veeser, H. Aram. "Introduction." *The New Historicism*. Ed. Veeser. New York: Routledge, 1989. ix–xvi.

Vendler, Helen. "Lionel Trilling and the Immortality Ode." *Salmagundi* 41 (1978): 66–86.

Viscomi, Joseph. *Blake and the Idea of the Book*. Princeton, NJ: Princeton UP, 1993.

Waelder, Robert. "The Principle of Multiple Function: Observations on Over-Determination." *Psychoanalytic Quarterly* 5 (1936): 45–62.

Waldoff, Leon. *Keats and the Silent Work of Imagination*. Urbana: U of Illinois P, 1984.

———. "The Quest for Father and Identity in 'The Rime of the Ancient Mariner.'"
Psychoanalytic Review 58 (1971): 439–53.

Wallen, Martin. *Coleridge's "Ancient Mariner": An Experimental Edition of Texts and Revisions,
1798–1828*. Barrytown, NY: Station Hill Literary Editions, 1993.

Warminski, Andrzej. "Missed Crossing: Wordsworth's Apocalypses." *MLN* 99 (1984):
983–1006.

Warren, Robert Penn. "A Poem of Pure Imagination: An Experiment in Reading." 1946.
Rev. rpt. *Selected Essays*. New York: Random House, 1958. 198–305.

Wasserman, Earl R. *The Finer Tone*. Baltimore: Johns Hopkins UP, 1953.

———. "Keats and Benjamin Bailey on the Imagination." *MLN* 68 (1953): 361–65.

———. *The Subtler Language: Critical Readings of Neoclassic and Romantic Poems*. Baltimore:
Johns Hopkins P, 1959.

Watkins, Daniel P. "History as Demon in Coleridge's *The Rime of the Ancient Mariner*."
PLL 24 (1988): 23–33.

———. *Keats's Poetry and the Politics of the Imagination*. Rutherford, NJ: Fairleigh Dickinson
UP, 1989.

Weiskel, Thomas P. *The Romantic Sublime: Studies in the Structure and Psychology of Transcendence*. Baltimore: Johns Hopkins UP, 1976.

Williams, Anne. "Wordsworth's *Intimations Ode:* The Fortunate Fall." 1981. Rev. rpt. *Prophetic Strain: The Greater Lyric in the Eighteenth Century*. Chicago: U of Chicago P, 1984.
140–51.

Williams, Raymond. *Culture and Society, 1780–1950*. New York: Columbia UP, 1958.

———. *Problems in Materialism and Culture*. London: Verso, 1982.

Wimsatt, W. K., Jr., and Monroe C. Beardsley. "The Intentional Fallacy." 1946. Rev.
rpt. Wimsatt, *The Verbal Icon: Studies in the Meaning of Poetry*. Lexington: UP of Kentucky, 1954. 3–18.

Wimsatt, W. K. "Battering the Object." 1970. *Day of the Leopards: Essays in Defense of Poems*.
New Haven, CT: Yale UP, 1976. 183–204.

———. "Genesis: An Argument Resumed." 1968. *Day of the Leopards*. 11–39.

Wolfson, Susan J. *Formal Charges: The Shaping of Poetry in British Romanticism*. Stanford, CA:
Stanford UP, 1997.

———. *The Questioning Presence: Wordsworth, Keats, and the Interrogative Mode in Romantic Poetry*.
Ithaca, NY: Cornell UP, 1986.

Wordsworth, Jonathan. *William Wordsworth: The Borders of Vision*. Oxford: Clarendon P,
1982.

Wordsworth, William. *The Fourteen-Book "Prelude" by William Wordsworth*. Ed. W. J. B. Owen. Ithaca, NY: Cornell UP, 1985.

———. *The Letters of William and Dorothy Wordsworth*. Ed. Ernest de Sélincourt. 2d rev. ed. Chester L. Shaver et al. 8 vols. Oxford: Clarendon P, 1967–93.

———. *"Lyrical Ballads" and Other Poems, 1797–1800, by William Wordsworth*. Ed. James Butler and Karen Green. Ithaca, NY: Cornell UP, 1992.

———. *"Poems, in Two Volumes," and other Poems, 1800–1807*. Ed. Jared Curtis. Ithaca, NY: Cornell UP, 1983.

———. *The Poetical Works of William Wordsworth*. Rev. ed. Ernest de Sélincourt and Helen Darbishire. 5 vols. Oxford: Clarendon P, 1952–59.

———. *The Prose Works of William Wordsworth*. Ed. W. J. B. Owen and Jane Worthington Smyser. 3 vols. Oxford: Clarendon P, 1974.

———. *The Thirteen-Book "Prelude" by William Wordsworth*. Ed. Mark L. Reed. Ithaca, NY, and London: Cornell UP, 1991.

Young, Robert. "The Eye and Progress of His Song: A Lacanian Reading of *The Prelude*." *Oxford Literary Review* 3, no. 3 (1979): 78–98. Rev. rpt. *William Wordsworth's "The Prelude,"* ed. Harold Bloom. New York: Chelsea House, 1986.

Index

Certain key words occur so frequently in the text that they cannot be indexed usefully here: desire, irony, lyric, mastery, narrator, narrative, poet, reader, self-consciousness, speaker, subject, subjectivity, time, understanding.

Romantic Poems, Poets, and Narrators

was designed and composed by Christine Brooks

at The Kent State University Press

in 10/13.5 Baskerville Old Style with display text in Bodoni Book

on an Apple Power Macintosh system using Adobe PageMaker;

printed on 50# Turin Book stock;

Smyth sewn and bound over binder's boards in Arristox cloth,

and wrapped with dust jackets printed in two colors

by Thomson-Shore, Inc. of Dexter, Michigan;

and published by

The Kent State University Press

KENT, OHIO 44242 USA